The edition of *The Complete Works of Frances Ridley Havergal* has five parts:

Volume I *Behold Your King: The Complete Poetical Works of Frances Ridley Havergal*

Volume II *Whose I Am and Whom I Serve: Prose Works of Frances Ridley Havergal*

Volume III *Loving Messages for the Little Ones: Works for Children by Frances Ridley Havergal*

Volume IV *Love for Love: Frances Ridley Havergal: Memorials, Letters and Biographical Works*

Volume V *Songs of Truth and Love: Music by Frances Ridley Havergal and William Henry Havergal*

David L. Chalkley, Editor   Dr. Glen T. Wegge, Music Editor

Frances Ridley Havergal's formal education ended when she was 17, with one term at a young women's school in Düsseldorf, Germany, yet she was a true scholar all her life. Fluent in German and French and nearly so in Italian, she read and loved the Reformers in Latin, German, and French. Knowledge was never an end in itself, only a means to know better her Lord and Saviour and to help to bring others to know Him. The Bible was her only Book, and she studied the Hebrew and Greek texts of Scripture, memorized nearly all the New Testament and large portions of the Old Testament, and loved the Author with all her being.

Frances was brought to a saving knowledge of Christ when she was 14, and the rest of her life was consecrated to her Saviour, the Lord Jesus. Keenly aware of her own sinfulness and inability, her sole desire was to please and glorify Him alone. Very finely gifted, she was truly diligent with her gifts: her poetry is among the finest in the English language, after George Herbert; her prose works are deeply beneficial; a musician to the core, she left behind important compositions. Like her works, her life richly touched the ones near her and countless many who met or heard her. The Lord Jesus Christ was her alone, only beauty, and she glowed Him and His truth. Never wanting attention to herself, Frances' desire of her heart was for herself and for others to know her King, the Lord Jesus Christ. Her works are a gold-mine of help and enrichment. There is life in these pages: her works truly glorify the Lord, truly benefit His people, and powerfully reach those who do not yet know Him.

The Music of Frances Ridley Havergal by Glen T. Wegge, Ph.D.

This Companion Volume to the Havergal edition is a valuable presentation of F.R.H.'s scores, most or nearly all of F.R.H.'s scores very little if any at all seen, or even known of, for nearly a century. What a valuable body of music has been unknown for so long and is now made available to many. Dr. Wegge completed his Ph.D. in Music Theory at Indiana University at Bloomington, and his diligence and thoroughness in this volume are obvious. First an analysis of F.R.H.'s compositions is given, an essay that both addresses the most advanced musicians and also reaches those who are untrained in music; then all the extant scores that have been found are newly typeset, with complete texts for each score and extensive indices at the end of the book. This volume presents F.R.H.'s music in newly typeset scores diligently prepared by Dr. Wegge, and Volume V of the Havergal edition presents the scores in facsimile, the original 19th century scores. (The essay—a dissertation—analysing her scores is given the same both in this Companion Volume and in Volume V of the Havergal edition.)

Dr. Wegge is also preparing all of these scores for publication in performance folio editions.

The Havergal Trust   P.O.Box 649   Kirksville, Missouri 63501

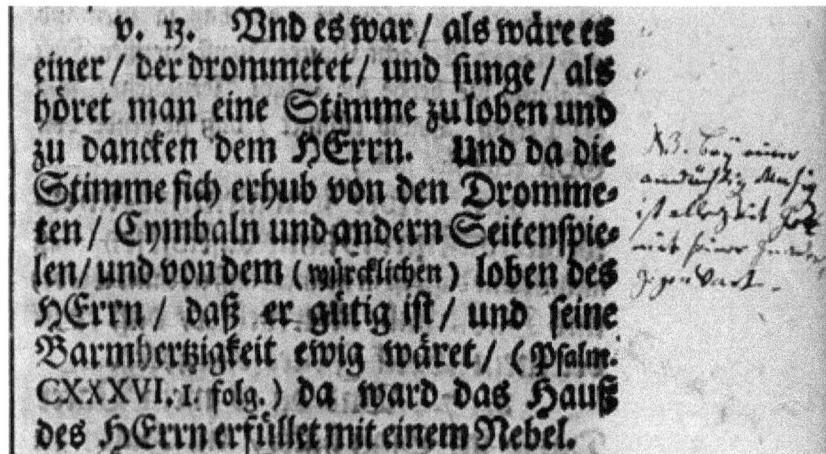

II Chronicles 5:13 *"It came even to pass, as the trumpeters and singers were as one, to make one sound to be heard in praising and thanking the Lord; and when they lifted up their voice with the trumpets and cymbals and instruments of musick, and praised the Lord, saying, For he is good; for his mercy endureth for ever: that then the house was filled with a cloud, even the house of the Lord."*

       Johann Sebastian Bach wrote this note beside II Chronicles 5:13 in his Calov Bible: "In devotional music, God is always present with His grace."

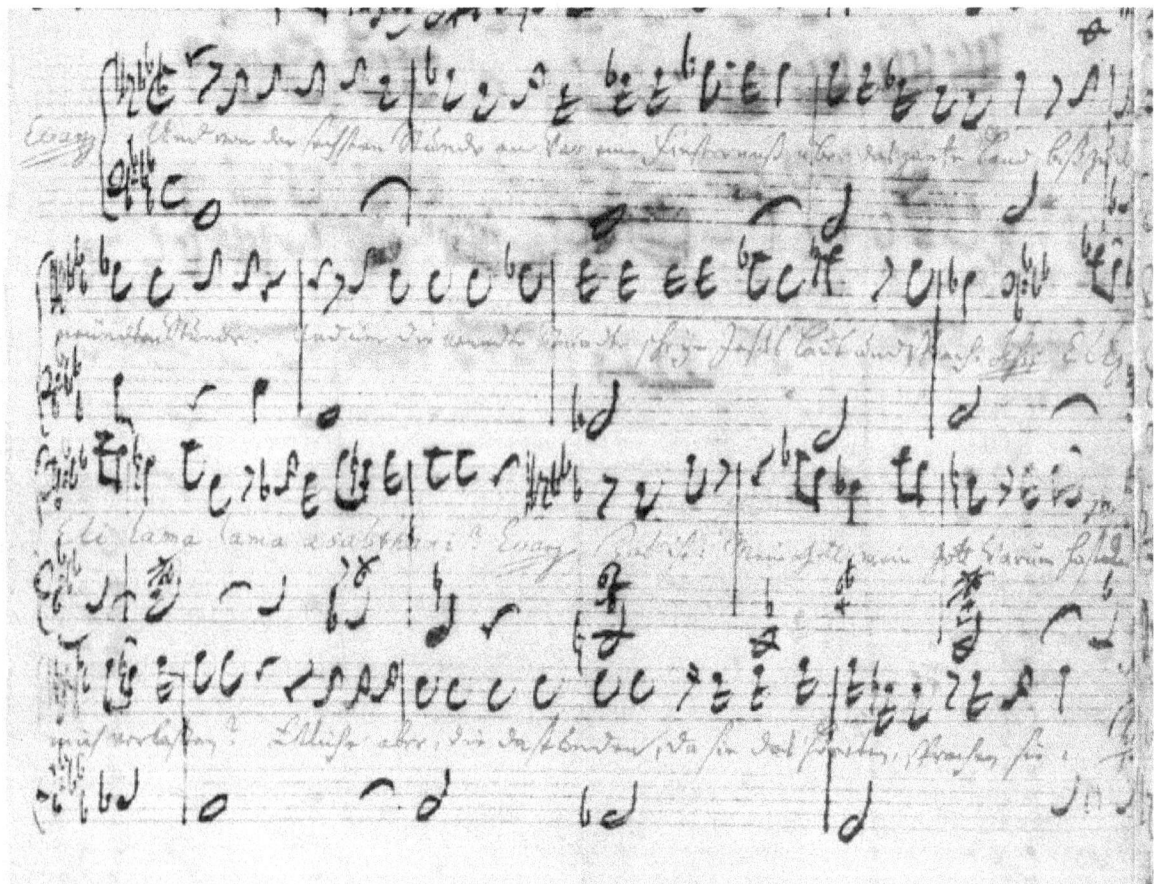

Johann Sebastian Bach's St. Matthew Passion *has Matthew 26:1 to 27:66 set to music, with observations, responses, and German hymns placed among the verses of Scripture. This is a part of Bach's fair copy autograph of the* St. Matthew Passion, *the setting of Matthew 27:46. "And about the ninth hour Jesus cried with a loud voice, saying, Eli, Eli, lama sabachthani? that is to say, My God, my God, why hast thou forsaken me?"*

THE

CHORALE BOOK

FOR ENGLAND.

German Hymns Translated by
Catherine Winkworth.

The German Hymn Tunes Edited by
William Sterndale Bennett and Otto Goldschmidt

A Facsimile Copy of the Original 1863 Edition Published by
Longman, Green, Longman, Roberts, and Green, London

Taken from the New Edition of
The Complete Works of Frances Ridley Havergal.

" Knowing her intense desire that Christ should be magnified, whether
by her life or in her death, may it be to His glory
that in these pages she, being dead,
' Yet speaketh!' "

THE CHORALE BOOK FOR ENGLAND.
German Hymns Translated by Catherine Winkworth
Set to German Hymn Tunes Edited by William Sterndale Bennett and Otto Goldschmidt
Copyright © 2017 by the Havergal Trust.

ISBN 978-1-937236-60-1   Library of Congress Control Number: 2017901562

Printed in the United States of America   *This book is printed on acid-free paper.*

Cover Design by Glen T. Wegge.

Winkworth, Catherine, William Sterndale Bennett, and Otto Goldschmidt
The Chorale Book for England, prose, poetry, and music taken from the edition of the complete works of Frances Ridley Havergal. 1. Winkworth, Catherine, 1827–1878, William Sterndale Bennett, 1816–1875, and Otto Goldschmidt, 1829–1907. 2. Christian Life. 3. Christian Poetry, English. 4. Music. I. Title

This is taken from *The Complete Works of Frances Ridley Havergal.*
David L. Chalkley, General Editor.   Dr. Glen T. Wegge, Music Editor.

The Chorale Book for England is a profoundly rich, valuable book, both the words and the music. This edition was originally prepared to be the section entitled "to fill up the leaf withal," the very last part of *Songs of Truth and Love Music by Frances Ridley Havergal and William Henry Havergal*, which is Volume V of *The Complete Works of Frances Ridley Havergal*. Each of the five volumes of the Havergal edition ends with a section named "to fill up the leaf withal" (the phrase and the concept learned from William Tyndale), and usually (not always, but nearly always) the section "to fill up the leaf withal" contained pieces not by F.R.H. but by others, pieces relevant to her life or her work, or pieces that she would have valued. F.R.H. and Catherine Winkworth almost certainly knew of each other and valued each other's works, and possibly may have met or corresponded, though we do not know now. Although no record of this is extant or can be found now, almost certainly Frances Ridley Havergal owned, used, and knew well *The Chorale Book for England* and Winkworth's *Lyra Germanica*. Frances was utterly fluent in German, spent much time in Germany and Switzerland, and sang German hymns in churches there; moreso, she truly loved the Lord Who is praised and worshipped in these hymns, and she loved the true music from which these German hymn scores are an example. Not that F.R.H.'s use and love of this book is so relevant: this book is true music as God created and meant music to be, and true worship, from Him alone, to Him alone. The Havergal edition was never about Frances Ridley Havergal, but about the object of her love and worship, the subject of her poetry, prose, and music, the Lord Jesus Christ. Worthy is the Lamb. The Lamb is all the glory in Emanuel's land, the kingdom of God.

"By Thy Cross and Passion."

"He hath given us rest by His sorrow,
and life by His death."—John Bunyan.

I.

What hast Thou done for me, O mighty Friend,
    Who lovest to the end!
Reveal Thyself, that I may now behold
    Thy love unknown, untold,
Bearing the curse, and made a curse for me,
That blessed and made a blessing I might be.

II.

Oh, Thou wast crowned with thorns, that I might
    A crown of glory fair;   [wear
"Exceeding sorrowful," that I might be
    Exceeding glad in Thee;
"Rejected and despised," that I might stand
Accepted and complete on Thy right hand.

III.

Wounded for my transgression, stricken sore,
    That I might "sin no more";
Weak, that I might be always strong in Thee;
    Bound, that I might be free;
Acquaint with grief, that I might only know
Fulness of joy in everlasting flow.

IV.

Thine was the chastisement, with no release,
    That mine might be the peace;
The bruising and the cruel stripes were Thine,
    That healing might be mine;
Thine was the sentence and the condemnation,
Mine the acquittal and the full salvation.

V.

For Thee revilings, and a mocking throng,
    For me the angel-song;
For Thee the frown, the hiding of God's face,
    For me His smile of grace;
Sorrows of hell and bitterest death for Thee,
And heaven and everlasting life for me.

VI.

Thy cross and passion, and Thy precious death,
    While I have mortal breath,
Shall be my spring of love and work and praise,
    The life of all my days;
Till all this mystery of love supreme
Be solved in glory—glory's endless theme.

            F.R.H. January, 1877
            Seventh Day of *Loyal Responses*

Ezekiel 33:10, Isaiah 53:6.

"Therefore, O thou son of man, speak unto
the house of Israel; Thus ye speak, saying, If our
transgressions and our sins be upon us, and we pine
away in them, how should we then live?"
    "All we like sheep have gone astray; we have
turned every one to his own way; and the Lord hath
laid on Him the iniquity of us all."

On Thee the Lord
    My mighty sins hath laid;
And against Thee Jehovah's sword
    Flashed forth its fiery blade.
The stroke of justice fell on Thee,
    That it might never fall on me.

        Frances Ridley Havergal   1877

This single verse of six lines was in a set of "Verses on
Texts." Though Zechariah 13:7 was not mentioned,
this also brings that Scripture to mind:
    "Awake, O sword, against my shepherd, and
against the man that is my fellow, saith the Lord of
hosts: smite the shepherd, and the sheep shall be
scattered: and I will turn mine hand upon the little
ones."

Behold Your King.

"Behold, and see if there be any sorrow like unto
My sorrow."—Lamentations 1:12.

Behold your King! Though the moonlight steals
    Through the silvery sprays of the olive tree,
No star-gemmed sceptre or crown it reveals,
    In the solemn shade of Gethsemane.
      Only a form of prostrate grief,
      Fallen, crushed, like a broken leaf!
Oh, think of His sorrow! that we may know
The depth of love in the depth of woe.

Behold your King! Is it nothing to you,
    That the crimson tokens of agony
From the kingly brow must fall like dew,
    Through the shuddering shades of Gethsemane?
      Jesus Himself, the Prince of Life,
      Bows in mysterious mortal strife;
Oh, think of His sorrow! that we may know
The unknown love in the unknown woe.

Behold your King, with His sorrow crowned,
    Alone, alone in the valley is He!
The shadows of death are gathering round,
    And the Cross must follow Gethsemane.
      Darker and darker the gloom must fall,
      Filled is the Cup, He must drink it all!
Oh, think of His sorrow! that we may know
His wondrous love in His wondrous woe.

        F.R.H.   Good Friday, 1879

"Unto you therefore which believe,
He is precious."—I Peter 2:7.

Christ is precious, oh most precious,
    gift by God the Father sealed;
Pearl of greatest price and treasure,
    hidden, yet to us revealed;
His own people's crown of glory,
    and resplendent diadem;
More than thousand worlds, and dearer
    than all life and love to them.

"Ye know that ye were not redeemed
    with corruptible things, . . . but with
    the precious blood of Christ, as of a
    lamb without blemish and without
    spot."—I Peter 1:18,19.

Now, in reverent love and wonder,
    touch the theme of deepest laud,
Precious blood of Christ that bought us
    and hath made us nigh to God!
His own blood, O love unfathomed!
    shed for those who loved Him not;
Mighty fountain always open,
    cleansing us from every spot.

        the second and fourth verses of
        "Precious Things" by F.R.H.
        September, 1874

An Easter Prayer.

Oh let me know
The power of Thy resurrection;
    Oh let me show
Thy risen life in calm and clear reflection;
    Oh let me soar
Where Thou, my Saviour Christ, art gone
    In mind and heart   [before;
Let me dwell always, only, where Thou art.

    Oh let me give
Out of the gifts Thou freely givest;
    Oh let me live
With life abundantly because Thou livest;
    Oh make me shine
In darkest places, for Thy light is mine;
    Oh let me be
A faithful witness for Thy truth and Thee.

    Oh let me show
The strong reality of gospel story;
    Oh let me go
From strength to strength, from glory unto
    Oh let me sing   [glory,
For very joy, because Thou art my King;
    Oh let me praise
Thy love and faithfulness through all my days.

        F.R.H.   February 12, 1879

For more than twelve years, Dr. Glen T. Wegge has been involved in the work to complete the Havergal edition. Without payment of money, with remarkable diligence, patience, persistence, and hard work, he has labored to prepare for publication all of the music in the Havergal edition, and also to complete and publish his own book, *The Music of Frances Ridley Havergal*, a Companion Volume to this edition of *The Complete Works of Frances Ridley Havergal*. He has also done so much to bring to completion (in countless hours of work) all of the other books in the Havergal edition. The patience and support of his wife, Denise, are also appreciated. So much thought, diligence, hard work, countless hours, a servant's heart, a labor of love. My estimate or guess is that Glen has worked approximately 1,500 hours on the Havergal edition, without pay. His work is remarkable both in quantity and in quality, first-rate, sterling work. How many times ? (the Lord knows how many times) has he gone back again and again to fix a text or an illustration until it was just right. Most of the details of his work were known only to Glen and me, much now forgotten, but God sees and knows every trace. How compassionately and richly He has blessed us in all of this.

For much or most of the past 100 years, few if any have realized the value of Frances' music, and Glen (who completed his Ph.D. in music theory at Indiana University at Bloomington and is so finely gifted and prepared to do this work) is the first one to analyze and present her music in such a scholarly way. He began his work on this in very difficult circumstances, and his diligence, persistence, and servant's heart are a true example for believers. Glen is worthy of strong gratitude from all those who will be encouraged and enriched by F.R.H.'s poetry, prose, and music.

The Lord reward him as I cannot, as no man can reward.

This is all the Lord's doing. Thanks be to God for His indescribable gift to us in Christ.

David Chalkley

The Complete Works of Frances Ridley Havergal is dedicated to the glory of the Lord Jesus Christ, laying this at His feet and asking Him to bless to others what He has provided,

"for Jesus' sake only"

and is gratefully inscribed to two people:

> Miss Janet Grierson,
> Mr. Stanley Ward.

Miss Grierson's Biography and her other work on F.R.H. are the most important work on Frances since Maria V. G. Havergal, and she has been invaluably helpful in the preparation of this edition.

Mr. Stanley Ward has been deeply interested in Frances since the 1960's, and his kindness, insights, and help have been truly and profoundly important to this edition.

Thanks be to God for His indescribable gift to us in Christ.

This is the end of the *St. John Passion* by J. S. Bach.

Ach Herr, lass dein lieb' Engelein
am letzten End' die Seele mein
in Abrahams Schooss tragen;
den Leib in sein'm Schlafkämmerlein
gar sanft, ohn ein'ge Qual und Pein,
ruhn bis am jüngsten Tage!
Alsdann vom Tod erwecke mich,
dass meine Augen sehen dich
in aller Freud', O Gottes Sohn,
mein Heiland und Genadenthron!
Herr Jesu Christ, erhöre mich, erhöre mich,
ich will dich preisen ewiglich!

Ah, Lord, let Thy dear angels
at my end my soul
in Abraham's bosom take;
the body in its small sleeping chamber
fully gentle without one torment or pain,
rest till at judgement day!
Then from death awaken me,
that my eyes see Thee
in all joy, O God's Son,
my Saviour and throne of grace.
Lord Jesus Christ, hear me, hear me!
I will praise Thee for ever.

"I will praise Thee, O Lord my God, with all my heart, and I will glorify Thy name for evermore." Psalm 86:12

CONTENTS

ILLUSTRATIONS

Jesus Christ, the Crucified

Words by Johann C. Schwedler
Music by Henri Abraham César Malan, harmonized by Lowell Mason

Hendon

2. What is faith's foundation strong?
   What awakes my heart to song?
   He Who bore my sinful load,
   Purchased for me peace with God,
       Jesus Christ, the Crucified.

3. Who is He that makes me wise
   To discern where duty lies?
   Who is He that makes me true
   Duty, when discerned to do,
       Jesus Christ, the Crucified.

4. Who defeats my fiercest foes?
   Who consoles my saddest woes?
   Who revives my fainting heart,
   Healing all its hidden smart?
       Jesus Christ, the Crucified.

5. Who is life in life to me?
   Who the death of death will be?
   Who will place me on His right,
   With the countless hosts of light?
       Jesus Christ, the Crucified.

6. This is that great thing I know;
   This delights and stirs me so;
   Faith in Him Who died to save,
   Him Who triumphed o'er the grave:
       Jesus Christ, the Crucified.

This is sung to Malan's "Hendon," the same score that is widely sung for the Consecration Hymn in the United States.

The Chorale Book for England.

The Chorale Book for England (London: Longman, Green, Longman, Roberts, and Green, 1863) is a collection of 200 German hymns translated into English by Catherine Winkworth, with German hymn scores edited by William Sterndale Bennett and Otto Goldschmidt.

Catherine Winkworth (1827–1878) translated German hymns and poems of worship into English and published them in the two volumes of *Lyra Germanica*, the first volume—called "Series I"—in 1853, and "Series II" in 1858. From the two volumes of *Lyra Germanica*, and also other sources, 200 hymns were published in *The Chorale Book for England* with "the fine old German chorales to which they are sung in their own country by vast congregations" (Winkworth's words in her Preface to Series II of *Lyra Germanica*, describing *The Chorale Book for England* then in preparation). Her translations of German hymns and verse into English are remarkably fine, a treasure chest of gems.

William Sterndale Bennett (1816–1875), for so long very obscure, sadly and inappropriately so, was a true colleague and friend of Mendelssohn, a very finely gifted composer, pianist, conductor, and teacher. He was (I personally think) the most important English composer of the 19th century before Sullivan and Elgar (William Henry Havergal was primarily a church musician, Bennett primarily a concert musician). Otto Goldschmidt (1829–1907) was a German pianist and composer who studied under Mendelssohn at Leipzig, later was Professor of Piano and Vice-Principal of the Royal Academy of Music in London, and founded and conducted the London Bach Choir. These men were unquestionably two of the finest musicians in England at that time.

The Chorale Book for England, so very obscure now, is—both words and music—a gold-mine, true worship, from Christ alone, to Him alone.   David Chalkley

Catherine Winkworth published the first volume of *Lyra Germanica* in 1855 (London: Longman, Brown, Green, and Longmans, 1855), and the "Second Series" in 1858. These were her translations of German hymns into English, a treasure of true worship, glorifying God and enriching His people. The *Lyra Germanica* Series I had 103 hymns, arranged around the church calendar; Series II had 121 hymns, arranged according to subjects. *The Chorale Book for England* was a set of German hymns translated by C.W. in her *Lyra Germanica* (and also other hymns not in the *Lyra Germanica*), with music scores—chiefly from German hymnbooks—edited by William Sterndale Bennett and Otto Goldschmidt, published in 1862. Here is true worship, glorifying God and edifying and enriching His people.

Catherine Winkworth also wrote the volume *Christian Singers of Germany* (a richly valuable collection of biographical essays on German hymnwriters with translated hymns) which was published in 1869. Other works published by her were the *Life of Amelia Wilhelmina Sieveking* From the German, Edited, with the Author's Sanction, by Catherine Winkworth (London: Longman, Green, Longman, Roberts, & Green, 1863), the first half translated by C.W., the second half translated by another lady unnamed, the whole edited by C.W.; the *Life of Pastor* [Theodore] *Fliedner* of Kaiserswerth Translated from the German (with the author's sanction) by Catherine Winkworth (London: Longmans, Green, and Co., 1867); and *Prayers from the Collection of the Late Baron Bunsen* Selected and Translated by Catherine Winkworth (London: Longmans, Green, and Co., 1871).

Her eldest sister, Susanna Winkworth (1820–1884), was also a valuable translator of German works into English, translating *Theologica Germanica* [a treatise likely written in the 14th century, so valued by Martin Luther and published by him in 1516] Edited by Dr. Pfeiffer from the Only Manuscript Yet Known, Translated from the German by Susanna Winkworth (her "Historical Introduction by the Translator" dated 1854). Susanna also translated and published other valuable works from the church in Germany: *The History and Life of the Reverend Doctor John Tauler* with Twenty-Five of His Sermons Translated from the German with Additional Notices of Tauler's Life and Times by Susanna Winkworth (Translator's Preface Manchester: Nov. 29th, 1856); *Signs of the Times: Letters to Ernst Moritz Arndt on the Dangers to Religious Liberty in the Present State of the World* by Christian Charles Josias Bunsen, Translated from the German by Susanna Winkworth (London: Smith, Elder & Co., 1856) and other German works translated by Susanna Winkworth.

Memorials of Two Sisters: Susanna and Catherine Winkworth was published by their niece Margaret J. Shaen (London: Longman, Green, and Co., 1908).

The following memorial article after the death of Catherine Winkworth was found in an 1878 issue of *The Sunday Magazine*: For Family Reading (London : Daldy, Isbister, & Co., 1878), page 792:

MISS CATHERINE WINKWORTH

We ought to have mentioned the name of Catherine Winkworth in our Memorial Record of last month—for she died on the 1st of July at Monnetier, near Geneva, somewhat suddenly, of heart disease—but we were in expectation of receiving more ample materials than we then possessed for a biographical notice. Miss Winkworth, who during the latter years of her life resided at Clifton, Bristol, was chiefly known to the public generally as an accomplished and sympathetic translator of hymns from the German. Her two volumes entitled "Lyra Germanica," the first published in 1855, the second in 1858, have passed through many editions, and have enabled thousands of English readers to form a more adequate conception than they could otherwise have obtained of the tone and character of the devotional poetry of Protestant Germany. The hymns in the first of these volumes are taken chiefly from the collection formed by the late Baron Bunsen, whose friendly encouragement greatly stimulated Miss Winkworth's efforts in this field of labour, and with whose family she cherished a lifelong intimacy. Her translations generally represent the original with combined fidelity and grace, and many of them may be pronounced as perfect as translations can be. A considerable number of them have found a place in selections of hymns for public worship in use among various sections of the Christian Church. A writer, who had the advantage of intimate personal acquaintance with Miss Winkworth, states that "her interest in poetry and literature was universal," and that "her knowledge of German poetry of all kinds and periods was minute and extensive." Of her thoroughness and capability in the department of hymnology which she had made especially her own, we have had an opportunity of judging also from her critical and biographical volume entitled "The Christian Singers of Germany," published in 1869, and from her book of "German Chorales," with music arranged by Messrs. Sterndale Bennett and Otto Goldschmidt. Miss Winkworth also published in 1863 the "Life of Amelia Sieveking," and in 1867 a "Life of Pastor Fliedner," the latter being a translation and the former partly so. Both these works are of deep interest, and we well remember the pleasure afforded us by the biography of Miss Sieveking when it first appeared. It is a book which deserves to be still more widely known. In the more limited but still important and extensive sphere of her own neighbourhood, Miss Winkworth took an active and influential part in philanthropic work, and especially in movements for promoting the higher education of women. In such work her sister, Miss Susannah Winkworth, was associated with her, and the name of this lady, who is the translator of Bunsen's "God is History," and of the "Theologica Germanica," has not unnaturally often been mistaken for that of the author of "Lyra Germanica." The writer, already alluded to, to whom we are indebted for some of the facts given in the sketch, observes with regard to Catherine Winkworth, that although latterly her multifarious labours began to tell on her, "it was not in her nature to withdraw from any purpose towards which by thought and counsel she could give substantial aid—a characteristic which will be gratefully cherished by the many private friends who have reason to remember what she was to them in times of sorrow or of difficulty. For amongst her other gifts she was singularly endowed with the power of silent insight and unobtrusive sympathy. And while her sweet, deep voice, her ready smile, her full and penetrating eye, carried light and warmth wherever she came, her balance of mind and clear, calm judgment were an unfailing stay to many a friend in hours of trial and perplexity. The same qualities, united as they were with remarkable fairness and candour, were no less valuable in business of a more public kind." A beautiful spirit has thus passed away from us, but the sweet fragrance of the good work she did for thoughtful and devout hearts will long remain. [1]

[1] *The Sunday Magazine*: For Family Reading (London : Daldy, Isbister, & Co., 1878) page 792.

Catherine Winkworth (1827–1878), the translator of German hymns and poems of worship in the two volumes of Lyra Germanica *and then* The Chorale Book for England. *Her labor of love has been so richly beneficial to believers in her day and since.*

Sir William Sterndale Bennett (1816–1875).

Though he has been very obscure for a century, I have long thought that W.S.B. was the most important composer and musician of England in the 19th century, likely the foremost or one of the foremost between Purcell and Elgar. So finely gifted as a pianist, composer, musician, he was a true friend and colleague of Felix Mendelssohn, warmly regarded and valued, and if Mendelssohn had not died so young, Bennett's career might have proceeded very differently. Mendelssohn wrote that he thought Bennett was "the most promising young musician I know" both in England and Germany, and encouraged him to come to Leipzig to study. After Bennett's performance of his own Piano Concerto No. 3 at one of the Leipzig Gewandhaus concerts, Schumann wrote that he was the most musical ("*musikalisch*") of all Englishmen.

Schumann also called him "an angel of a musician" (a play on the two words "Anglisch" and "angel"), and dedicated his *Symphonic Etudes* Op. 13 to Bennett. He was invited to be the conductor of the Leipzig Gewandhaus Orchestra, a position he declined. In 1854 he gave the first public performance in England of Bach's *St. Matthew Passion*. Those who knew him well realized his remarkable, rare gifts, and these can be glimpsed in a number of his compositions. He composed a Symphony in G-minor, Op. 43; Piano Concertos in D-minor, E-flat major, C-minor, F-minor; *The May Queen*, Cantata, Op. 39; *The Woman of Samaria*, Sacred Cantata, Op. 44; chamber music, solo piano music, songs, anthems, etc. Much of his adult life was occupied in teaching and other duties (Professor at Cambridge University, Conductor of the Philharmonic Society, Principal of the Royal Academy of Music, etc.), and he did not compose nearly as much as his gifts merited. He founded the Bach Society, and in 1854 gave the first public British performance of J. S. Bach's *St. Matthew Passion*. William Sterndale Bennett was honored with the Gold Medal of the Royal Philharmonic Society in 1871. More than 30 years after his death, his son J. R. Sterndale Bennett published the biography *The Life of William Sterndale Bennett* (Cambridge: Cambridge University Press, 1907), which gives many valuable details, among them the clear, remarkably strong regard of Felix Mendelssohn for W.S.B. So unjustly forgotten today (both Sterndale Bennett and this *Chorale Book for England*), his preparation of this book is invaluable, true gold.   D.C.

Otto Goldschmidt and Jenny Lind as newlyweds.

Otto Moritz David Goldschmidt (1829–1907) was a pianist, conductor, and composer. He was the piano accompanist of the famous Swedish soprano Jenny Lind, and they were married in 1852, living in Dresden and later settling in England in 1858. In 1861 he was elected an Honorary Member of the London Philharmonic Society, and he was elected an Honorary Member of the Royal Philharmonic Society in 1869. Otto Goldschmidt was a Professor of Piano and later the Vice-Principal of the Royal Academy of Music (under William Sterndale Bennett) in London; he also was the founder of the London Bach Choir, which he conducted 1875–1885. Goldschmidt and the London Bach Choir gave the first performance in England of J. S. Bach's *Mass in B-minor*, BWV 232, on April 26, 1876, and they later gave the first London performances of Bach's *Magnificat*, BWV 243, and his Cantata *Ein Feste Burg*, BWV 80. He conducted a music festival in Düsseldorf in 1863, and one in Hamburg in 1866.

Born in Hamburg, Goldschmidt was a student of Felix Mendelssohn at the Leipzig Conservatory. Mendelssohn gave this testimonial of his student: "The last named [Mendelssohn] presented his student the following testimonial: Mr. Goldschmidt has demonstrated a fine talent for piano playing in a gratifying, cultured way, and also in the composition for his instrument has demonstrated not insignificant gifts" (quoted Marx 2003, page 158).[1]

---

[1] ". . . Mendelssohn. Letztgenannter stellte seinem Studenten folgendes Zeugnis aus: *Herr Goldschmidt hat ein schönes Talent zum Piano-fortespiel auf erfreulicher Weise ausgebildet, u. auch in der Composition für sein Instrument nicht unbedeutende Anlagen gezeigt.*" (*Hamburger Mendelssohn-Vorträge* edited by Hans Joachim Marx ISBN 3767214156 page 158).

After Mendelssohn's death, Goldschmidt went to Paris in 1848, wanting to study under Chopin. He had private piano lessons with Clara Schumann. He must have been a fine pianist, as he was the accompanist of Jenny Lind, likely the most famous and wealthiest woman singer of her time. He taught piano lessons to Queen Victoria's third daughter, the Princess Helena. His compositions include the oratorio *Ruth* (1867, performed at the Hereford music festival that year), Op. 20; a cantata *Music* for soprano and female voices (1898), Op. 27; a Piano Concerto, Op. 10; a Piano Trio, Op. 12; Twelve Grandes Etudes for the piano, Op. 13; *Ruth, A Sacred Pastoral*, Op. 20 (London, 1870); Psalm 130, Sacred Cantata; duets for two pianos, studies and various pieces for piano, songs, part songs, etc.

Goldschmidt had already been interested in publishing a collection of German hymn tunes when Catherine Winkworth and William Sterndale Bennett were working on *The Chorale Book for England*, and he "was so deeply interested in the project that he offered to join Dr. Bennett in it; whereupon Dr. Bennett wrote to Catherine as follows:—" [1]

DR. STERNDALE BENNETT *to* CATHERINE

EASTBOURNE, *Aug. 5th*, 1859.

I had recently a conversation with Mr. Otto Goldschmidt (who requested to see me purposely) upon the subject of the work which we have in hand, and I found that he was anxious to undertake a somewhat similar work, had he not been made aware that I had already started with it. He has been most polite towards me in the matter, as you will see in a letter which I enclose, his great object being, however, to persuade us to enlarge the character of this work. He offers his co-operation, in case we can arrange it, and I am to see him this evening and talk his ideas over with him. I have already explained to him that I am bound to Mr. Longman and yourself to carry out your plans if you see no reason to alter them, and I assure you that I am quite in a humour to fulfil my task to the very best of my ability.

I send you the first catalogue sheet of the twenty-five Chorales which are finished, and I shall certainly do as many more in the next days, that I may have done a fair portion of my work before I even enter into the joint work with Mr. Goldschmidt. I do not disguise that I consider his co-operation would be most desirable, from his being a first-rate German musician, as well as having a keen feeling in this exquisite branch of music.

A tender shoot.

A tender shoot has started
    Up from a root of grace,
as ancient seers imparted
    From Jesse's holy race;
It blooms without a blight,
Blooms in the cold bleak winter
Turning our darkness into light.

This shoot, Isaiah taught us,
    From Jesse's root should spring;
The Virgin Mary brought us
    The branch of which we sing:
Our God of endless might
Gave her this child to save us,
Thus turning darkness into light.

Words by Otto Goldschmidt,
translated by W. Bartholomew

Otto Goldschmidt set this poem to his own music, a carol anthem for a capella chorus.

[1] This quotation, and the following two paragraphs quoted from a letter by Bennett to Winkworth, were found in *Memorials of Two Sisters: Catherine and Susanna Winkworth* by their niece Margaret J. Shaen (London: Longmans, Green, and Co., 1908), pages 208–209.

This is the hymn "O Haupt voll Blut und Wunden," first in the original German words by Paul Gerhardt, next in the English translation by James Waddell Alexander, then in the translation by Catherine Winkworth published as hymn number 51 in *The Chorale Book for England*, and finally in a different translation by Catherine Winkworth published in her *Lyra Germanica* Series I in 1855.

1. O Haupt voll Blut und Wunden,
Voll Schmerz und voller Hohn,
O Haupt, zum Spott gebunden
Mit einer Dornenkron',
O Haupt, sonst schön gezieret
Mit höchster Ehr' und Zier,
Jetzt aber höchst schimpfieret:
Gegrüßet sei'st du mir!

2. Du edles Angesichte,
Davor sonst schrickt und scheut
Das große Weltgewichte,
Wie bist du so bespeit!
Wie bist du so erbleichet!
Wer hat dein Augenlicht,
Dem sonst kein Licht nicht gleichet,
So schändlich zugericht't?

3. Die Farbe deiner Wangen,
Der roten Lippen Pracht
Ist hin und ganz vergangen;
Des blaßen Todes Macht
Hat alles hingenommen,
Hat alles hingerafft,
Und daher bist du kommen
Von deines Leibes Kraft.

4. Nun, was du, Herr, erduldet,
Ist alles meine Last;
Ich hab' es selbst verschuldet,
Was du getragen hast.
Schau her, hier steh' ich Armer,
Der Zorn verdienet hat;
Gib mir, o mein Erbarmer,
Den Anblick deiner Gnad'!

5. Erkenne mich, mein Hüter,
Mein Hirte, nimm mich an!
Von dir, Quell aller Güter,
Ist mir viel Gut's getan.
Dein Mund hat mich gelabet
Mit Milch und süßer Kost;
Dein Geist hat mich begabet
Mit mancher Himmelslust.

6. Ich will hier bei dir stehen,
Verachte mich doch nicht!
Von dir will ich nicht gehen,
Wenn dir dein Herze bricht;
Wenn dein Haupt wird erblaßen
Im letzten Todesstoß,
Alsdann will ich dich faßen
In meinen Arm und Schoß.

7. Es dient zu meinen Freuden
Und kommt mir herzlich wohl,
Wenn ich in deinem Leiden,
Mein Heil, mich finden soll.
Ach, möcht' ich, o mein Leben,
An deinem Kreuze hier
Mein Leben von mir geben,
Wie wohl geschähe mir!

8. Ich danke dir von Herzen,
O Jesu, liebster Freund,
Für deines Todes Schmerzen,
Da du's so gut gemeint.
Ach gib, daß ich mich halte
Zu dir und deiner Treu'
Und, wenn ich nun erkalte,
In dir mein Ende sei!

9. Wenn ich einmal soll scheiden,
So scheide nicht von mir;
Wenn ich den Tod soll leiden,
So tritt du dann herfür;
Wenn mir am allerbängsten
Wird um das Herze sein,
So reiß mich aus den Ängsten
Kraft deiner Angst und Pein!

10. Erscheine mir zum Schilde,
Zum Trost in meinem Tod,
Und laß mich sehn dein Bilde
In deiner Kreuzesnot!
Da will ich nach dir blicken,
Da will ich glaubensvoll
Dich fest an mein Herz drücken.
Wer so stirbt, der stirbt wohl.

Tune: "Herzlich tut mich" by Hans Leo Haßler, 1601.   Text: Paul Gerhardt (1607–1676).

O Haupt voll Blut und Wunden.
A Passion Hymn.

O sacred Head! now wounded,
   with grief and shame weighed down,
now scornfully surrounded
   with thorns, Thine only crown;
O sacred Head! what glory,
   what bliss till now was Thine!
Yet though despised and gory,
   I joy to call Thee mine.

O noblest Brow, and dearest!
   In other days the world
all feared, when Thou appearedst.
   What shame on Thee is hurled!
How art Thou pale with anguish,
   with sore abuse and scorn;
how does that visage languish,
   which once was bright as morn.

The blushes late residing
   upon that holy cheek,
the roses once abiding
   upon those lips so meek,
Alas! they have departed;
   wan death has rifled all!
for weak and broken-hearted,
   I see Thy body fall.

What Thou, my Lord, hast suffered
   was all for sinners' gain.
Mine, mine was the transgression,
   but Thine the deadly pain.
Lo! here I fall, my Saviour,
   'tis I deserve Thy place.
Look on me with Thy favour,
   vouchsafe me to Thy grace.

Receive me, my Redeemer,
   my Shepherd, make me Thine.
Of every good the fountain,
   Thou art the spring of mine.
Thy lips with love distilling,
   and milk of truth sincere,
with heaven's bliss are filling
   the soul that trembles here.

Beside Thee, Lord, I've taken
   my place — forbid me not!
Hence will I ne'er be shaken,
   though Thou to death be brought.
If pain's last paleness holds Thee,
   in agony opprest,
then, then will I enfold Thee
   within this arm and breast!

The joy can ne'er be spoken
   above all joys beside,
when in Thy body broken
   I thus with safety hide.
My Lord of life, desiring
   Thy glory now to see,
beside the cross expiring,
   I'd breathe my soul to Thee.

What language shall I borrow
   to thank Thee dearest Friend,
for this Thy dying sorrow,
   Thy pity without end?
Oh! make me Thine forever,
   and should I fainting be,
Lord, let me never, never
   outlive my love to Thee.

And when I am departing,
   Oh! part not Thou from me.
When mortal pangs are darting,
   come, Lord, and set me free.
And when my heart must languish
   amidst the final throe,
release me from mine anguish
   by Thine own pain and woe.

Be near me when I'm dying,
   Oh! show Thy cross to me,
and for my succour flying,
   come, Lord, and set me free.
These eyes, new faith receiving,
   from Jesus shall not move,
for he who dies believing
   dies safely through Thy love.

A Passion Hymn by Paul Gerhardt (1607–1676),
translated by James Waddell Alexander (1804–1859).

O Haupt voll Blut und Wunden
Good Friday.

Ah wounded Head that bearest
   Such bitter shame and scorn,
That now so meekly wearest
   The mocking crown of thorn!
Erst reigning in the highest
   In light and majesty,
Dishonour'd here Thou diest,
   Yet here I worship Thee.

Thou noble Face, whose anger
   Shall make a world to quail,
That glance is quench'd in languor
   To which the sun were pale;
How hath its brightness vanish'd!
   Those gracious eyes, how dim!
What foe their light hath banish'd,
   Who dared to scoff at Him?

All lovely hues have faded
   That glow'd with warmth and life
As He endures unaided
   The last and mortal strife;
The Mighty One of valour
   Must yield Him as a prey,
Death triumphs in his pallor
   O'er all His strength to-day.

Ah Lord, this cruel burden
   Of right belongs to me;
Of my misdeeds the guerdon [1]
   Hath all been laid on Thee;
I cast me down before Thee,
   Wrath were my rightful lot,
Yet hear me, I implore Thee,
   Redeemer, spurn me not!

My Guardian, deign to own me,
   My Shepherd, I am Thine;
What goodness hast Thou shewn me,
   O Fount of Love Divine!

How oft Thy lips have fed me
   On earth with angels' food!
How oft Thy Spirit led me
   To stores of heavenly good!

Ah would that I were bidden
   To share Thy cross and woes!
There all true joy lies hidden,
   Thence all true comfort flows.
Ah well for me, if lying
   Here at Thy feet, my Life,
I too with Thee were dying,
   And thus might end my strife!

My soul doth melt within me,
   O Jesus, dearest Friend,
That Thou shouldst bear to win me
   Such woes, for such an end!
Ah make me cling the firmer
   To One so true to me,
And sink without a murmur
   To sleep at last in Thee.

Yes, when I hence betake me,
   Lord, do not Thou depart;
Oh! never more forsake me
   When death is at my heart,
And faith and hope are sinking,
   O'erwhelm'd with dread dismay;
Thou barest all unshrinking,—
   O chase my fears away!

Appear then, my Defender,
   My Comfort, ere I die!
This life I can surrender
   If but I see Thee nigh;
My dim eyes shall behold Thee,
   Upon Thy cross shall dwell,
My heart by faith enfold Thee;
   Who dieth thus, dies well!

Paul Gerhardt, 1659.
Translated by Catherine Winkworth.
This is hymn number 51 in *The Chorale Book for England.*

[1] guerdon: reward, or payment

Good Friday. Morning.
He was wounded for our transgressions, He was bruised for our iniquities; the chastise-
ment of our peace was upon Him, and with His stripes we are healed.
From the Lesson. Isaiah 53:5.

6,6,8,6

O Haupt voll Blut und Wunden.

Paul Gerhardt. 1659.
Translated by Catherine Winkworth, 1855.

Ah wounded Head! Must Thou
 Endure such shame and scorn!
The blood is trickling from Thy brow
 Pierced by the crown of thorn.
 Thou Who wast crown'd on high
 With light and majesty,
In deep dishonour here must die,
 Yet here I welcome Thee!

Thou noble countenance!
 All earthly lights are pale
Before the brightness of that glance,
 At which a world shall quail.
 How is it quenched and gone!
 Those gracious eyes how dim!
Whence grew that cheek so pale and wan?
 Who dared to scoff at Him?

All lovely hues of life,
 That glow'd on lip and cheek,
Have vanish'd in that awful strife;
 The Mighty One is weak.
 Pale death has won the day,
 He triumphs in this hour
When Strength and Beauty fade away,
 And yield them to his power.

Ah Lord, Thy woes belong,
 Thy cruel pains, to me,
The burden of my sin and wrong
 Hath all been laid on Thee.
 Behold me where I kneel,
 Wrath were my rightful lot,
One glance of love yet let me feel!
 Redeemer, spurn me not!

My Guardian, own me Thine;
 My Shepherd, bear me home:
O Fount of mercy, Source Divine,
 From Thee what blessings come!

How oft Thy mouth has fed
 My soul with angels' food,
How oft Thy Spirit o'er me shed
 His stores of heavenly good!

Ah would that I could share
 Thy cross, Thy bitter woes!
All true delight lies hidden there,
 Thence all true comfort flows.
 Ah well were it for me
 That I could end my strife,
And die upon the cross with Thee,
 Who art my Life of life!

My soul is all o'erfraught,
 O Jesus, dearest Friend,
With thankful love to Him Who sought
 Such woe for such an end.
 Grant me as true a faith,
 As Thou art true to me,
That so the icy sleep of death
 Be but a rest in Thee.

Yes, when I must depart,
 Depart Thou not from me;
When Death is creeping to my heart,
 Bear Thou mine agony.
 When faith and courage sink,
 O'erwhelm'd with dread dismay,
Come Thou Who ne'er from pain didst shrink,
 And chase my fears away.

Come to me ere I die,
 My comfort and my shield;
Then gazing on Thy cross can I
 Calmly my spirit yield.
 On Thee, when life is past,
 My darkening eyes shall dwell,
My heart in faith shall hold Thee fast;
 Who dieth thus, dies well.

This was translated by Catherine Winkworth (1827–1878), and was published in the first volume ("Series I") of
Lyra Germanica in 1855.

THE

CHORALE BOOK

FOR ENGLAND;

A COMPLETE HYMN-BOOK FOR PUBLIC AND PRIVATE WORSHIP, IN
ACCORDANCE WITH THE SERVICES AND FESTIVALS OF
THE CHURCH OF ENGLAND.

THE HYMNS FROM THE

LYRA GERMANICA AND OTHER SOURCES,

TRANSLATED BY

CATHERINE WINKWORTH;

THE TUNES FROM THE SACRED MUSIC

OF THE

LUTHERAN, LATIN, AND OTHER CHURCHES,

FOR FOUR VOICES, WITH HISTORICAL NOTES, ETC., ETC.,

COMPILED AND EDITED BY

WILLIAM STERNDALE BENNETT,

PROFESSOR OF MUSIC IN THE UNIVERSITY OF CAMBRIDGE,

AND

OTTO GOLDSCHMIDT.

LONDON:

LONGMAN, GREEN, LONGMAN, ROBERTS, AND GREEN.

ALSO TO BE HAD OF

MESSRS COCK, HUTCHINGS, AND CO., 63, NEW BOND STREET.

1863.

TRANSLATOR'S PREFACE.

Note: *The Chorale Book for England* was printed with the "long s" (ʃ) where the small letter s would be printed in our day. The "long s" was commonly used in the 18th century, but less and less in the 19th, and virtually never in the 20th century (except in antiquarian books or specially typeset texts). The "long s" looks similar to our small letter f: see the second word ("preʃent") of the first paragraph in this "Translator's Preface." When a word ends with s in this text, a small s is used. For an example, the second word of the second sentence of the first paragraph was typeset "conʃtitutes" (typeset "constitutes" in our day).

THE preʃent volume fulfils the promiʃe which was made in the Second Series of the Lyra Germanica, that the hymns contained there ʃhould be brought out in another edition, accompanied by their proper tunes. It conʃtitutes, however, at the ʃame time, an independent work, with an object different from that of the two preceding volumes of tranʃlations from the German hymnology. The Lyra Germanica was intended chiefly for uʃe as a work of private devotion; the Chorale Book for England is intended primarily for uʃe in united worʃhip in the church and family, as alʃo in meetings for the practice of church muʃic. This aim has throughout governed the choice of the hymns and tunes, and the form given to them; many beautiful hymns contained in the Lyra Germanica have thus been excluded, becauʃe their length or their purely reflective character rendered them ill-adapted for congregational ʃinging, while a large number of new tranʃlations—about one-third of the whole—have been introduced, either for the ʃake of their tunes, or to ʃupply neceʃʃary requirements of our ʃervices. Theʃe have been ʃelected from various ʃources, chiefly from ʃome very early German hymn-books, from the collections of Tucher and Wackernagel, from the new Bavarian hymn-book of the Lutheran Church, and from the Evangeliʃches Kirchengeʃangbuch, Stuttgart, 1855, publiʃhed by the Church Conference held in Eiʃenach in 1853.

With regard to the form of the hymns, conʃiderable difficulty has ariʃen on two points;—the great length of many of them, and the peculiarity of their metres involving the conʃtant uʃe of diʃʃyllable rhymes. It has ʃeemed beʃt, in many caʃes, conʃiderably to curtail the longer hymns, to bring them within limits which, though they may ʃtill appear long to thoʃe accuʃtomed to the Engliʃh allowance of four verʃes only, may yet, it is thought, be uʃed without inconvenience. The hymn may frequently be found in its complete form in the Lyra Germanica. This courʃe has, however, been deemed inadmiʃʃible, where the hymn was very well known, or its meaning would have been ʃeriouʃly injured by abbreviation, and it has then been omitted altogether, or given at full length, as is the caʃe with Luther's verʃion of the Lord's Prayer, his Chriʃtmas Carol, and the fine old hymn on the Seven Words of our Lord on the Croʃs, here aʃʃigned to Good Friday.

As a rule, the hymn and tune have been conʃidered as one and indiviʃible, and the original metres therefore ʃtrictly preʃerved for the ʃake of the tunes, which would not admit of any deviation without detriment to their characteriʃtic beauty. This has neceʃʃitated the frequent uʃe of the double rhymes, which the ʃtructure of the German language renders as common, and indeed inevitable, in German, as monoʃyllabic rhymes are with us. The comparatively ʃmall number of the former in our language preʃents a ʃerious obʃtacle to rendering the German hymns into Engliʃh with the force and ʃimplicity they poʃʃeʃs in their own tongue, and without which they cannot become truly naturalized among us; yet it is one which muʃt be encountered if the tunes alʃo are to be introduced with them, as they ought to be, and in their proper form. In this work the queʃtion has been dealt with in detail, according to the ʃpecial character of each hymn and tune; in ʃome few inʃtances, moʃtly of comparatively modern date, where the tune admitted without injury of adaptation to ʃingle rhymes, it has been thus arranged; in the greater number, the verʃions previouʃly given in the Lyra Germanica have been remodelled to ʃuit the muʃic. Apart from the rhymes, it will be obʃerved that theʃe hymns poʃʃeʃs a great variety of metres, ʃome of which will at firʃt, no doubt, ʃtrike an Engliʃh ear as ʃtrange. But it muʃt be remembered that by far the greater part of theʃe hymns and tunes date from the earlier ages of German hymnology, when hymns were always written to be ʃung, not read; for this reaʃon the long and monotonous lines which mark the compoʃitions of a later period and of a more didactic character, were inʃtinctively avoided, and metres of more complex movement, and capable of conveying more variety of fentiment, were invented. Thefe metres will be found to follow a ftrict rule of their own, both in the varying number of feet, and the frequent alternation of Trochaic and Iambic lines; and it is believed that when the ear has once learnt to perceive this, and to affociate them with the appropriate rhythm of their tune, there is no reafon why they fhould not become naturalized in England. A few, included here for the fake of the tunes only, may probably always retain an alien found to us; but thefe are very few indeed, and, in general, it would certainly be greatly to the advantage of our hymn-books if we could widen the range both of form and thought which is now given to this clafs of compofitions.

At the prefent time, when the whole fubject of church mufic and congregational finging is receiving far more attention than ever before, it feems peculiarly defirable to feize the opportunity to enrich our own hymnology from the ftores of a country fo pre-eminently diftinguifhed in this way. That thefe hymns and tunes firft fprang up on a foreign foil is no reafon why they fhould not take root among us; all who ufe our Common Prayer know well how the unity of Chriftian fentiment is felt to fwallow up all diverfity of national origin. In truth, any embodiment of Chriftian experience and devotion, whether in the form of hymn or prayer or meditation, or whatever fhape art may give it, if it do but go to the heart of our common faith, becomes at once the rightful and moft precious inheritance of the whole Chriftian Church. Much more, then, where the country is fo nearly akin to our own, may we feel that it is at once our privilege and our duty to appropriate all that fhe can beftow on us, and to hope that her gifts will find a welcome and a home here.

C. W.

Clifton, September, 1862.

EDITORS' PREFACE.

In laying before the public the "Chorale Book for England," the Editors defire that it fhould be accompanied by fome obfervations explanatory of its contents, and alfo of the principles by which they have been guided in its compilation.

This work is bafed upon the tranflation of German hymns by Mifs C. Winkworth, well known under the title of "Lyra Germanica," and contains[1] hymns and tunes chiefly of German origin, and belonging more efpecially to the 16th and two following centuries. Had the "Chorale Book" however been reftricted to a republication of the "Lyra Germanica" with mufic, it would not have comprifed all that is requifite to illuftrate the beauty of German Hymnology and to fit the work for ufe in the Church of England. It will be found therefore that, in addition to the principal contents of the "Lyra Germanica," much frefh matter has been brought forward.

Though the "Chorale Book" contains hymns for all the feftivals and fervices of the Church of England, the Editors have abftained, with one exception,[2] from inferting either hymns or tunes of Englifh origin: to do fo would have detracted from the fpecial character which they believe the work to poffefs, as the firft introduction into England of all that ranks as the effence of German Hymnology in *words and mufic united.*

During the 16th and 17th centuries Hymnology was in its height in Germany, and bore its moft precious bloffoms; hymn and tune were then juftly confidered indivifible, and, though the beauty and popularity of a tune would caufe frefh hymns to be written for it, the tune ftill continued to be known by the name of the original hymn with which it was affociated.

---

[1] Whenever in this work the term *hymn* occurs, it is applied to the words as diftinguifhed from the mufic.

[2] Tune No. xcii.

In accordance with·this precedent, the fame original connection between hymn and tune has—with few exceptions—been maintained in this book.[1]

Many hymns rightly forming part of a German hymn-book, which in a great meafure takes the place in Germany of the Book of Common Prayer in England, have for obvious reafons been excluded from this compilation, and the Editors have thus been enabled to limit the number to two hundred, believing, at the fame time, that none have been omitted which are effential to the purpofe in view.

While the "Chorale Book" contains no Englifh tunes, it neverthelefs includes fome already well known in this country, fuch as the "Old Hundredth," the "Veni Creator," that called "Luther's Hymn,"[2] and others. The origin of every tune, as far as it can be traced, as alfo the names of the authors of the hymns, are given in the various Indexes at the end of the work, to which the reader is referred. It may however be defirable to give here a fhort fketch of the growth of hymnology on the continent, and more particularly in Germany, fince the Reformation.

When Luther took up the caufe of the Reformation, and had to remodel the fervices of the Church, he believed he could not better enhance their beauty than by appealing to his nation's love for fong, and foftering the practice of congregational finging (Gemeinbegefang). With this view he made tranflations from the Latin hymns previoufly in ufe in the Church, paraphrafed feveral of the Pfalms and Canticles of Holy Scripture, himfelf wrote many new hymns, and requefted his friends to contribute others. As to mufic, he availed himfelf in many cafes of tunes already exifting in the Church, which he fparingly modified to fuit his new metres; of other tunes the origin is unknown, and of thofe afcribed to Luther, three only can be traced with any certainty to him as the compofer;[3] two of which have been received into this work, No. 124, and No. VI. in the Appendix.

The firft important German hymn-book, preceded in the fame year by

[1] In thefe cafes the term *Original Tune* is ufed, with the quotation of the firft line of the correfponding hymn in German above it; whenever the fame tune appears in the book again, it is quoted with the firft line of the Englifh tranflation. In the few exceptional cafes alluded to, the German name of the tune has been given, and the Pfalms of Goudimel have been quoted as they ftand in his edition.

[2] See tunes XC, CI, LXXI.

[3] C. von Winterfeld „Der evangelifche Kirchengefang ꝛc." Vol. 1. p. 160.

feveral fmaller books, publifhed under the name of "Enchiridion," Erfurt, &c. &c., appeared under the aufpices of Luther in the year 1524. It was edited by his friend, Johann Walther,[1] and was accompanied by a preface from the pen of Luther himfelf.

Walther's work (printed with the mufic for five voices, the melody in the Tenor, as ufual at that time), with fucceffive additions, went through feveral editions (1537 and 1551), and was followed in rapid fequence by numerous fimilar works, of which thofe publifhed at Wittenberg, Nürnberg, and Strasburg, are the moft important.[2] Every new book brought frefh additions, and by the end of the 16th century the number of hymns introduced into the Church was counted by hundreds. Among the tunes of this century and the early part of the next, the Editors would efpecially name V, XIII, XXVI, XXXIX, CVI, CXVII.

The firft metrical verfions of the Pfalms were publifhed in France and Switzerland about the fame period. Among the beft known, though not the earlieft in appearance, is that edited (with the mufic for four voices) by Goudimel (1565). This work was introduced into Germany by Dr Lobwaffer—the Pfalms metrically tranflated by him—in 1573, and its contents foon found their way as a whole or in parts into the Lutheran Church.

Several of Goudimel's Pfalm tunes are believed to be of fecular origin, and

[1] Choirmafter („Sängermeifter") of the Palatine of Saxony.

[2] We find Luther further contributing to hymn-books or fupplying them with a preface in that of Kluge, Wittenberg, 1543, and the one printed by Babft, Leipzig, 1545.

the fame fhould be ftated with regard to fome among the fineft tunes of the 16th century appropriated to the Lutheran fervice. It fpeaks well for the character of the fecular mufic of that period, that any of its melodies fhould have taken a place in the Church, and fhould have retained it undifputed to the prefent day. (See XI, XL, LXXXV.)

As another fource from which the Lutheran Church gladly drew, the Editors muft name the rich ftore of the early Moravian hymn-books; fpecimens from which, as well as tunes from Goudimel's edition of the Pfalms, will be found in this work.

About the fame time Lutheran hymn-books were introduced into Scandinavia, where, efpecially in Sweden, the hymns and tunes of Germany, with numerous additions of home growth, have remained up to the prefent time the ftock of the national hymn-book. Courland, Livonia, and Finland alfo received thefe facred ftrains into their fervice, and ftill retain them, and it fhould be mentioned here that a Lutheran hymn-book was printed and publifhed in the Icelandic language at Skalholt in Iceland, in the year 1594, of which a fixth edition appeared in 1691.[1]

Towards the middle of the following century (the 17th) Mufic enters into a new phafe. Until then its fole purpofe was to ferve the Church, through the medium of the human voice and the organ. But now inftrumental mufic, though at firft fubordinate, begins to make its appearance. Secular Cantatas, forerunners of the Opera, are produced on feftive occafions at the courts, particularly of Italy; and German muficians, like thofe of other countries, who had gone to Italy for ftudy or other purpofes, on their return fpread the influence which they had themfelves received.

In Proteftant Germany, Church mufic gradually became lefs an object of ambition to compofers; fewer tunes, and moft of them inferior in quality and vigour to thofe of the firft century after the Reformation, fprung up; nor did the nation at large any longer fet its feal upon them by adopting or rejecting them, as before. In the hymn-books of the latter part of the 17th and beginning of the 18th century we alfo find fome of the beft old tunes omitted, others deprived of the triple time ($\frac{3}{4}$) peculiar to them, others again without their diftinct rhythm, all levelled to a general ftandard of lifelefs uniformity.

Before paffing on to the laft period which calls for notice in this place, the Editors would direct the attention of readers to the moft prominent tune-compofer of the 17th century, Johann Crüger (1598—1662), of whofe writing many fpecimens will be found in this work; alfo to the tunes compofed by Schein, H. Albert, and Schop, and laftly to the celebrated hymn and tune of G. Neumark,[2] „ Wer nur ben lieben Gott läßt walten" (No. 134).

In the beginning of the 18th century, Freylinghaufen of Halle publifhed a hymn-book which foon became widely circulated. Further reference being made to it in another place, few words refpecting it will fuffice here. Among the numerous tunes publifhed for the firft time in that work, and of which the individual authors are not known, fome are very fine, though differing in character from thofe of an earlier date.

[1] Winterfeld, „ Zur Gefchichte heiliger Tonkunft." Vol. II.

[2] The tune became fo popular, that within 100 years after its appearance no lefs than 400 hymns had been written to be fung to it.

With the exception of one or two tunes moft probably compofed by Bach, one by Kühnau, one by Layriz[1] of a ftill more recent date, and fome few others, which need not be fpecified, Freylinghaufen's work in its feveral enlarged editions is the lateft fource from which materials for the " Chorale Book for England " have been drawn; nor could it be otherwife, as from that time facred tunes of real worth rarely make their appearance; and with the diminifhed intereft which Religion commanded in Germany towards the clofe of the 18th century, the diftinctive outward feature of its Church, the

[1] Kühnau and Layriz have both compiled very good Chorale books.

hymn-book, alfo decays. The old ftandard hymns are improved, as it is termed, by recafting them; the tunes difappear from the hymn-books and are collected feparately for the ufe of the organift, and, the control of the congregation having thus ceafed, it is with the organift and the precentor alone that the refponfibility for their correct performance refts in future.[a] If we further remember

[a] One of the immediate confequences was the predominance of the organ in the fervice at the expenfe of the finging of the congregation. This led eventually to a practice in every refpect to be deprecated, and which we ftill find all over Germany, that of introducing between every line of the hymn an Interlude performed by the organift.

the many Principalities of which Germany is made up, each with fovereign authority in Church as well as State, and each poffeffing its own diftinct hymn-book, we can hardly wonder at the unfettled and unfatisfactory ftate into which the congregational finging of Germany fell.

Of late years however Chriftian men interefted in the fervices of the Church have raifed their voices, trying to revive the intereft of the Proteftant part of the German nation in their congregational mufic, and urging a complete revifion of the exifting hymn-books. Recent publications, the refult of thefe efforts, clearly fhow, that owing to the defire to fee thefe tunes re-introduced with their exact rhythm and harmony as originally compofed, too little allowance is made either for the progrefs of mufic or for the mufical feelings prevalent in our own time. Much however had to be remedied, and thefe praifeworthy endeavours have not only already borne fruit, but will doubtlefs continue to do fo.

In this fketch, fome brief mention of John Sebaftian Bach, the great mafter, whofe name, in the minds of all interefted in the fubject, is fo clofely affociated with the Chorales of Germany, muft neceffarily find a place.

While during the 17th century the ftrictly congregational Church mufic declined, the facred Cantata (fubfequently expanding into the Oratorio) arofe; not only did the folemn feftival of the Paffion offer the opportunity for cultivating it, as we find from Bach's "Paffionsmufik," the text of which, with flight modifications, was fet to mufic by his predeceffors and contemporaries, Keyfer, Matthefon, and Handel; but the other feftivals alfo recommended themfelves to Bach for the exercife of his great powers, and Cantatas of his compofition exift for nearly every Sunday in the year, many of which in all probability were performed during or after the evening fervice, from the Organ gallery of St Thomas's, Leipzic, by an orcheftra and choir under his direction.

Bach, fully alive to the beauty of the tunes and hymns of his country, adopted the practice, in which he was followed by his fucceffors, Mendelffohn and others, of introducing Chorales into all his numerous facred works, either to their own words or to new ones fuiting better the fubject of the Cantata, thereby doubtlefs bringing it more readily home to the appreciation of the congregation, well acquainted with the old familiar tunes.

How Bach harmonized thefe Chorales is well known, and need not be dwelt upon here, but his introduction of them in the manner defcribed has much contributed to the confufion of the titles of hymns, which has continued to the prefent time.

After J. S. Bach's death, his fon, Ph. E. Bach, undertook to extract the Chorales from his father's work, and to publifh them in a feparate collection. One hundred of thefe, edited by him, appeared in 1765. A fecond volume containing another hundred was publifhed in 1769 (though not with Ph. E. Bach's name as editor). Then followed in 1784 an edition compiled by Kirnberger, and fubfequently feveral others, all with the title, "Joh. Seb. Bach's Vierftimmige Choralgefänge."

They are well known, and the impreffion generally prevails that Bach is the author of the tunes, which is not furprifing, confidering the manner in which thefe compilations, with the fingle exception of the moft recent one by Erck, have been publifhed. After what has been ftated, this erroneous belief requires no further refutation, but it fhould be mentioned, that a few tunes, probably juftly afcribed to Bach, and contained in the " Choralgefänge," have been inferted by the Editors in the " Chorale Book."

Under the circumftances the correctnefs of the verfion of the tunes given in the following work muft not be judged of from a comparifon with thofe in Bach's works, or elfewhere in the compofitions of Mendelffohn and other great mafters. Thefe mafters could handle fuch Chorales freely for their own pur- pofes, but the Editors were bound to go back to the fources, from which their melodies might be obtained not only moft accurately, but alfo in the form moft fuitable for their object. They have therefore drawn either from the works in which the tunes originally appeared, or from thofe of Winterfeld, Tucher, and others of high ftanding into which they had been literally copied.

In determining the form in which to admit thefe tunes, the Editors were naturally befet with doubts, in confequence of the unfettled ftate of hymnology in Germany at the prefent moment. For while one party there in- fifts on retaining the tunes even more than the hymns in the ftate of lifelefs uniformity into which they have fallen, the other calls for their complete reftitution to .their original form.

Without going into detail, the Editors wifh to ftate that they deemed it beft to felect the middle path. They have treated the tunes *individually*, not *collectively;* thofe written in ¾ time (as, for example, V, LX, LXII, LXXXII, CXV, etc.) they have feen no right or reafon to change, and in every cafe they have endeavoured to give the tune as nearly as poffible ac- cording to its original verfion, and in a fhape which might at the fame time juftify the hope of its being accepted by the Englifh public. This however refers only to the *rhythmical* flow of the tune, not to the *melody* itfelf, which in no inftance has been touched by the Editors, but is given according to the beft-authenticated verfions.[1]

A few words have ftill to be faid refpecting the harmonization of the tunes in this work. The Editors have in many cafes retained the harmonies of the authors of the tunes, and in general have ftriven to preferve as far as poffible the character belonging to the period of their compofition; thus the melodies of the 16th and 18th century called for different ftyles of harmony, clearly indicated by their different flow in refpect of diftances. In all cafes, however, the Editors have endeavoured to combine folemnity with fimplicity, and to give

---

[1] A few fpecimens of tunes are given in the Appendix to illuftrate the form in which thofe of an early date were originally publifhed, and in which it is defired in fome quarters to re- introduce them. They will be found divided not into the mufical bars of modern mufic, but according to the length of the lines of the poetry, which would appear the only way to render legibly tunes containing recurring mixtures of common and triple time, in Germany now called „ Rhytmifcher Wechfel."

harmonies, which, though offering no difficulty in execution, fhould yet ap- proach the ftrength and purity peculiar to the beft Church mufic of all times.

The Editors cannot bring this Preface to a clofe without pointing to the names of the meritorious inquirers into the interefting fubject of Hymnology, who have of late years appeared in Germany, and without whofe writings they believe no fatisfactory hymn-book of modern times could be compiled; they mean G. von Tucher, P. Wackernagel, Layriz, and others, but par- ticularly C. von Winterfeld, who, in his remarkable work on the „ Evan= gelifche Kirchengefang,"* and other fmaller writings, has vindicated the real importance of this facred branch of mufic, and fhown its hiftorical bafis and de- velopment in a manner at once to raife it in general eftimation and to guide all who follow him in this difficult path. To his memory the grateful thanks of the Editors are due, and from his works, as well as from thofe previoufly

---

* Der evangelifche Kirchengefang, und fein Verhältniß zur Kunft des Tonfatzes. Dargeftellt von Carl v. Winterfelb. 3 vols. Leipzig, 1843—47.

named, they have drawn freely—as was their duty—and as feemed beſt for this work.

That the "Chorale Book for England" may be received into the new fphere for which it is intended, and that its facred ftrains may contribute to the comfort of the troubled foul, the fanctification of home, and the glory of God's name in His Church on earth, is the earneft prayer of thofe who compiled it.

London, November, 1862.

TABLE OF CONTENTS.

INTRODUCTION.

I. THE CHURCH.

I. HOLY SEASONS.

2. SERVICES.

II. THE CHRISTIAN LIFE.

III. SPECIAL OCCASIONS.

IV. THE CLOSE.

PRAISE AND THANKSGIVING.

(v.—„Allein Gott in der Höh sei Ehr.")

I.

Original Tune.

All glo-ry be to God on High,
To us no harm shall now come nigh,

Who hath our race be-friend-ed!
The feud at last is end-ed;

God show-eth His good-will toward men,

And peace shall dwell on earth a-gain;

Oh thank Him for His good-ness.

2

We praise, we worship Thee, we trust,
  And give Thee thanks for ever,
O Father, that Thy rule is just
  And wise, and changes never:
Thy boundless power o'er all things reigns,
Done is whate'er Thy will ordains;
    Well for us that Thou rulest!

3

O Jesu Christ, our God and Lord,
  Son of Thy heavenly Father,
O Thou who hast our peace restored
  And the lost sheep dost gather,
Thou Lamb of God, to Thee on high
From out our depths we sinners cry,
    Have mercy on us, Jesus!

4

O Holy Ghost, Thou precious Gift,
  Thou Comforter unfailing,
O'er Satan's snares our souls uplift,
  And let Thy power availing
Avert our woes and calm our dread,
For us the Saviour's blood was shed,
    We trust in Thee to save us!

(xxix.—„Es ist das Heil uns kommen her.")

2.

All praise and thanks to God most High, The Fa-ther, whose is per-fect love;
The God who do-eth won-drous-ly, The God who from His Throne a-bove

My ſoul with rich-eſt ſo-lace fills,

The God who ev'-ry ſor-row ſtills;

(Index of Tunes, xc.)   3.

Tune.—" Ye ſervants of the Lord, who ſtand."

Lo, heaven and earth, and ſea and air,

Their Mak-er's glo-ry all de-clare;

And thou, my ſoul, a-wake and ſing,

To Him Thy praiſ-es al-ſo bring.

Give glo-ry now to Him, our God!

Through Him the glorious Source of Day
Drives all the clouds of night away;
The pomp of ſtars, the moon's ſoft light,
Praiſe Him through all the ſilent night.

  Behold, how He hath everywhere
  Made earth ſo wondrous rich and fair;
  The foreſt dark, the fruitful land,
  All living things do ſhow His hand.

Behold, how through the boundleſs ſky
The happy birds all ſwiftly fly;
And fire and wind and ſtorm are ſtill
The ready ſervants of His will.

  Behold the waters' ceaſeleſs flow,
  For ever circling to and fro;
  The mighty ſea, the bubbling well,
  Alike their Maker's glory tell.

My God, how wondrouſly doſt Thou
Unfold Thyſelf to us e'en now!
O grave it deeply on my heart
What I am, Lord, and what Thou art!

2

The hoſt of heaven thy praiſes tell,
  All powers and thrones bow down to Thee,
And all who in Thy ſhadow dwell,
  Alike in earth and air and ſea,
Declare and laud their Maker's might,
Whoſe wiſdom orders all things right:
  Give glory then to Him, our God!

3

And for the creatures He hath made,
  Our God will ceaſeleſsly provide,
His grace will be their conſtant aid,
  And guard them round on every ſide;
His kingdom ye may ſurely truſt,
There all is equal, all is juſt;
  Give glory then to Him, our God!

4

I ſought Him in my hour of need,
  I cried,—Lord God, now hear my prayer!
For death He gave me life indeed,
  And hope and comfort for deſpair;
For this my thanks ſhall endleſs be,
O thank Him, thank Him too with me;
  Give glory now to Him, our God!

5

The Lord is never far away,
  Is never fundered from His flock,
He is their refuge and their ftay,
  He is their peace, their truft, their rock ;
And with a mother's watchful love
He guides them wherefoe'er they rove :
  Give glory then to Him, our God !

6

Ah yes ! till life hath reached its bound,
  My faithful God, I'll worfhip Thee !
The chorus of Thy praife fhall found
  From henceforth over land and fea.
Oh foul and body, now rejoice,
My heart, fend forth a gladfome voice ;
  Give glory now to Him, our God !

7

All ye who name Chrift's holy name,
  Give all the glory to our God !
Ye who the Father's power proclaim,
  Give all the glory to our God !
All idols under foot be trod,
The Lord is God, the Lord is God !
  Give glory evermore to Him !

(LI.)—"In natali Domini."

4.

Com - eth fun - fhine af - ter rain, Af - ter mourn - ing
joy a - gain, Af - ter hea - vy bit - ter grief
Dawn - eth fure - ly fweet re - lief! And my
foul, who from her height Sank to realms of
woe and night, Wing - eth now to heav'n her flight.

4

Though to-day may not fulfil
All thy hopes, have patience ftill,
For perchance to-morrow's fun
Sees thy happier days begun ;
  As God willeth march the hours,
  Bringing joy at laft in fhowers,
  When whate'er we afk'd is ours.

5

Now as long as here I roam,
On this earth have houfe and home,
Shall this wondrous gleam from Thee
Shine through all my memory.
  To my God I yet will cling,
  All my life the praifes fing
  That from thankful hearts outfpring.

6

Every forrow, every fmart,
That the Eternal Father's heart
Hath appointed me of yore,
Or hath yet for me in ftore,
  As my life flows on, I'll take
  Calmly, gladly for His fake,
  No more faithlefs murmurs make.

7

I will meet diftrefs and pain,
I will greet e'en Death's dark reign,
I will lay me in the grave,
With a heart ftill glad and brave ;
  Whom the Strongeft doth defend,
  Whom the Higheft counts His friend,
  Cannot perifh in the end.

2

Bitter anguifh have I borne,
Keen regret my heart hath torn,
Sorrow dimm'd my weeping eyes,
Satan blinded me with lies ;
  Yet at laft am I fet free,
  Help, protection, love, to me
  Once more true companions be.

3

None was ever left a prey,
None was ever turn'd away,
Who had given himfelf to God,
And on Him had caft his load.
  Who in God his hope hath placed
  Shall not life in pain outwafte,
  Fulleft joy he yet fhall tafte.

(LXXVIII.—„O baß ich taufenb Zungen hätt'.")

5.

Original Tune.

Oh would, my God, that I could praife Thee
How many a fong my lips fhould raife Thee,

With thou-fand tongues, by day and night!
Who or-der'ft all things here a-right;

My thank-ful heart would ev-er be

Tell-ing what God hath done for me.

(Index of Tunes, LXXVIII.)

6.

Tune.—"Oh would, my God, that I could praife Thee."

I praife Thee, O my God and Fa-ther,
The blef-ings that we dai-ly ga-ther,

For all I am and all I have,
Ev'n from our cra-dle to our grave;

For Thy rich grace hath scat-ter'd here What-e'er we need to help and cheer.

2

O all ye powers that He implanted,
　Arife, keep filence thus no more,
Put forth the ftrength that He hath granted,
　Your nobleft work is to adore ;
O foul and body, make ye meet
With heartfelt praife your Lord to greet.

3

　Ye foreft leaves fo green and tender,
　　That dance for joy in fummer air ;
　Ye meadow graffes bright and flender,
　　Ye flowers fo wondrous fweet and fair ;
　Ye live to fhow His praife alone,
　Help me to make His glory known.

4

O all things that have breath and motion,
　That throng with life earth, fea, and fky,
Now join me in my heart's devotion,
　Help me to raife His praifes high,
My utmoft powers can ne'er aright
Declare the wonders of His might.

5

　But I will tell, while I am living,
　　His goodnefs forth with every breath,
　And greet each morning with thanksgiving,
　　Until my heart is ftill in death,
　Nay, when at laft my lips grow cold,
　His praife fhall in my fighs be told.

6

O Father, deign Thou, I befeech Thee,
　To liften to my earthly lays ;
A nobler ftrain in heaven fhall reach Thee,
　When I with angels hymn Thy praife,
And learn amid their choirs to fing
Loud hallelujahs to my King.

2

I praife Thee, Saviour, whofe compaffion
　Hath brought Thee down to fuccour me ;
Thy pitying heart fought my falvation,
　Though keeneft woes were heaped on Thee,
Wrought me from bondage full releafe,
Made me Thine own, and gave me peace.

3

Thee too I praife, O Holy Spirit,
　By whofe deep teachings I am made
A heavenly kingdom to inherit,
　Who art my Comforter, my aid ;
Whate'er of good by me is done
Is of Thy grace and light alone.

4

And as my life is onward gliding,

With each fresh scene anew I mark

How Thou art holding me and guiding,

Where all seems troubled, strange, and dark;

When cares oppress and hopes depart,

Thy light hath never failed my heart.

5

Shall I not then be filled with gladness,

Shall I not praise Thee evermore?

And triumph o'er all fears and sadness,

E'en when my cup of woe runs o'er?

Though heaven and earth may pass away,

I know Thy word stands fast for aye.

(LXXIV.—„Nun lob' mein' Seel' den Herren.")

7.

Original Tune.

My soul, now praise thy Mak - er! Let all with-in me bless His name,
Who mak-eth thee par - tak - er Of mer-cies more than thou dar'st claim!

For - get Him not, whose meek - ness Still bears with all thy sin,

Who heal-eth all thy weak - ness, Re-news thy life with - in,

Whose grace and care are end - less, And sav'd thee thro' the past;

Who leaves no suff' - rer friend - less, But rights the wrong'd at last!

2

He shows to man His treasure

Of judgment, truth, and righteousness,

His love beyond our measure,

His yearning pity o'er distress;

Nor treats us as we merit,

But lays His anger by,

The humble contrite spirit

Finds His compassions nigh;

And high as heaven above us,

As break from close of day,

So far, since He doth love us,

He puts our sins away.

3

For as a tender father

Hath pity on his children here,

He in His arms will gather

All who are His in childlike fear;

He knows how frail our powers,

Who but from dust are made,

We flourish as the flowers,

And even so we fade,

A storm-wind o'er them passes,

And all their bloom is o'er,—

We wither like the grasses,

Our place knows us no more.

4

His grace alone endureth,

And children's children yet shall prove

How God with strength assureth

The hearts of all that seek His love.

In heaven is fixed His dwelling,

His rule is over all,

Angels in might excelling,

Bright hosts, before Him fall!

Praise Him who ever reigneth,

All ye who hear His word;

Nor our poor hymns disdaineth,—

My soul, O praise the Lord!

(LXVI.—„Meine Hoffnung stehet feste.")

8.

Original Tune.

All my hope is ground - ed sure - ly
I can trust His aid se - cure - ly,

On the ev-er-liv-ing God,
He shall be my high-est Good;
For this Rock fears no shock,
And our trust will nev-er mock.

2

Tell me, if no dread e'er seizes
  You, who lean on some frail man?
Can you build on waves and breezes?
  Dare you trust your wisest plan?
Soon 'tis past, cannot last,
Nought that earth has standeth fast.

3

But His goodness still shall flourish
  Evermore, nought changes here;
Man and beast His hand doth nourish
  Day by day through all the year;
Morn and eve, doth He give
All they need to all that live.

4

Are we not by gifts surrounded
  More than we dare ask of good?
For His mercies are unbounded,
  Flowing like a mighty flood;
Earth and air to us bear
Tokens of His loving care.

5

Let not then His gifts upbraid us,
  Who His very Son hath given;
Thank, O thank Him who hath made us
  From the dust, yet heirs of heaven.
God is our shield and tower,
Great in wisdom, love, and power.

I. THE CHURCH.

I. HOLY SEASONS.

2. SERVICES.

(LXII.—„Lobe den Herren, den mächtigen König der Ehren.")

9.

Praise to the Lord! the Al-migh-ty,
O. my soul, praise Him, for He is the thy

King of cre-a-tion! All ye who
health and sal-va-tion!

hear, Now to His tem-ple draw near,

Join me in glad a-do-ra-tion!

2

Praise to the Lord! who o'er all things so wondrously reigneth,
Shelters thee under His wings, yea so gently suftaineth;
Haft thou not feen
How thy defires have been
Granted in what He ordaineth?

3

Praise to the Lord! who doth profper thy work and defend thee,
Surely His goodnefs and mercy here daily attend thee;
Ponder anew
What the Almighty can do,
If with His love He befriend thee!

4

Praise to the Lord! Oh let all that is in me adore Him!
All that hath life and breath, come now with praifes before Him!
Let the Amen
Sound from His people again,
Gladly for aye we adore Him!

(LX.—„Laffet uns den Herren preifen.")

10.

Shall I not fing praife to Thee, Shall I not give thanks, O Lord?
Since for us in all I fee How Thou keep-eft watch and ward; How the tru-eft, ten-d'reft love

Ev-er fills Thy heart, my God, Help-ing, cheer-ing, on their road All who in Thy fer-vice move.

All things elfe have but their day, God's love on-ly lafts for aye.

2

As the eagle o'er her neft
  Spreads her fheltering wings abroad,
So from all that would moleft
  Doth Thine arm defend me, Lord ;
From my youth up e'en till now
  Of the being Thou didft give,
  And the earthly life I live,
Faithful Guardian ftill wert Thou.
All things elfe have but their day,
God's love only lafts for aye.

3

When I fleep my Guardian wakes,
  And revives my wearied mind ;
Every morning on me breaks
  With fome mark of love moft kind ;
Had my God not ftood my Friend,
  Had His countenance not been
  Here my guide, I had not feen
Many a trial reach its end.
All things elfe have but their day,
God's love only lafts for aye.

4

As a father ne'er withdraws
  From a child his all of love,
Though it often break his laws,
  Though it carelefs, wilful, prove :
Even fo my loving Lord
  Doth my faults with pity fee ;
  With His rod He chaftens me,
Not avenging with His fword.
All things elfe have but their day,
God's love only lafts for aye.

5

When His ftrokes upon me lignt,
  Bitterly I feel their fmart,
Yet are they, if feen aright,
  Tokens that my Father's heart
Yearns to bring me back again
  Through thefe croffes to His fold,
  From the world that fain would hol
Soul and body in its chain.
All things elfe have but their day,
God's love only lafts for aye.

6

All my life I ftill have found,
  And I will forget it never,
Every forrow hath its bound,
  And no crofs endures for ever.
After all the winter's fnows
  Comes fweet fummer back again ;
Patient fouls ne'er wait in vain,
Joy is given for all their woes.
All things elfe have but their day,
God's love only lafts for aye.

7

Since then neither change nor end
  In Thy love can e'er have place,
Father ! I befeech Thee fend
  Unto me Thy loving grace.
Help Thy feeble child, and give
  Strength to ferve Thee day and night,
  Loving Thee with all my might,
While on earth I yet muft live ;
So fhall I, when Time is o'er,
Praife and love Thee evermore.

PUBLIC WORSHIP.

(Lxx.—„Nun banket alle Gott.")

11.

Original Tune.

Now thank we all our God, With heart and hands and voi-ces,
Who won-drous things hath done, In whom His world re-joi-ces ;

Who from our mo-ther's arms Hath blefs'd us on our way

With count-lefs gifts of love, And ftill is ours to-day.

2

Oh may this bounteous God
Through all our life be near us,
With ever joyful hearts
And blefled peace to cheer us ;
And keep us in His grace,
  And guide us when perplex'd,
  And free us from all ills
In this world and the next.

3

All praife and thanks to God
The Father now be given,
  The Son, and Him who reigns
With them in higheft heaven,
The One eternal God,
  Whom earth and heaven adore,
For thus it was, is now,
  And fhall be evermore !

(LXI.—„Liebſter Jeſu, wir ſind hier.")

12.
Original Tune.

Bleſſ - ed Je - ſus, at Thy word We are ga - ther'd
Let our hearts and ſouls be ſtirr'd Now to ſeek and

all to hear Thee; By Thy teach - ings ſweet and
love and fear Thee;

ho - ly Drawn from earth to love Thee ſole - ly.

2

All our knowledge, ſenſe, and ſight
  Lie in deepeſt darkneſs ſhrouded,
Till Thy Spirit breaks our night
  With the beams of truth unclouded;
Thou alone to God canſt win us,
Thou muſt work all good within us.

3

Glorious Lord, Thyſelf impart!
  Light of light from God proceeding,
Open Thou our ears and heart,
  Help us by Thy Spirit's pleading,
Hear the cry Thy people raiſes,
Hear, and bleſs our prayers and praiſes!

(XXXVII.—„Herr Jeſu Chriſt Dich zu uns wend.")

13.
Original Tune.

Lord Je - ſus Chriſt, be pre - ſent now! And let Thy

Ho - ly Spi - rit bow All hearts in love and fear to-

day, To hear the truth and keep Thy way.

2

Open our lips to ſing Thy praiſe,
Our hearts in true devotion raiſe,
Strengthen our faith, increaſe our light,
That we may know Thy name aright:

3

Until we join the hoſt that cry
" Holy, Holy art Thou moſt High,"
And 'mid the light of that bleſt place
Shall gaze upon Thee face to face.

4

Glory to God, the Father, Son,
And Holy Spirit, Three in One!
To Thee, O bleſſed Trinity,
Be praiſe throughout eternity!

(Index of Tunes, LXXVI.)

14.

Tune.—" Now that the fun doth fhine no more."

A - bide a - mong us with Thy grace, Lord Je - fus, ev - er - more,

Nor let us e'er to fin give place, Nor grieve Him we a - dore.

2

Abide among us with Thy word,
Redeemer whom we love,
Thy help and mercy here afford,
And life with Thee above.

3

Abide among us with Thy ray,
O Light that l'ghten'ft all,
And let Thy truth preferve our way,
Nor fuffer us to fall.

4

Abide with us to blefs us ftill,
O bounteous Lord of peace ;
With grace and power our fouls fulfill,
Our faith and love increafe.

5

Abide among us as our fhield,
O Captain of Thy hoft ;
That to the world we may not yield,
Nor e'er forfake our poft.

6

Abide with us in faithful love,
Our God and Saviour be,
Thy help at need, Oh let us prove,
And keep us true to Thee.

(XCVIII.—„ Unſer Herrſcher, Unſer König.")

15.

O - pen now Thy gates of beau - ty, Zi - on,
Where my foul in joy - ful du - ty Waits for

let me en - ter there, Oh, how blefs - ed
Him who an - fwers pray'r ;

is this place, Fill'd with fo - lace, light, and grace.

2 Yes, my God, I come before Thee,
   Come Thou alfo down to me ;
   Where we find Thee and adore Thee
   There a heaven on earth muft be.
To my heart oh enter Thou,
Let it be Thy temple now.

3 Here Thy praife is gladly chanted,
   Here Thy feed is duly fown,
   Let my foul where it is planted,
   Bring forth precious fheaves alone,
So that all I hear may be
Fruitful unto life in me.

4 Thou my faith increafe and quicken,
   Let me keep Thy gift divine
   Howfoe'er temptations thicken ;
   May Thy word ftill o'er me fhine,
As my pole-ftar through my life,
As my comfort in my ftrife.

5 Speak, O God, and I will hear Thee,
   Let Thy will be done indeed ;
   May I undifturbed draw near Thee
   While Thou doft Thy people feed ;
Here of Life the Fountain flows,
Here is balm for all our woes.

16.

Tune.—" O bleſt the houſe, whate'er befall."

Thee, Fount of bleſſ - ing, we a - dore! Lo! we un-
lock our lips once more Be - fore Thy deep of
ho - li - neſs, Oh deign to hear us now and bleſs.

2
The Lord, the Maker, with us dwell,
In ſoul and body ſhield us well,
And guard us with His ſleepleſs might
From every ill by day and night!

3
The Lord, the Saviour, Light Divine,
Now cauſe His face on us to ſhine,
That ſeeing Him, with perfect faith
We truſt His love for life and death!

4
The Lord, the Comforter, be near,
Imprint His image deeply here,
From bonds of ſin and dread releaſe,
And give us His unchanging peace!

5
O Triune God! Thou vaſt abyſs!
Thou ever-flowing Fount of bliſs,
Flow through us, heart and ſoul and will
With endleſs praiſe and bleſſing fill!

(xxi.—„Der Tag bricht an und zeiget ſich.")

17.

Once more the day - light ſhines a - broad, O
bre - thren, let us praiſe the Lord, Whoſe grace and mer - cy
thus have kept The night - ly watch while we have ſlept.

2 To Him let us together pray
With all our heart and ſoul to-day,
That He would keep us in His love,
And all our guilt and ſin remove.

3 Eternal God! Almighty Friend,
Whoſe deep compaſſions have no end,
Whoſe never-failing ſtrength and might
Have kept us ſafely through the night:

4 Now ſend us from Thy heavenly throne
Thy grace and help through Chriſt Thy Son,
That with Thy ſtrength our hearts may glow,
And fear nor man nor ghoſtly foe.

5 Lord God! oh, hear us, we implore!
Be Thou our Guardian evermore,
Our mighty Champion and our Shield
That goeth with us to the field.

6 We offer up ourſelves to Thee,
That heart and word and deed may be
In all things guided by Thy mind,
And in Thine eyes acceptance find.

7 Thus, Lord, we bring, through Chriſt Thy Son,
Our morning offering to Thy throne;
Now be Thy precious gift outpour'd,
And help us for Thine honour, Lord!

(1.—„Ach bleib' bei uns Herr Jeſu Chriſt.")

18.

Original Tune.

Lord Je - ſu Chriſt, with us a - bide, For round us

falls the ev'-ning tide; Nor let Thy Word,

our glo-rious light, For us be ev-er veil'd .. in night.

2

In thefe dark days that yet remain,
May we Thy Sacraments maintain,
And keep Thy Word ftill free and pure,
And fteadfaft in the faith endure.

(LXVII.—„Meinen Jefum laſs ich nicht.")

19.

Light of light, en-light-en me
Sun of grace, the fha-dows flee,

Now a-new the day is dawn-ing;
Bright-en Thou my Sab-bath morn-ing,

With Thy joy-ous fun-fhine bleft

Hap-py is my day of reft!

2

Fount of all our joy and peace,
To Thy living waters lead me,
Thou from earth my foul releafe
And with grace and mercy feed me;
Blefs Thy word that it may prove
Rich in fruits that Thou doft love.

3

Kindle Thou the facrifice
That upon my lips is lying;
Clear the fhadows from mine eyes,
That, from every error flying,
No ftrange fire may in me glow
That Thine altar doth not know.

4

Let me with my heart to-day,
Holy, Holy, Holy, finging,
Rapt awhile from earth away,
All my foul to Thee upfpringing,
Have a foretafte inly given
How they worfhip Thee in Heaven.

5

Reft in me and I in Thee,
Build a Paradife within me;
Oh reveal Thyfelf to me,
Bleffed Love, who diedft to win me;
Fed from Thine exhauftlefs urn,
Pure and bright my lamp fhall burn.

6

Hence all care, all vanity,
For the day to God is holy;
Come, Thou glorious Majefty,
Deign to fill this temple lowly;
Nought to-day my foul fhall move,
Simply refting in Thy love.

ADVENT.

20.

Tune.—" From heaven above to earth I come."

Ye heav'ns, oh hafte your dews to fhed, Ye clouds, rain

glad - nefs on our head, Thou earth, be - hold the

time of grace, And blof - fom forth in right - eouf - nefs!

2
O living Sun, with joy break forth,
And pierce the gloomy clefts of earth ;
Behold, the mountains melt away
Like wax beneath Thine ardent ray !

3
O Life-dew of the Churches, come,
And bid this arid defert bloom !
The forrows of Thy people fee,
And take our human flefh on Thee.

4
Refrefh the parch'd and drooping mind,
The broken limb in mercy bind,
Us finners from our guilt releafe,
And fill us with Thy heavenly peace.

5
O wonder ! night no more is night !
Comes then at laft the long'd-for light ?
Ah yes, Thou fhineft, O true Sun,
In whom are God and man made one !

21.

Original Tune.

Ah ! Lord, how fhall I meet Thee, How wel-come Thee a - right ?
All na - tions long to greet Thee, My hope, my fole de - light !

Brigh - ten the lamp that burn - eth But dim - ly in my breaft,

And teach my foul, that yearn - eth To hon - our fuch high gueft.

4
O ye fad hearts that ficken
 With hope deferred, and fee
The gloom around you thicken,
 The joys ye hoped for flee,—
Defpair not, He is near you,
 Yea, at the very door,
Who beft can help and cheer you,
 He will not linger more.

5
Nor fin fhall make you fearful,
 Afhamed to fee His face,
The contrite heart and tearful
 He covers with His grace ;
He comes to heal the fpirit
 That mourneth fin-oppreffed,.
And raife us to inherit
 With Him our proper reft.

6
He comes to judge the nations,
 A terror to His foes,
A light of confolations
 And bleffed hope to thofe
Who love the Lord's appearing :
 O glorious Sun, now come,
Send forth Thy beams of cheering
 And guide us fafely home !

2
Thy Zion ftrews before Thee
 Her faireft buds and palms,
And I too will adore Thee
 With fweeteft fongs and pfalms ;
My foul breaks forth in flowers
 Rejoicing in Thy fame,
And fummons all her powers
 To honour Jefus' name.

3
Nought, nought, dear Lord, could move Thee
 To leave Thy rightful place
Save love, for which I love Thee ;
 A love that could embrace
A world where forrow dwelleth,
 Which fin and fuffering fill,
More than the tongue e'er telleth ;—
 Yet Thou couldft love it ftill !

22.

Tune.—" My inmoſt heart now raiſes."

A - riſe, the king - dom is at hand, The
A - riſe with joy, ye faith - ful band, To

King is draw - ing nigh; Ye Chriſ - tians, haſ - ten forth,
greet the Lord moſt High!

With ho - ly ar - dours greet your King, And glad Ho -

ſan - nas to Him ſing, Nought elſe your love is worth.

(LVI.—„Komm, Heiden Heiland! Löſegeſt.")

23.

Original Tune.

Re - deem - er of the na - tions, come! Ran - ſom of

earth, here make Thy home! Bright Sun, oh dart Thy flame to

earth, For ſo ſhall God in Chriſt have birth!

2

Look up, ye drooping hearts, to-day!
    The King is very near,
Oh caſt your griefs and fears away,
    For lo! your Help is here;
    And comfort rich and ſweet
In many a place for us is ſtored,
Where in His ſacraments and word
    Our Saviour we can meet.

3

Look up, ye ſouls weigh'd down with care!
    The Sovereign is not far;
Look up, faint hearts, from your deſpair,
    Behold the Morning Star!
    The Lord is with us now,
Who ſhall the ſinking ſpirit feed
With ſtrength and comfort at its need,
    To whom e'en Death ſhall bow.

4

Hope, O ye broken hearts, at laſt!
    The King comes on in might,
He loved us in the ages paſt
    When we ſat wrapp'd in night;
    Now are our ſorrows o'er,
And fear and wrath to joy give place,
Since God hath made us in His grace
    His children evermore.

5

O rich the gifts Thou bringeſt us,
    Thyſelf made poor and weak;
O love beyond compare that thus
    Can foes and ſinners ſeek!
    For this to Thee alone
We raiſe on high a gladſome voice,
And evermore with thanks rejoice
    Before Thy glorious throne.

2

Thou comeſt from Thy kingly throne,
O Son of God, the Virgin's Son!
Thou Hero of a twofold race,
Doſt walk in might earth's darkeſt place.

3

Thou ſtoopeſt once to ſuffer here,
And riſeſt o'er the ſtarry ſphere;
Hell's gates at thy deſcent were riven,
Thy aſcent is to higheſt Heaven.

4

One with the Father! Prince of might!
O'er nature's realm aſſert Thy right,
Our ſickly bodies pine to know
Thy heavenly ſtrength, Thy living glow.

5

How bright Thy lowly manger beams!
Down earth's dark vale its glory ſtreams,
The ſplendour of Thy natal night
Shines through all time in deathleſs light.

(XXXIII.—„Gott sei Dank durch alle Welt.")

24.

Original Tune.

Let the earth now praise the Lord, Who hath tru-ly kept His word,

And the sin-ner's help and Friend Now at last to us doth send.

(LXIV.—„Macht hoch die Thür, die Thor'macht weit.")

25.

Original Tune.

Lift up your heads, ye migh-ty gates, Be-hold the King of glo-ry waits;

The King of kings is draw-ing near, The Sa-viour of the world is here;

Life and sal-va-tion doth He bring, Wherefore re-joice and glad-ly sing:

We praise Thee, Fa-ther, now! Cre-a-tor, wise art Thou!

(XXXVIII.—„Herr nun laß in Friede.")

26.

Once He came in bless-ing, All our ills re-dress-ing, Came in like-ness low-ly,

2

What the fathers most desired,
What the prophets' heart inspired,
What they long'd for many a year,
Stands fulfill'd in glory here.

3

Abram's promised great reward,
Zion's Helper, Jacob's Lord,
Him of twofold race behold,
Truly come, as long foretold.

4

Welcome, O my Saviour, now!
Hail! my portion, Lord, art Thou!
Here too in my heart, I pray,
Oh prepare Thyself a way.

5

Enter, King of Glory, in!
Purify the wastes of sin
As Thou hast so often done;
It belongs to Thee alone.

6

As Thy coming was in peace,
Noiseless, full of gentleness,
Let the same mind dwell in me
That was ever found in Thee.

7

Bruise for me the serpent's head,
That, set free from doubt and dread,
I may cleave to Thee in faith,
Safely kept through life and death:

8

And when Thou dost come again
As a glorious King to reign,
I with joy may see Thy face,
Freely ransom'd by Thy grace.

2

The Lord is just, a Helper tried,
Mercy is ever at His side,
His kingly crown is holiness,
His sceptre, pity in distress,
The end of all our woe He brings;
Wherefore the earth is glad and sings:
   We praise Thee, Saviour, now,
   Mighty in deed art Thou!

3

Oh blest the land, the city blest,
Where Christ the Ruler is confest!
Oh happy hearts and happy homes
To whom this King in triumph comes!
The cloudless Sun of joy He is,
Who bringeth pure delight and bliss:
   O Comforter Divine,
   What boundless grace is Thine!

4

Fling wide the portals of your heart,
Make it a temple set apart
From earthly use for Heaven's employ,
Adorn'd with prayer and love and joy;
So shall your Sovereign enter in,
And new and nobler life begin:
   To Thee, O God, be praise,
   For word and deed and grace!

5

Redeemer, come! I open wide
My heart to Thee,—here, Lord, abide!
Let me Thy inner presence feel,
Thy grace and love in me reveal,
Thy Holy Spirit guide us on
Until our glorious goal is won!
   Eternal praise and fame
   We offer to Thy name.

Son of God most ho-ly, Bore the cross to save us, Hope and free-dom gave us.

2

Still He comes within us,
Still His voice would win us
From the sins that hurt us;
Would to Truth convert us
From our foolish errors,
Ere He comes in terrors.

3

Thus if thou hast known Him,
Not ashamed to own Him,
Nor dost love Him coldly,
But wilt trust Him boldly,
He will now receive thee,
Heal thee, and forgive thee.

4

But through many a trial,
Deepest self-denial,
Long and brave endurance,
Must thou win assurance
That His own He makes thee,
And no more forsakes thee.

5

He who thus endureth
Bright reward secureth;
Come then, O Lord Jesus,
From our sins release us.
Let us here confess Thee,
Till in heaven we bless Thee.

(Ch.—„Wach auf, Wach auf du sich're Welt.")

27.

Original Tune.

A - wake, thou care-less world, a - wake! That fi-nal Judg-ment day will sure-ly come; Know what the
What Heav'n hath fix'd no Time can shake, Time nev-er more shall sweep a - way thy doom.

Lord Him-self hath spo-ken Shall come at last and not de-lay: Though heav'n and earth shall pass a-way, His stead-fast Word can ne'er be bro-ken.

2 Awake! thou careless world, awake!
For none can tell how soon our God may please
   That suddenly that day should break,
No human wisdom fathoms depths like these:
      O flee earth's base delights and pride,
         For as the bird is in the snare,
         Or ever of its foe aware,
      So comes that day so long denied.

3 Yet He in love delayeth long
That awful day, and grants the sinner space
   To turn away from sin and wrong,
And mourning seek in time His love and grace.
      He holdeth back that best of days
         Until the righteous shall approve
         Their faith and hope, their constant love;
      So gentle us-ward are His ways!

4 And those found faithful then shall see
That glorious morning dawn in love and joy,
   Their Saviour comes to set them free,
Their Judge Himself shall all their bonds destroy;
      He the true Joshua then shall bring
         His people with a mighty hand
         Into their promised fatherland,
      Where songs of victory they shall sing.

5 Arise, and let us night and day
Watch for our Lord, and study o'er His word,
   And in the Spirit ever pray,
That we be ready when His call is heard;
      Arise, and let us haste to meet
         The Bridegroom standing at the door,
         That with the angels evermore
      We too may worship at His feet.

(XLVII.—„ Ich steh' in Angst, und Pein.")

28.

Original Tune.

A dread hath come on me, I know not where to flee, My pow'rs can nought a-vail me; My trem-bling limbs grow weak, My lips re-fuse to speak, My heart and fens-es fail me:

2

For thinking on that found
That once shall pierce the ground
  And make its flumb'rers tremble,—
" Arife ! the Day of Doom
Is come at laft,—is come !
  Before the Judge affemble ! "

3

Ah God ! no tempeft's fhock.
That cleaves the folid rock
  Could make my fpirit fhiver
As doth that awful tone ;
Were my heart fteel or ftone
  'T would hear that voice and quiver.

4

I eat, or wake, or fleep,
I talk, or fmile, or weep,
  Yet ftill that voice of thunder
Is founding through my heart,—
" Forget not what thou art,
  The doom thou lieft under ! "

5

For daily do I fee
How many deaths there be,
  How fwiftly all things wither ;
How ficknefs fills the grave,
Or fire, or fword, or wave
  Is fweeping thoufands thither.

6

My turn will foon be here,
The end is drawing near,
  I hear its warning plainly ;
Death knocketh at my door
And tells me all is o'er,
  And I would fly him vainly.

7

Ah ! who in this my ftrait
Will be mine Advocate ?
  Will all things leave me friendlefs ?
My wealth and power are duft,
This Judge is ever juft,
  His righteous doom is endlefs.

8

Lord Jefus Chrift ! 't is Thou
Alone canft help me now,
  But 't was for this Thou cameft,
To fave us in this hour ;—
Then fhow Thy mercy's power,
  For they are fafe Thou claimeft.

9

Speak Thou for me ! Thou art
The refuge of my heart ;
  With gladnefs let me hear Thee ;
Bid me to Thee afcend,
Where praife fhall never end,
  And love fhall aye be near Thee.

CHRISTMAS.

(LIX.—„ Laßt uns alle fröhlich fein.")

29.

Original Tune.

‖: Let us all with glad-fome voice Praife the God of hea-ven,:‖

Who to bid our hearts re-joice His own Son hath giv-en.

(CIV.—„Vom Himmel hoch da komm' ich her.")

30.

2
‖:Down to this sad earth He comes,
Here to serve us deigning,:‖
That with Him in yon fair homes
We may once be reigning.

3
‖:We are rich; for He was poor,
Gaze upon this wonder!:‖
Let us praise God evermore,
Here on earth, and yonder!

4
‖:Look on all who sorrow here,
Lord, in pity bending,:‖
Grant us now a glad New Year,
And a blessed ending!

Original Tune.

From heaven a-bove to earth I come

To bear good news to ev'-ry home;

Glad tid—ings of great joy I bring,

Where-of I now will say and sing:

2
To you this night is born a child
Of Mary, chosen mother mild ;
This little child, of lowly birth,
Shall be the joy of all your earth.

3
'Tis Christ, our God, who far on-high
Hath heard your sad and bitter cry ;
Himself will your Salvation be,
Himself from sin will make you free.

4
He brings those blessings, long ago
Prepared by God for all below ;
Henceforth His kingdom open stands
To you, as to the angel bands.

5
These are the tokens ye shall mark,
The swaddling clothes and manger dark ;
There shall ye find the young child laid,
By whom the heavens and earth were made.

6
Now let us all with gladsome cheer
Follow the shepherds, and draw near
To see this wondrous gift of God,
Who hath His only Son bestow'd.

7
Give heed, my heart, lift up thine eyes !
Who is it in yon manger lies ?
Who is this child, so young and fair ?
The blessed Christ-child lieth there.

8
Welcome to earth, Thou noble guest,
Through whom e'en wicked men are blest !
Thou com'st to share our misery,
What can we render, Lord, to Thee !

9
Ah Lord, who hast created all,
How hast Thou made Thee weak and small,
That Thou must choose Thy infant bed
Where ass and ox but lately fed !

10
Were earth a thousand times as fair,
Beset with gold and jewels rare,
She yet were far too poor to be
A narrow cradle, Lord, for Thee.

11
For velvets soft and silken stuff
Thou hast but hay and straw so rough,
Whereon Thou King, so rich and great,
As 'twere Thy heaven, art throned in state.

12
Thus hath it pleased Thee to make plain
The truth to us poor fools and vain,
That this world's honour, wealth, and might
Are nought and worthless in Thy sight.

13
Ah ! dearest Jesus, Holy Child,
Make Thee a bed, soft, undefiled,
Within my heart, that it may be
A quiet chamber kept for Thee.

14
My heart for very joy doth leap,
My lips no more can silence keep ;
I too must raise with joyful tongue
That sweetest ancient cradle-song—

15
Glory to God in highest heaven,
Who unto man His Son hath given !
While angels sing with pious mirth
A glad New Year to all the earth.

(CVIII.—„Warum follt' ich mich denn grämen.")

31.

All my heart this night re-joi-ces, As I hear,

Far and near, Sweet-eft an-gel voi-ces; "Chrift is born," their

choirs are fing'-ing, Till the air Ev'-ry-where Now with joy is ring-ing.

2 Hark ! a voice from yonder manger,
     Soft and fweet,
     Doth entreat,
" Flee from woe and danger;
Brethren, come, from all doth grieve you
     You are freed,
     All you need
I will furely give you."

3 Come then, let us haften yonder;
     Here let all,
     Great and fmall,
Kneel in awe and wonder.
Love Him who with love is yearning;
     Hail the Star
     That from far
Bright with hope is burning !

4 Ye who pine in weary fadnefs,
     Weep no more,
     For the door
Now is found of gladnefs.
Cling to Him, for He will guide you
     Where no crofs,
     Pain or lofs,
Can again betide you.

5 Hither come, ye heavy-hearted,
     Who for fin
     Deep within,
Long and fore have fmarted ;
For the poifon'd wounds you're feeling
     Help is near,
     One is here
Mighty for their healing !

6 Hither come, ye poor and wretched ;
     Know His will
     Is to fill
Every hand outftretched ;
Here are riches without meafure,
     Here forget
     All regret,
Fill your hearts with treafure.

7 Thee, dear Lord, with heed I 'll cherifh,
     Live to Thee,
     And with Thee
Dying, fhall not perifh ;
But fhall dwell with Thee for ever,
     Far on high,
     In the joy
That can alter never.

(XXX.—„Freut euch ihr lieben Chriften.")

32.

Original Tune.

Re-joice, re-joice, ye Chrif-tians, With all your hearts this morn ! Oh hear the blefs-ed tid-ings, "The Lord, the Chrift, is

born," Now brought us by the an-gels That ftand a-bout God's throne ; Oh love-ly are the voi-ces

That make fuch tid-ings known, That make fuch tid-ings known.

2

Oh hearken to their finging,
     " This Child fhall be your Friend,
The Father fo hath will'd it,
     That thus your woes fhould end ;
The Son is freely given,
     That in Him ye may have
The Father's grace and blefling,
‖: And know He loves to fave. :‖

3

Nor deem the form too lowly
     That clothes Him at this hour ;
For know ye what it hideth ?
     'Tis God's almighty power.
Though now within the manger
     So poor and weak He lies,
He is the Lord of all things,
‖: He reigns above the skies. :‖

4

Sin, Death, and Hell, and Satan
  Have loſt the victory ;
This Child ſhall overthrow them,
  As ye ſhall ſurely ſee ;
Their wrath ſhall nought avail them,
  Fear not, their reign is o'er ;
This Child ſhall overthrow them,—
‖: Oh hear and doubt no more." :‖

(xxxi.—„ Freuet euch ihr Chriſten alle.“)

33.
Original Tune.

To be ſung only at the beginning and end of the Hymn.

Hal - le - lu-jah, Hal - le - lu-jah, Hal - le - lu-jah, Hal-le - lu-jah, Hal-le - lu-jah, Hal-le-lujah, Halle-lujah, Hal-le-lu-jah, Hal-le-lu-jah, Hal-le-lu-jah, Halle - lu - jah, Hal-le-lu-jah.

O re-joice, ye Chriſtians, loud-ly, For your joy is now be-gun;

Wond-rous things our God hath done; Tell a-broad His good-neſs proud-ly,

Who our race hath hon-our'd thus That He deigns to dwell with us:

Joy, O joy, be-yond all glad-neſs! Chriſt hath done a-way with ſad-neſs!

Hence, all ſor-row and re-pin-ing, For the Sun of grace is ſhin-ing.

2

See, my ſoul, thy Saviour chooſes
  Weakneſs here and poverty,
  In ſuch love He comes to thee,
Nor the hardeſt couch refuſes ;
  All He ſuffers for thy good,
  To redeem thee by His blood :
Joy, then, joy beyond all gladneſs !
Chriſt hath done away with ſadneſs !
  Hence, all ſorrow and repining,
  For the Sun of grace is ſhining.

3

Lord, how ſhall I thank Thee rightly ?
  I acknowledge that from Thee
  Every bleſſing flows to me.
Let me not forget it lightly,
  But to Thee through all things cleave ;
  So ſhall heart and mind receive
Joy, yea, joy beyond all gladneſs !
Chriſt hath done away with ſadneſs !
  Hence, all ſorrow, all repining,
  For the Sun of grace is ſhining !

4

Jeſu, guard and guide Thy members,
  Fill Thy brethren with Thy grace,
  Hear their prayers in every place,
Quicken now life's fainteſt embers ;
  Grant all Chriſtians, far and near,
  Holy peace, a glad New Year !
Joy, O joy, beyond all gladneſs !
Chriſt hath done away with ſadneſs !
  Hence, all ſorrow, all repining,
  For the Sun of grace is ſhining !

(CXIX.—„ Wir Chriſtenleut.")

34.
Original Tune.

We Chriſ - tians may re - joice to - day,

When Chriſt was born to com - fort and to

ſave us; Who thus be - lieves

no long - er grieves, For none are loſt who graſp the hope He gave us.

2

O wondrous joy, that God moſt high
Should take our fleſh, and thus our race ſhould honour ;
A virgin mild hath borne this Child,
Such grace and glory God hath put upon her.

3

Sin brought us grief, but Chriſt relief,
When down to earth He came for our ſalvation ;
Since God with us is dwelling thus,
Who dares to ſpeak the Chriſtian's condemnation ?

4

Then hither throng, with happy ſong
To Him whoſe birth and death are our aſſurance ;
Through whom are we at laſt ſet free
From ſins and burdens that ſurpaſſed endurance.

5

Yes, let us praiſe our God and raiſe
Loud hallelujahs to the ſkies above us ·
The bliſs beſtowed to-day by God,
To ceaſeleſs thankfulneſs and joy ſhould move us.

(Index of Tunes, XXVIII.)

35.
Tune.—" Ere yet the dawn hath fill'd the ſkies."

Thee, O Im - man - u - el, we praiſe, The

Prince of Life and Fount of Grace, The Morn - ing

Heav'nly Flower,

Star, the Heav'n - ly Flower, The Vir - gin's

Son, the Lord of Power. Hal - le - lu - jah.

2

With all Thy saints, Thee, Lord, we sing,
Praise, honour, thanks to Thee we bring,
That Thou, O long-expected guest,
Hast come at last to make us blest!
                    Hallelujah.

3

Since first the world began to be,
How many a heart hath long'd for Thee;
Long years our fathers hoped of old
Their eyes might yet Thy Light behold:
                    Hallelujah.

4

The prophets cried; "Ah, would He came
To break the fetters of our shame:
That help from Zion came to men,
Israel were glad, and prosper'd then!"
                    Hallelujah.

5

Now art Thou here; we know Thee now,
In lowly manger lieth Thou;
A child, yet makest all things great,
Poor, yet is earth Thy robe of state.
                    Hallelujah.

6

From Thee alone all gladness flows,
Who yet shalt bear such bitter woes;
Earth's light and comfort Thou shalt be,
Yet none shall watch to comfort Thee.
                    Hallelujah.

7

All heavens are Thine, yet Thou dost come
To sojourn in a stranger's home;
Thou hangest on Thy mother's breast
Who art the joy of spirits blest.
                    Hallelujah.

8

Now fearless I can look on Thee,
From sin and grief Thou sett'st me free;
Thou bearest wrath, Thou conquerest Death,
Fear turns to joy Thy glance beneath.
                    Hallelujah.

9

Thou art my Head, my Lord Divine,
I am Thy member, wholly Thine,
And in Thy Spirit's strength would still
Serve Thee according to Thy will.
                    Hallelujah

10

Thus will I sing Thy praises here
With joyful spirit year by year;
And they shall sound before Thy throne,
Where time nor number more are known.
                    Hallelujah.

(Index of Tunes, CXVII.)

36.

EPIPHANY.   *Tune.*—"O Morning Star! how fair and bright."

How bright-ly beams the Morn - ing Star! What sud - den ra - diance
Bright-ness of God, that breaks our night And fills the dark - en'd

1st Time.   2nd Time.

from a - far Doth glad us with its shin - ing,
souls with light Who long for truth were   pin - ing!

Thy Word, Je - su, In - ly feeds us, Right - ly leads us, Life be - stow-ing;

Praise, oh praise such love o'er - flow - ing.

2 Thou here my Comfort, there my Crown,
   Thou King of Heaven, who camest down
      To dwell as man beside me;
   My heart doth praise Thee o'er and o'er,
   If Thou art mine I ask no more,
      Be wealth or fame denied me;
   Thee I seek now; None who proves Thee,
         None who loves Thee
         Finds Thee fail him;
   Lord of life, Thy powers avail him!

3 Through Thee alone can I be blest,
   Then deep be on my heart imprest
      The love that Thou hast borne me;
   So make it ready to fulfil
   With burning zeal Thy holy will,
      Though men may vex or scorn me;
   Saviour, let me Never lose Thee,
         For I choose Thee,
         Thirst to know Thee;
   All I am and have I owe Thee!

4 O God, our Father far above,
   Thee too I praise, for all the love
      Thou in Thy Son dost give me;
   In Him am I made one with Thee,
   My Brother and my Friend is He;
      Shall aught affright or grieve me?
   He is Greatest, Best, and Highest,
         Ever nighest
         To the weakest;
   Fear no foes, if Him thou seekest!

5 O praise to Him who came to save,
   Who conquer'd death and burst the grave;
      Each day new praise resoundeth
   To Him the Lamb who once was slain,
   The Friend whom none shall trust in vain,
      Whose grace for aye aboundeth;
   Sing, ye Heavens, Tell the story
         Of His glory,
         Till His praises
   Flood with light Earth's darkest places.

(XLIV.—„Ich dank' Dir lieber Herre.")

37.

O Je-su, King of Glo-ry! Our Sov'-reign and our
Thy throne is fix'd in Hea-ven, Thy king-dom hath no

Friend !
end : Oh now to all men, far and near,

Lord, make it known, we pray, That as in Heaven all

crea-tures here May know Thee and o-bey.

2

The Eastern sages bringing
  Their tribute-gifts to Thee,
Bear witness to Thy Kingdom,
  And humbly bow the knee ;
To Thee the Morning Star doth lead,
  To Thee th' inspired Word,
We hail Thee, Saviour in our need,
  We worship Thee, the Lord.

3

Ah look on me with pity,
  Though I am weak and poor,
Admit me to Thy kingdom
  To dwell there blest and sure.
Oh rescue me from all my woes,
  And shield me with Thine arm
From Sin and Death, the mighty foes
  That daily seek our harm.

4

And bid Thy Word within us
  Shine as the fairest Star ;
Keep sin and all false doctrine
  From all Thy people far :
Let us Thy name aright confess,
  And with Thy Christendom,
Our King and Saviour own and bless
  Through all the world to come.

(Index of Tunes, LV.)

38.

Tune.—" Jesus Christ, my sure Defence."

Rise, O Sa-lem, rise and shine !
He-rald of a morn di-vine,

Lo ! the Gen-tiles hail thy wak--ing;
See the day-spring o'er us break--ing,

Tell--ing God has call'd to mind Those who long in dark-ness pined.

2

Ah, how blindly did we stray,
  Ere this sun our earth had brightened !
Heaven we sought not, for no ray
  Had our 'wilder'd eyes enlighten'd ;
All our looks were earthward bent,
All our strength on earth was spent.

3

But the day-spring from on high
  Hath arisen with beams unclouded,
And we see before it fly
  All the heavy gloom that shrouded
This sad earth, where sin and woe
Seem'd to reign o'er all below.

4

Thy appearing, Lord, ſhall fill
All my thoughts in ſorrow's hour;
Thy appearing, Lord, ſhall ſtill
All my dread of death's dark power;
Whether joy or tears be mine,
Through them ſtill Thy light ſhall ſhine.

5

Let me, when my courſe is run,
Calmly leave a world of ſadneſs
For the place that needs no ſun,
For Thou art its light and gladneſs,
For the manſions fair and bright,
Where Thy ſaints are crown'd with light.

(Index of Tunes, IV.)

39.

Tune.—" What ſhall I, a ſinner, do?"

Is thy heart a-thirſt to know That the King of heav'n and earth Deigns to dwell with man be-low, Yea, hath ſtoop'd to mor-tal birth? Search the Word with ceaſe-leſs care Till thou find this trea-ſure there.

2

With the ſages from afar
Journey on o'er ſea and land,
Till thou ſee the Morning Star
O'er thy heart unchanging ſtand,
Then ſhalt thou behold His face
Full of mercy, truth, and grace.

3

For if Chriſt be born within,
Soon that likeneſs ſhall appear
Which the heart had loſt through ſin,
God's own image fair and clear,
And the ſoul ſerene and bright
Mirrors back His heavenly light.

4

Jeſus, let me ſeek for nought
But that Thou ſhouldſt dwell in me;
Let this only fill my thought,
How I may grow liker Thee,
Through this earthly care and ſtrife,
Through the calm eternal life.

5

With the wiſe who know Thee right,
Though the world accounts them fools,
I will praiſe Thee day and night;
I will order by Thy rules
All my life, that it may be
Fill'd with praiſe and love of Thee.

(XIII.—„Aus tiefer Noth ſchrei ich zu Dir.")

LENT.

40.

Original Tune.

Out of the depths I cry to Thee, Lord, hear me, I im-plore Thee! If Thou re-mem-b'reſt
Bend down Thy gra-cious ear to me, Let my prayer come be-fore Thee!
each miſ-deed, If each ſhould have its right-ful meed, Who may a-bide Thy pre-ſence?

2

Our pardon is Thy gift, Thy love
And grace alone avail us;
Our works could ne'er our guilt remove,
The ſtricteſt life muſt fail us,
That none may boaſt himſelf of aught,
But own in fear Thy grace hath wrought
What in him ſeemeth righteous.

3

And thus my hope is in the Lord,
And not in mine own merit;
I reſt upon His faithful word
To them of contrite ſpirit,
That He is merciful and juſt—
Here is my comfort and my truſt,
His help I wait with patience.

4

And though it tarry till the night,
And round till morning waken,
My heart ſhall ne'er miſtruſt His might,
Nor count itſelf forſaken.
Do thus, O ye of Iſrael's ſeed,
Ye of the Spirit born indeed,
Wait for our God's appearing.

5

Though great our ſins and ſore our woes,
His grace much more aboundeth;
His helping love no limit knows,
Our utmoſt need it ſoundeth;
Our kind and faithful Shepherd, He
Who ſhall at laſt ſet Iſrael free
From all their ſin and ſorrow.

(XCVII.—„ Straf mich nicht in Deinem Zorn.")

41.

Original Tune.

Not in an - ger, migh - ty God, Not in an - ger smite us;
We must per - ish if Thy rod Just - ly should re - quite us. We are nought, Sin hath brought, Lord, Thy wrath up -

on us, Yet have mer - cy on us!

2

Show me now a Father's love,
And His tender patience,
Heal my wounded soul, remove
These too sore temptations;
I am weak,
Father, speak
Thou of peace and gladness,
Comfort Thou my sadness.

3

Weary am I of my pain,
Weary with my sorrow,
Sighing still for help in vain,
Longing for the morrow;
Why wilt Thou
Tarry now?
Wilt Thou friendless leave me,
And of hope bereave me?

4

Hence, ye foes! He comes in grace,
God hath deign'd to hear me;
I may come before His face,
He is inly near me;
He o'erthrows
All my foes,
Death and hell are vanquish'd,
In whose bonds I languish'd.

5

Father, hymns to Thee we raise,
Here and once in heaven;
And the Son and Spirit praise,
Who our bonds have riven;
Evermore
We adore
Thee whose grace hath stirr'd us,
And whose pity heard us.

(IX.—„ An Dir allein, an Dir hab' ich gesündigt.")

42.

Original Tune.

A - gainst Thee on - ly have I sinn'd, I own it, And done this e - vil in Thy sight;

My guilt de - serves Thy wrath, and Thou hast shown it,— Ah! see my grief, my wretch - ed plight.

2

My secret prayers and sighs Thou hearest plainly,
My tears are ever known to Thee;
Ah God, my God, and shall I seek Thee vainly?
How long wilt Thou be far from me?

3

Lord, not according to my guilt requite me,
But deal with me in tender grace;
Thy patience and long-suffering still invite me,
I come: Ah hide Thou not Thy face!

4

Make me to sing once more of joy and gladness,
Father of mercies, hear my voice!
For Thy name's sake, oh raise me from this sadness,
Thou, God, dost love that we rejoice.

5

Teach me Thy law, with spirit glad and fervent
Let me go forth upon my way;
Thou art my God, I am Thy willing servant
To do Thy pleasure day by day.

6

Oh haste Thou, my Defence, be now beside me!
Behold, the Lord hath heard my prayer!
Now on a plainer path His hand shall guide me,
My soul is safe beneath His care

(LXXXVII.—Pfalm 8, Goudimel.)

43.

Am I on earth a lone and friend-lefs ftran-ger? When fhall thefe days be paft of fear and dan-ger,
When fhall I find fome re-fpite, fome re-lief, From this un-fleep-ing pain, this haunt-ing grief?

2

The joyful fun may bring another morning,
I wake to care, to confcience' voice of warning ;
The foft moon comes with filent night and fleep,
And bringeth nought to me but time to weep.

3

My heart and foul faint, fmitten by Thine arrow,
Keen as a fire that pierceth to the marrow ;
From morn to eventide where'er I flee
I find no hiding-place, great God, from Thee.

4

Vain are my prayers, vainly I weep my errors,
While Thou doft ftrive againft me with Thy terrors ;
The zeal of Thy juft anger and Thy might
Have plunged my foul in blackeft depths of night.

5

Oh that I had a dove's fwift wings ! I'd hie me
To fome far mountain-top where none came nigh me !
Yet could I not efcape His mighty hand
Before whom all things bare and open ftand.

6

Nay, all He fends me let me fuffer rather,
Though ftill His angry ftorms around me gather ;
A willing heart and patient mind, O God,
I bring to Thy fevere but righteous rod.

7

Much have I finn'd, and utterly I perifh,
If memory of my fin Thou ftill will cherifh ;
Yet, Lord of Hofts, doth not Thy Word proclaim
The Merciful is Thy moft glorious name !

(XXXVI.—„ Herr, ich habe mißgehanbelt.")

44.

Original Tune.

Lord, to Thee I make con-fef-fion, I have
finn'd and gone a-ftray, I have mul-ti-plied tranf-gref-fion,
Cho-fen for my-felf my way : Forced at laft to fee my
er-rors, Lord, I trem-ble at Thy ter-rors.

2

But from Thee how can I hide me,
Thou, O God, art everywhere ;
Refuge from Thee is denied me,
Or by land or fea or air ;
Nor death's darknefs can enfold me
So that Thou fhouldft not behold me.

3

Yet though confcience' voice appall me,
Father, I will feek Thy face ;
Though Thy child I dare not call me,
Yet accept me to Thy grace ;
Do not for my fins forfake me,
Let not yet Thy wrath o'ertake me.

4

For Thy Son hath fuffer'd for me,
And the blood He fhed for fin,
That can heal me and reftore me,
Quench this burning fire within ;
'Tis alone His crofs can vanquifh
Thefe dark fears and foothe this anguifh.

5

Then on Him I caft my burden,
Sink it in the depths below !
Let me feel Thy inner pardon,
Wafh me, make me white as fnow.
Let Thy Spirit leave me never,
Make me only Thine for ever !

45.

Tune.—"Am I on earth alone, a friendlefs ftranger?"

Here, O my God, low at Thy feet I bend me,

Rea - dy to fuf - fer what - fo - e'er Thou fend me,

Yet look on me, great God, with pi - ty - ing eyes,

Re - ward me not for mine in - i - qui - ties.

2

My heart hath cherifh'd fin, and fear'd no morrow,
Loved the broad, eafy road that ends in forrow ;
Till now I learn, O fin, how keen thy fmart,
O wrath of God, how terrible thou art !

3

Can I efcape no more ? will no one find me
Some help to break the heavy chains that bind me ?
Will man nor creature fhow me any place
Where I may flee and hide me from God's face ?

4

Nay, I muft flee to Him who can deliver,
In whom our life and hope are hid for ever ;
What all the world muft unaccomplifh'd leave,
Thou, for Thou art Almighty, canft achieve.

5

Think on the covenant Thou haft never broken,
Think on the fteadfaft word Thyfelf haft fpoken,
Know that I am a God, Thy promife faith,
Who hath no pleafure in a finner's death.

6

Then let the arms of love be thrown around me ;
Have pity on me, Thou who thus haft found me,
Call back Thy fheep that, wandering far aftray,
Was loft in fin, nor knew the homeward way.

7

O God, moft merciful ! my thankful fpirit
Adores the goodnefs that I did not merit ;
'T is meet in praifing Thee my time I fpend,
Here, and above, where praife fhall never end.

PASSION-WEEK.

46.

Original Tune.

O Lamb of God, moft ftain - lefs !
Pa - tient through all Thy for - rows,

Who on the crofs didft lan - guifh,
Though mock'd a - mid Thine an - guifh ;

Our fins Thou bar - eft for us,

2

O Lamb of God moft ftainlefs !

Who on the crofs didft languifh,

Patient through all Thy forrows,

Though mock'd amid Thine anguifh ;

Our fins Thou bareft for us,

Elfe had defpair reign'd o'er us :

Have mercy upon us, O Jefu !

3

O Lamb of God, moft ftainlefs !

Who on the crofs didft languifh,

Patient through all Thy forrows,

Though mock'd amid Thine anguifh ;

Our fins Thou bareft for us,

Elfe had defpair reign'd o'er us :

Grant us Thy peace to-day, O Jefu !

Elfe had de - fpair reign'd o'er us :

Have mer - cy up - on us, O Je - fu !

(Index of Tunes, LXIII.)

47.

Tune.—" Deal with me, God, in mercy now."

O Love, who form - edft me to wear
Who fought - eft me with ten - der care

The im - age of Thy God - head here ;
Through all my wand' - rings wild and drear ;

O Love, I give my - felf to Thee,

Thine ev - er, on - ly Thine to be.

2

O Love, who ere life's earlieft dawn
On me Thy choice haft gently laid ;
O Love, who here as man waft born
And like to us in all things made ;
O Love, I give myfelf to Thee,
Thine ever, only Thine to be.

3

O Love, who once in Time waft flain,
Pierced through and through with bitter woe ;
O Love, who wreftling thus didft gain
That we eternal joy might know ;
O Love, I give myfelf to Thee,
Thine ever, only Thine to be.

4

O Love, of whom is truth and light,
The Word and Spirit, life and power,
Whofe heart was bared to them that fmite,
To fhield us in our trial hour ;
O Love, I give myfelf to Thee,
Thine ever, only Thine to be.

5

O Love, who thus haft bound me faft,
Beneath that gentle yoke of Thine ;
Love, who haft conquer'd me at laft
And rapt away this heart of mine ;
O Love, I give myfelf to Thee,
Thine ever, only Thine to be.

6

O Love, who loveft me for aye,
Who for my foul doft ever plead ;
O Love, who didft my ranfom pay,
Whofe power fufficeth in my ftead ;
O Love, I give myfelf to Thee,
Thine ever, only Thine to be.

7

O Love, who once fhalt bid me rife
From out this dying life of ours ;
O Love, who once above yon fkies
Shalt fet me in the fadelefs bowers :
O Love, I give myfelf to Thee,
Thine ever, only Thine to be.

48.
Tune—"O Thou, of God the Father."

When o'er my sins I sorrow, Lord, I will
And hence my com-fort bor-row, That Thou wast

look   to   Thee,   Yea, Lord, Thy pre-cious blood was spilt For
slain   for   me!

me, O most un-wor-thy, To take a-way my guilt.

Then let Thy woes, Thy patience,
My heart with strength inspire
To vanquish all temptations,
And spurn all low desire;
This thought I fain would cherish most—
What pain my soul's redemption
To Thee, O Saviour, cost!

3

Whate'er may be the burden,
The cross here on me laid;
Be shame or want my guerdon,
I'll bear it with Thine aid;
Give patience, give me strength to take
Thee for my bright example,
And all the world forsake.

4

And let me do to others
As Thou hast done to me,
Love all men as my brothers,
And serve them willingly,
With ready heart, nor seek my own,
But as Thou, Lord, hast help'd us
From purest love alone.

5

And let Thy cross upbear me
With strength, when I depart;
Tell me that nought can tear me
From my Redeemer's heart,
But since my trust is in Thy grace
Thou wilt accept me yonder,
Where I shall see Thy face!

49.
Original Tune.

Christ the Life of all the liv-ing, Christ the
Who Thy-self for us once giv-ing To the

Death of death our foe, Pa-tient-ly didst yield Thy breath
dark-est depths of woe,

But to save my soul from death; Thou-sand, thou-sand

thanks shall be, Bless-ed Je-sus, brought to Thee.

2

Thou, ah Thou, hast taken on Thee
Bitter strokes, a cruel rod,
Pain and scorn were heap'd upon Thee
O Thou sinless Son of God,
Only thus for me to win
Rescue from the bonds of sin;
Thousand, thousand thanks shall be,
Blessed Jesus, brought to Thee.

3

Thou didst bear the smiting only
That it might not fall on me;
Stoodest falsely charged and lonely,
That I might be safe and free;
Comfortless that I might know
Comfort from Thy boundless woe;
Thousand, thousand thanks shall be,
Blessed Jesus, brought to Thee.

4

That Thou wast so meek and stainless
Doth atone for my proud mood;
And Thy death makes dying painless,
All Thy ills have wrought our good;
Yea, the shame Thou didst endure
Is my honour and my cure;
Thousand, thousand thanks shall be,
Blessed Jesus, brought to Thee.

5

Then for all that wrought our pardon,
For Thy sorrows deep and sore,
For Thine anguish in the garden,
I will thank Thee evermore;
Thank Thee with my latest breath
For Thy sad and cruel death,
For that last most bitter cry,
And shall praise Thee, Lord, on high.

(III.—„Ach Jesu dein Sterben.")

50.
Original Tune.

Ah Je - sus, the me - rit Of all that Thou haft borne Mak - eth me in - he - rit

After the last verse.

The crown that hath no thorn! A - men.

2
Ah then, teach me duly
To worfhip at Thy crofs,
Owning inly, truly,
The Love that bore our lofs.

3
To fin, there, oh let me
From henceforth daily die;
Nor in death forget me,
Then grant me life on high.

GOOD FRIDAY.

(XL:—„Herzlich thut mich verlangen."
„O Haupt voll Blut und Wunden.")

51.

Ah wound - ed Head that bear - eft Such
That now fo meek - ly wear - eft The

bit - ter fhame and fcorn, Erft reign - ing in the
mock - ing crown of thorn!

high - eft In light and ma - jef - ty, Dif -

hon - our'd here Thou di - eft, Yet here I wor - fhip Thee.

2
Thou noble Face, whofe anger
Shall make a world to quail,
That glance is quench'd in languor
To which the fun were pale;
How hath its brightnefs vanifh'd!
Thofe gracious eyes how dim!
What foe their light hath banifh'd,
Who dared to fcoff at Him?

3
All lovely hues have faded
That glow'd with warmth and life
As He endures unaided
The laft and mortal ftrife;
The Mighty One of valour
Muft yield Him as a prey,
Death triumphs in his pallour
O'er all His ftrength to-day.

4
Ah Lord, this cruel burden
Of right belongs to me;
Of my mifdeeds the guerdon
Hath all been laid on Thee;
I caft me down before Thee,
Wrath were my rightful lot,
Yet hear me, I implore Thee,
Redeemer, fpurn me not!

5
My Guardian, deign to own me,
My Shepherd, I am Thine;
What goodnefs haft Thou fhown me,
O Fount of Love Divine!
How oft Thy lips have fed me
On earth with angels' food!
How oft Thy Spirit led me
To ftores of heavenly good!

6
Ah would that I were bidden
To fhare Thy crofs and woes!
There all true joy lies hidden,
Thence all true comfort flows.
Ah well for me, if lying
Here at Thy feet, my Life,
I too with Thee were dying,
And thus might end my ftrife!

7
My foul doth melt within me,
O Jefus, deareft Friend,
That Thou fhouldft bear to win me
Such woes, for fuch an end!
Ah make me cling the firmer
To One fo true to me,
And fink without a murmur
To fleep at laft in Thee.

8
Yes, when I hence betake me,
Lord, do not Thou depart;
Oh! never more forfake me
When death is at my heart,
And faith and hope are finking,
O'erwhelm'd with dread difmay;
Thou bareft all unfhrinking,—
Oh chafe my fears away!

9
Appear then, my Defender,
My Comfort, ere I die!
This life I can furrender
If but I fee Thee nigh;
My dim eyes fhall behold Thee,
Upon Thy crofs fhall dwell,
My heart by faith enfold Thee;
Who dieth thus, dies well!

(XLI.—„Herzliebster Jesu was haft Du verbrochen.")

52.
Original Tune.

A-las, dear Lord, what law then haft Thou bro-ken,

That such sharp fen-tence should on Thee be fpo-ken? Of what great

crime haft Thou to make con-fef-fion— What dark tranf-gref-fion?

5 There was no fpot in me by fin untainted,
Sick with its venom all my heart had fainted;
My heavy guilt to hell had well-nigh brought me,
Such woe it wrought me.

6 O wondrous love! whofe depths no heart hath founded,
That brought Thee here by foes and thieves furrounded;
All worldly pleafures, heedlefs, I was trying,
While Thou wert dying!

7 O mighty King! no time can dim Thy glory!
How fhall I fpread abroad Thy wondrous ftory?
How fhall I find fome worthy gift to proffer?
What dare we offer?

8 For vainly doth our human wifdom ponder—
Thy woes, Thy mercy ftill tranfcend our wonder.
Oh how fhould I do aught that could delight Thee!
Can I requite Thee?

9 Yet unrequited, Lord, I would not leave Thee,
I can renounce whate'er doth vex or grieve Thee,
And quench with thoughts of Thee and prayers moft lowly,
All fires unholy.

10 But fince my ftrength alone will ne'er fuffice me
To crucify defires that ftill entice me,
To all good deeds, oh let Thy Spirit win me,
And reign within me!

11 I'll think upon Thy mercy hour by hour,
I'll love Thee fo that earth muft lofe her power;
To do Thy will fhall be my fole endeavour
Henceforth for ever.

12 Whate'er of earthly good this life may grant me
I'll rifk for Thee,—no fhame, no crofs fhall daunt me;
I fhall not fear what man can do to harm me,
Nor death alarm me.

13 But worthlefs is my facrifice, I own it,
Yet, Lord, for love's fake Thou wilt not difown it;
Thou wilt accept my gift in Thy great meeknefs,
Nor fhame my weaknefs.

14 And when, dear Lord, before Thy throne in heaven
To me the crown of joy at laft is given,
Where fweeteft hymns Thy faints for ever raife Thee,
I too fhall praife Thee!

2 They crown His head with thorns, they fmite, they fcourge Him,
With cruel mockings to the crofs they urge Him,
They give Him gall to drink, they ftill decry Him,—
They crucify Him.

3 Whence come thefe forrows, whence this mortal anguifh
It is my fins for which my Lord muft languifh;
Yes, all the wrath, the woe He doth inherit,
'T is I do merit!

4 What ftrangeft punifhment is fuffer'd yonder!—
The Shepherd dies for fheep that loved to wander!
The Mafter pays the debts His fervants owe Him,
Who would not know Him.

(XVII.—„Da Jesus an dem Kreuze ftund.")

53.
Original Tune.

When on the crofs the Sav-iour hung, And that fore load that on Him weigh'd With bit-ter pangs His

na-ture wrung, Seven words a-mid His pain He faid: Oh let them well to heart be laid!

2
"Father, forgive thefe men," He fpake;
"For lo! they know not what they do,
Nor of my fufferings vengeance take!"
And when we fin in error too,
For us, dear Lord, this prayer renew!

3
He thought upon the thief, and faid,—
"Thou fhalt behold my Paradife
With me, ere yet this day be fled."
Lord, fee us too with pitying eyes,
And raife us from our miferies!

4
His mother ftood befide Him there;
"Behold thy fon! Oh let her find
A fon, O John, in thy true care."
Lord, care for thofe we leave behind,
Nor let the world prove all unkind!

5
Once more He faith,—"I thirft, I thirft!"
O Prince of Life! that we might be
Refcued from death, Thou dar'ft the worft.
So doft Thou long to fet us free!
Not fruitlefs be that thirft in Thee!

6

Again, " My God, My God," He cried,
" Ah why doſt Thou forſake me thus ? "
Thou art forſaken at this tide,
To win acceptance, Lord, for us ;
Oh comfort deep and marvellous !

7

He ſaith,—" Lo ! it is finiſh'd now ! "
Saviour, Thy perfect work is done !
O make us faithful, Lord, as Thou,
No trial and no croſs to ſhun
Till all Thou lay'ſt on us be done.

8

And laſt,—" My Father, to Thine hands
My parting ſoul I now commend."
Lord, when my ſpirit trembling ſtands
Upon life's verge, this cry I ſend
To Thee, and with Thy words I end.

9

Whoſo ſhall ponder oft theſe words
When long-paſt ſins his ſoul alarm,
Shall find the hope Thy croſs accords,
And in Thy grace a healing balm
That brings the wounded conſcience calm.

10

Lord Jeſu Chriſt, who diedſt for us,
This one thing grant us evermore ;
To ponder o'er Thy paſſion thus,
Till truer, deeper than before
We learn to love Thee and adore !

EASTER EVE.

(LXXXIV.—„ O Traurigkeit, O Herzeleib.")

54.
Original Tune.

O darkeſt woe ! Ye tears forth flow ! Has earth ſo ſad a wonder, That the Father's only Son Now lies buried yonder !

2

O ſon of man !
It was the ban
Of death on thee that brought Him
Down to ſuffer for thy ſins,
And ſuch woe hath wrought Him.

3

Behold thy Lord,
The Lamb of God,
Blood-ſprinkled lies before thee,
Pouring out His life that He
May to life reſtore thee.

4

O Ground of faith
Laid low in death !
Sweet lips now ſilent ſleeping !
Surely all that live muſt mourn
Here with bitter weeping.

5

Yea, bleſt is he
Whoſe heart ſhall be
Fix'd here, and apprehendeth
Why the Lord of glory thus
To the grave deſcendeth.

6

O Jeſu bleſt !
My help and reſt !
With tears I pray—Lord, hear me ;
Make me love Thee to the laſt,
In the grave be near me !

(XX.—„ Der Du Herr Jeſu Ruh und Raſt.")

55.

Lord Jeſus, who, our ſouls to ſave, Didſt reſt and ſlumber in the grave, Now grant us all in Thee to reſt, And here to live as ſeems Thee beſt.

2

Give us the ſtrength, the dauntleſs faith,
That Thou haſt purchaſed with Thy death,
And lead us to that glorious place
Where we ſhall ſee the Father's face.

3

O Lamb of God ! who once waſt ſlain,
We thank Thee for that bitter pain !
Let us partake Thy death, that we
May enter into life with Thee !

(Index of Tunes, LXXXIV.)

56.

Tune.—" O darkeft woe ! Ye tears, forth flow !"

Thou fore-op-preff'd, The Sab-bath reft In yon ftill grave art keep-ing! All Thy la-bour now is done, Paft is all Thy weep-ing!

2

The ftrife is o'er,
Nought hurts Thee more,
The heart at laft hath flumber'd,
That in confliĉt fore for us
Bore our fins unnumber'd.

3

Thou awful tomb,
Once fill'd with gloom !
How bleffed and how holy
Art thou now, fince in the grave
Slept the Saviour lowly !

4

How calm and bleft
The dead now reft
Who in the Lord departed !
All their works do follow them,
Yes, they fleep glad-hearted.

5

O lead us Thou
To reft e'en now,
With all who, forely anguifh'd
'Neath the burden of their fins,
Long in woe have languifh'd.

6

O Bleffed Rock !
Soon grant Thy flock
To fee Thy Sabbath morning !
Strife and pain will all be paft
When that day is dawning.

EASTER.

(XXVIII.—„ Erſchienen iſt der herrlich' Tag.")

57.

Ere yet the dawn hath fill'd the fkies Be-hold my Sa-viour Chrift a-rife, He chaf-eth from us fin and night, And brings us joy and life and light. Hal-le-lu-jah.

2 O ftronger Thou than Death and Hell,
Where is the foe Thou canft not quell ?
What heavy ftone Thou canft not roll
From off the prifon'd anguifh'd foul ?
              Hallelujah.

3 If Jefus lives, can I be fad ?
I know He loves me, and am glad ;
Though all the world were dead to me,
Enough, O Chrift, if I have Thee !
              Hallelujah.

4 He feeds me, comforts and defends,
And when I die His angel fends
To bear me whither He is gone,
For of His own He lofeth none.
              Hallelujah.

5 No more to fear or grief I bow,
God and the angels love me now ;
The joys prepared for me to-day
Drive fear and mourning far away ;
              Hallelujah.

6 Strong Champion ! For this comfort fee
The whole world brings her thanks to Thee ;
And once we too fhall raife above
More fweet and loud the fong we love :
              Hallelujah.

(XVI.—„ Chriſt iſt erſtanden.")

58.

Original Tune.

Chrift the Lord is rifen a-gain !

Chrift has bro-ken ev'-ry chain !

Hark, the an-gels shout for joy, Sing-ing ev-er-
more on high, Hal-le-lu-jah.

2

He who gave for us His life,
Who for us endured the ftrife,
Is our Pafchal Lamb to-day!
We too fing for joy, and fay:
　　　　　Hallelujah.

3

He who bore all pain and lofs
Comfortlefs upon the crofs,
Lives in glory now on high,
Pleads for us and hears our cry:
　　　　　Hallelujah.

4

He whofe path no records tell,
Who defcended into hell,
Who the ftrong man arm'd hath bound,
Now in higheft heaven is crown'd:
　　　　　Hallelujah.

5

He who flumber'd in the grave
Is exalted now to fave;
Now through Chriftendom it rings
That the Lamb is King of kings!
　　　　　Hallelujah.

6

Now He bids us tell abroad
How the loft may be reftored,
How the penitent forgiven,
How we too may enter heaven.
　　　　　Hallelujah.

7

Thou our Pafchal Lamb indeed,
Chrift, to-day Thy people feed;
Take our fins and guilt away,
That we all may fing for aye,
　　　　　Hallelujah.

(I.V:—„Jefus meine Zuverficht.")

59.
Original Tune.

Je-fus Chrift, my fure De-fence
Know-ing this, my con-fi-dence
And my Sa-viour, ev-er liv--eth;
Refts up-on the hope it giv--eth,
Though the night of death be fraught
Still with many an anx-ious thought.

2

Jefus, my Redeemer, lives!
　I too unto life muft waken;
He will have me where He is,
　Shall my courage then be fhaken?
Shall I fear? Or could the Head
Rife and leave its members dead?

3

Nay, too clofely am I bound
　Unto Him by hope for ever;
Faith's ftrong hand the Rock hath found,
　Grafped it, and will leave it never;
Not the ban of death can part
From its Lord the trufting heart.

4

What now fickens, mourns, and fighs,
　Chrift with Him in glory bringeth;
Earthly is the feed and dies,
　Heavenly from the grave it fpringeth;
Natural is the death we die,
Spiritual our life on high.

5

Then take comfort, nay, rejoice,
　For His members Chrift will cherifh;
Fear not, they will know His voice,
　Though awhile they feem to perifh,
When the final trump is heard,
And the deaf, cold grave is ftirred.

6

Laugh to fcorn the gloomy grave,
　And at death no longer tremble,
For the Lord, who comes to fave,
　Round Him fhall His faints affemble,
Raifing them o'er all their foes,
Mortal weaknefs, fear, and woes.

7

Only draw away your heart
　Now from pleafures bafe and hollow;
Would ye there with Chrift have part,
　Here His footfteps ye muft follow;
Fix your heart beyond the fkies,
Whither ye yourfelves would rife!

(xiv.—,, Chriſt lag in Todesbanden.'')

60.
Original Tune.

In Death's ſtrong graſp the Sav-iour lay, For our of-fen-ces

giv — en; But now the Lord is riſen to-day, And

brings us life from hea — ven; Where-fore let us all re-joice

And praiſe our God with cheer-ful voice, And

ſing loud Hal-le-lu — jahs. Hal-le-lu — jah!

2
No ſon of man could conquer Death,
   Such miſchief ſin had wrought us,
For innocence dwelt not on earth,
   And therefore Death had brought us
Into thraldom from of old,
And ever grew more ſtrong and bold,
   His ſhadow lay athwart us.—Hallelujah !

3
But Jeſus Chriſt, God's only Son,
   Hath come to conquer for us,
Hath put away our ſins, and won
   Death's power and title o'er us.
Now 'tis but his form is left,
For of his ſting he is bereft
   Since Jeſus will reſtore us.—Hallelujah !

4
It was a wondrous war, I trow,
   When Life and Death contended ;
But Life hath triumphed o'er the foe,
   The reign of Death is ended ;
Yea, 'tis as the Scripture ſaith,
That Chriſt in dying conquered Death,
   And from his realm aſcended.—Hallelujah !

5
Then let us keep the feaſt to-day
   That God Himſelf hath given ;
And His pure Word ſhall do away
   The old and evil leaven ;
Chriſt to-day will meet His own,
And faith will feed on Him alone,
   The Living Bread from heaven.—Hallelujah !

(xcii. Psalm 88, Ravenſcroft.)

61.

Wel-come, Thou vic-tor in the ſtrife, Now

wel-come from the cave! To-day we tri-umph

in Thy life A - round Thine emp - ty grave.

2

The dwellings of the juft refound
  With fongs of victory ;
For in their midft, Lord, Thou art found,
  And bringeft peace with Thee.

3

Oh fhare with us the fpoils, we pray,
  Thou diedft to achieve ;
We meet within Thy houfe to-day
  Our portion to receive :

4

We die with Thee ; oh let us live
  Henceforth to Thee aright ;
The bleffings Thou haft died to give,
  Be daily in our fight.

5

Fearlefs we lay us in the tomb,
  And fleep the night away,
If Thou art there to break the gloom,
  And call us back to day.

6

Death hurts us not ; his power is gone,
  And pointlefs all his darts ;
Now hath God's favour on us fhone,
  And joy fills all our hearts.

(Index of Tunes, cix.)

62.

Tune.—"Whate'er my God ordains is right."

O rif - en Lord! O con - qu'ring King!
To - day that peace of Eaf - ter bring

O Life of all the liv - ing!
Which comes but of Thy giv - ing!

Once Death, our foe, Had laid Thee low,

Now haft Thou rent his bonds in twain,

Now art Thou rifen who once waft flain!

2

Oh that to know Thy victory
  To us were inly granted,
And thefe cold hearts might catch from Thee
  The glow of faith undaunted ;
    Thy quenchlefs light,
    Thy glorious might
Still comfortlefs and lonely leave
The foul that cannot yet believe.

3

Then break through our hard hearts Thy way,
  O Jefus, Lord of glory !
Kindle the lamp of faith to-day,
  Teach us to fing before Thee
    For joy at length,
    That in Thy ftrength
We too may rife whom fin had flain,
And Thine eternal reft attain.

4

And when our tears for fin o'erflow,
  Do Thou in love draw near us,
Thy precious gift of peace beftow,
  Let Thy bright prefence cheer us,
    That fo may we,
    O Chrift, from Thee
Drink in the life that cannot die,
And keep true Eafter feafts on high.

ASCENSION.

63.

Tune.—" Hark ! a voice faith, All are mortal."

Con-qu'ring Prince and Lord of Glo-ry, Ma-jes-ty en-
All the heav'ns are bow'd be-fore Thee, Far be-yond them

throned in light ; Shall I fall not at Thy feet,
spreads Thy might ;

And my heart with rap-ture beat, Now Thy glo-ry

were made ?
is dif-play'd, Thine ere yet the worlds were made ?

64.

Tune.—" All praife and thanks."

Since Chrift has gone to heav'n His home,
And in this hope I o-ver-come

I too that home one day muft fhare ;
All doubt, all an-guifh, and def-pair ;

For where the Head is, well we know,

2

As I watch Thee far afcending
   To the right hand of the throne,
See the hoft before Thee bending,
   Praifing Thee in fweeteft tone,
Shall not I too at Thy feet
Here the angels' ftrain repeat,
And rejoice that heaven doth ring
With the triumph of my King ?

3

Power and Spirit are o'erflowing,
   On me alfo be they pour'd ;
Every hindrance overthrowing,
   Make Thy foes Thy footftool, Lord !
Yea, let earth's remoteft end
To Thy righteous fceptre bend,
Make Thy way before Thee plain,
O'er all hearts and fpirits reign.

4

Lo ! Thy prefence now is filling
   All Thy Church in every place ;
Fill my heart too, make me willing
   In this feafon of Thy grace ;
Come, Thou King of glory, come,
Deign to make my heart Thy home,
There abide and rule alone,
As upon Thy heavenly throne !

5

Thou art leaving me, yet bringing
   God and heaven moft inly near ;
From this earthly life upfpringing,
   As though ftill I faw Thee here,
Let my heart, tranfplanted hence,
Strange to earth and time and fenfe,
Dwell with Thee in heaven e'en now,
Where our only joy art Thou !

The mem - bers He hath left be - low
In time He sure - ly ga - thers there.

2

Since Chrift hath reached His glorious throne,
  And mighty gifts henceforth are His,
My heart can reft in heaven alone,
  On earth my Lord I daily mifs ;
I long to be with Him on high,
And heart and thoughts would hourly fly
  Where now my only treafure is.

3

From Thy afcenfion let fuch grace,
  Dear Lord, be ever found in me,
That fteadfaft faith may guide my ways
  With ftep unfault'ring up to Thee,
And at Thy voice I may depart
With joy to dwell where Thou, Lord, art :
  O Saviour, grant this prayer to me !

(Index of Tunes, LV.)

65.

Tune.—" Jefus Chrift, my fure Defence."

Heav'n - ward doth our jour - ney tend,
Towards our Pro - mifed Land we wend,

Here on earth we are but ftran - - gers,
Through a wil - der - nefs of dan - - gers;

Here we roam, a pil - grim band,

Yon - der is our na - tive land.

2

Heavenward ftretch, my foul, thy wings,
  Thou canft claim a heavenly nature ;
Cleave not to thefe earthly things,
  Thou canft reft not in the creature.
Every foul that God infpires,
Back to Him, its Source, afpires.

3

Heavenward ! doth His Spirit cry,
  Oft as in His word I hear Him ;
Pointing to the reft on high
  Where I fhall be ever near Him.
When His word fills all my thought,
Oft to heaven my foul is caught.

4

Heavenward ftill I long to hafte,
  When Thy fupper, Lord, is given ;
Heavenly ftrength on earth I tafte,
  Feeding on the Bread of Heaven ;
Such is e'en on earth our fare,
Who Thy marriage feaft will fhare.

5

Heavenward ! To that bleffed home
  Death at laft will furely lead me ;
All my trials overcome,
  Chrift with life and joy will feed me ;
Who Himfelf hath gone before
That we too might heavenward foar.

6

Heavenward ! This fhall be my cry
  While a pilgrim here I wander,
Paffing earth's allurements by
  For the love of what is yonder ;
Heavenward all my being tends,
Till in Heaven my journey ends.

(Index of Tunes, LIV.)

66.

Tune.—" Chrift the Life of all the living."

Lord, on earth I dwell fad-heart-ed, Here I oft muft mourn and figh: Take me, take me hence with Thee,
Where-fore haft Thou then de-part-ed, Why af-cend-eft Thou on high?

Or a-bide, Lord, ftill in me; Let Thy love and gifts be left, That I be not all be-reft.

2

Leave Thy heart ftill inly near me,
  Take mine hence where Thou art gone,
Open heaven to me, and hear me
  When to Thee I cry alone ;
When I cannot pray, oh plead
With Thy Father in my ftead ;
Seated now at God's right hand,
Help us here, Thy faithful band.

3

Worldly joys I caft behind me,
  Let me choofe the better part,
And though mortal chains yet bind me,
  Heavenly be my thoughts and heart ;
That my time through faith may be
Order'd for eternity ;
'Till we rife, all perils o'er,
Whither Thou haft gone before.

4

Then return, the promife keeping
  That was made to us of old ;
Raife the members that are fleeping
  Gnaw'd of death beneath the mould.
Judge the evil world that deems
Thy fure words but empty dreams ;
And for all our forrows paft
Let us know Thy joy at laft.

(LXV.—„ Mein Jefu, bem bie Seraphinen.")

67.

Original Tune.

My Je-fus, if the Se-ra-phim, The burn-ing hoft that near Thee ftand, How fhall thefe mor-tal eyes, now cloud-ed
Be-fore Thy Ma-jef-ty are dim, And veil their face at Thy com-mand,

And dim with e-vil's hate-ful night, En-dure to meet the blaze of light In which Thy throne is aye en-fhroud-ed ?

2 Yet grant the eye of faith, O Lord,
  To pierce within the Holy Place,
For I am faved and Thou adored,
  If I am quicken'd by Thy grace.
Behold, O King, my foul is bending
  In lowly love before Thy throne,
Oh fay, " I choofe thee for mine own,
  With faithful love thy courfe befriending."

3 Have mercy, Lord of love, for long
  My fpirit for Thy mercy fighs,
My inmoft foul hath found a tongue,
  " Be merciful, O God," fhe cries !
I know Thou wilt not bid me leave Thee,
  Thou canft not fhow Thyfelf a foe
To one for whom Thou bar'ft fuch woe,
  Whofe loft eftate fo fore could grieve Thee.

4 Then let Thy wifdom be my guide,
  Nor take Thy light from me away,
Thy grace be ever at my fide,
  That from Thy path I may not ftray ;
But feeling that Thy hand is o'er me,
  In fteadfaft faith my courfe fulfil,
And keep Thy word, and do Thy will,
Thy love within, Thy heaven before me !

5 Reach down and arm me with Thy hand,
  And ftrengthen me with inner might,
That I through faith may ftrive and ftand
  Though craft and force againft me fight ;
That fo may through me and within me
  The kingdom of Thy love be fpread,
That honours Thee, our glorious Head,
  And once a crown of light fhall win me.

6 To Thee I rife in faith on high,
  O bend Thou down in love to me !
Let nothing rob me of this joy,
  That all my foul is fill'd with Thee ;
As long as here I live, yea longer,
  Thee will I honour, fear, and love,
For when this heart hath ceafed to move
Than Death itfelf Thy Love is ftronger.

(Index of Tunes, xv.)

68.

Tune.—" My life is hid in Jefus."

Draw us to Thee, Lord Je-fus, And we will haf-ten on; For ftrong de-fire doth

feize us To go where Thou art gone.

2
Draw us to Thee; enlighten
These hearts to find Thy way,
That else the tempests frighten,
Or pleasures lure astray.

3
Draw us to Thee; and teach us
Even now that rest to find,
Where turmoils cannot reach us,
Nor cares weigh down the mind.

4
Draw us to Thee; nor leave us
Till all our path is trod,
Then in Thine arms receive us,
And bear us home to God.

WHITSUNTIDE.

(xxxiv.—„Heil'ger Geift, bu Tröfter mein.")

69.

Original Tune.

Ho-ly Ghoft! my Com-for-ter! Now from high-eft

heav'n ap-pear, Shed Thy gra-cious ra-diance here.

2
Come to them who suffer dearth,
With Thy gifts of priceless worth,
Lighten all who dwell on earth!

3
Thou the heart's most precious guest,
Thou of comforters the best,
Give to us, th' o'er-laden, rest!

4
Come, in Thee our toil is sweet,
Shelter from the noon-day heat,
From whom sorrow flieth fleet!

5
Blessed Sun! Oh let Thy rays
Fill with joy and warmth and grace
Every heart that truly prays.

6
What without Thy aid is wrought,
Skilful deed or wisest thought,
God will count but vain and nought.

7
Cleanse us, Lord, from sinful stain,
O'er the parchèd heart oh rain,
Heal the wounded from its pain.

8
Bend the stubborn will to Thine,
Melt the cold with fire divine,
Erring hearts aright incline.

9
Grant us, Lord, who cry to Thee,
Steadfast in the faith to be,
Give Thy gifts of charity:

10
May we live in holiness,
And in death find happiness,
And abide with Thee in bliss!

(Index of Tunes, CXVII.)

70.

Tune.—" O Morning Star! how fair and bright."

| 1st Time. | 2nd Time. |

O Ho-ly Spi-rit, en-ter in, A-mong thefe hearts Thy work be-gin, Thy tem-ple deign to make us;
Sun of the foul, Thou Light Di-vine, A-round and in us bright-ly fhine, To ftrength and glad-nefs wake us.

Where Thou fhin-eft Life from hea-ven There is giv-en, We be-fore Thee For that pre-cious gift im-plore Thee.

1 Left to ourfelves we fhall but ftray;
O lead us on the narrow way,
  With wifeft counfel guide us,
And give us fteadfaftnefs, that we
May henceforth truly follow Thee,
  Whatever woes betide us;
Heal Thou gently Hearts now broken,
  Give fome token
  Thou art near us,
Whom we truft to light and cheer us.

3 O mighty Rock, O Source of Life,
Let Thy dear Word, 'mid doubt and ftrife,
  Be fo within us burning
That we be faithful unto death,
In Thy pure love and holy faith,
  From Thee true wifdom learning;
Lord, Thy graces On us fhower,
  By Thy power
  Chrift confeffing,
Let us win His grace and bleffing.

4 O gentle Dew, from heaven now fall
With power upon the hearts of all,
  Thy tendernefs inftilling;
That heart to heart more clofely bound,
Fruitful in kindly deeds be found,
  The law of love fulfilling;
No wrath, no ftrife Here fhall grieve thee,
  We receive Thee,
  Where Thou liveft
Peace and love and joy Thou giveft.

5 Grant that our days, while life fhall laft,
In pureft holinefs be paft;
  Our minds fo rule and ftrengthen
That they may rife o'er things of earth,
The hopes and joys that here have birth;
  And if our courfe Thou lengthen,
Keep Thou pure, Lord, From offences,
  Heart and fenfes;
  Bleffed Spirit,
Bid us thus true life inherit!

(cui.—Crüger's tune: „Von Gott will ich nicht laſſen.")

71

O en - ter, Lord, Thy tem - ple, Be Thou my ſpi - rit's gueſt!
Who at my birth didſt give me A ſe - cond birth more bleſt.

Thou in the God - head, Lord, Though here to dwell Thou deign - eſt,

For ev - er e - qual reign - eſt, Art e - qual - ly a - dored.

2

O enter, let me know Thee,
   And feel Thy power within,
The power that breaks our fetters,
   And reſcues us from ſin ;
So waſh and cleanſe Thou me,
   That I may ſerve Thee truly,
   And render honour duly
With perfect heart to Thee.

3

'Tis Thou, O Spirit, teacheſt
   The ſoul to pray aright ;
Thy ſongs have ſweeteſt muſic,
   Thy prayers have wondrous might ;
Unheard they cannot fall,
   They pierce the higheſt heaven,
   Till He His help hath given
Who ſurely helpeth all.

4 Joy is Thy gift, O Spirit !
   Thou wouldſt not have us pine ;
In darkeſt hours Thy comfort
   Doth aye moſt brightly ſhine ;
Ah then how oft thy voice
   Hath ſhed its ſweetneſs o'er me,
   And open'd heaven before me,
And bid my heart rejoice !

5 All love is Thine, O Spirit !
   Thou hateſt enmity ;
Thou loveſt peace and friendſhip,
   All ſtrife wouldſt have us flee ;
Where wrath and diſcord reign
   Thy whiſper inly pleadeth,
   And to the heart that heedeth
Brings love and light again.

6 The whole wide world, O Spirit !
   Upon Thy hands doth rest,
Our wayward hearts Thou turneſt
   As it may ſeem Thee beſt ;
Once more Thy power make known !
   As Thou haſt done ſo often,
   Convert the wicked, ſoften
To tears the heart of ſtone.

7 With holy zeal then fill us,
   To keep the faith ſtill pure ;
And bleſs our lands and houſes
   With wealth that may endure ;
And make that foe to flee
   Who in us with Thee ſtriveth,
   From out our heart he driveth
Whate'er delighteth Thee.

8 Order our path in all things
   According to Thy mind,
And when this life is over,
   And muſt be all reſign'd,
Oh grant us then to die
   With calm and fearleſs ſpirit,
   And after death inherit
Eternal life on high.

(Lvii.—„Komm heiliger Geiſt, Herre Gott.")

72.
Original Tune.

Come, Ho - ly Spi - rit, God and Lord, Be all Thy

gra - ces now out - pour'd On the be - liev - er's mind and ſoul,

And touch our hearts with liv - ing coal. Thy Light this day ſhone forth fo clear, All tongues and na-tions gath-er'd near To learn that

faith, for which we bring Glad praife to Thee, and loud-ly, loud-ly fing,

Hal-le-lu-jah, Hal - le - lu-jah, Hal-le-lu-jah, Hal-le-lu-jah.

Thou Strong Defence, Thou Holy Light,
Teach us to know our God aright,
And call Him Father from the heart:
The Word of life and truth impart,
That we may love not doctrines ftrange,
Nor e'er to other teachers range,
But Jefus for our Mafter owr,
And put our truft in Him, in Him alone.
Hallelujah, Hallelujah!

3

Thou Sacred Ardour, Comfort Sweet,
Help us to wait with ready feet
And willing heart at Thy command,
Nor trial fright us from Thy band.
Lord, make us ready with Thy powers,
Strengthen the flefh in weaker hours,
That as good warriors we may force
Through life and death to Thee, to Thee our courfe.
Hallelujah, Hallelujah!

(Index of Tunes, LIV.)

73.
Tune.—" Chrift the Life of all the living."

Sweet - eft Fount of ho - ly glad - nefs, Fair - eft
Who a - like in joy and fad - nefs Leav - eft

light was ev - er fhed, Spi - rit of the High-eft God,
none un-vif - it - ed;

Lord, from whom is life be-ftow'd, Who up-hold - eft

ev' - ry - thing, Hear me, hear me, while I fing.

2

Thou art fhed like gentleft fhowers
From the Father and the Son,
Bringing to us quicken'd powers,
Pureft bleffing from their throne;
Suffer then, O noble Gueft,
That rich gift by Thee poffeft,
That Thou giveft at Thy will,
All my being now to fill.

3

Thou art ever true and holy,
Sin and falfehood Thou doft hate;
But Thou comeft where the lowly
And the pure Thy prefence wait;
Wafh me then, O Well of grace,
Every ftain and fpot efface,
Let me flee what Thou doft flee,
Grant me what Thou lov'ft to fee.

4

Well content am I if only
Thou wilt deign to dwell with me;
With Thee I am never lonely,
Never comfortlefs with Thee;
Thine for ever make me now,
And to Thee, my Lord, I vow
Here and yonder to employ
Every power for Thee with joy.

5

When I cry for help, oh hear me;
When I fink, oh hafte to fave;
When I die, be inly near me,
Be my hope e'en in the grave;
Bring me when I rife again
To the land that knows no pain,
Where Thy followers from Thy ftream
Drink for ever joys fupreme!

(LVIII.—„Komm, O komm bu Geist bes Lebens.")

74.
Original Tune.

Ho - ly Spi - rit, once a - gain
Nor Thy pow'r de - scend in vain,

Come, Thou true E - ter - nal God!
Make us ev - er Thine a - bode;

So shall Spi - rit, joy, and light

Dwell in us, where all was night.

2

Guide us, Lord, from day to day,
  Keep us in the paths of grace,
Clear all hindrances away
  That might foil us in the race;
When we ftumble hear our call,
Work repentance for our fall.

3

Witnefs in our hearts that God
  Counts us children through His Son,
That our Father's gentle rod
  Smites us for our good alone;
So when tried, perplex'd, diftreft,
In His love we ftill may reft.

4

Quicken us to feek His face
  Freely, with a trufting heart,
In our prayers oh breathe Thy grace,
  Go with us when we depart;
So fhall our requefts be heard,
And our faith to joy be ftirr'd.

5

Lord, preferve us in the faith,
  Suffer nought to drive us thence,
Neither Satan, fcorn, nor death;
  Be our God and our defence;
Though the flefh refift Thy will,
Let Thy word be ftronger ftill.

6

And at laft when we muft die,
  Oh affure the finking heart
Of the glorious realm on high
  Where Thou healeft every fmart,
Of the joys unfpeakable
Where our God would have us dwell.

TRINITY SUNDAY.

(CXX.—„Wir glauben all an einen Gott, Bater.")

75.
Original Tune.

We all be-lieve in One true God, Fa-ther, Son, and Ho-ly Ghoft,

Strong De-liv'-rer in our need, Praifed by all the heav'n-ly hoft,

By whofe might-y power a-lone All is made, and wrought, and done.

2

And we believe in Jefus Chrift,
  Son of man and Son of God;
Who, to raife us up to heaven,
  Left His throne, and bore our load;
By whofe crofs and death are we
Refcued from our mifery.

3

And we confefs the Holy Ghoft,
  Who from both for ever flows;
Who upholds and comforts us
  In the midft of fears and woes.
Bleft and holy Trinity,
Praife fhall aye be brought to Thee!

(xlii.—„Hochheilige Dreieinigkeit.") TRINITY.

76
Original Tune.

Moft High and Ho—ly Tri—ni—ty! O Thou, who of Thy mer—cy mild Oh let me love Thee day and night, With
Haft form'd me here in time to be Thy im—age and Thy lov—ing child,

all my foul, with all my might; Oh come, Thyfelf my foul pre—pare, And make Thy dwell—ing ev—er there.

2

Father! replenifh with Thy grace
This longing heart that would be Thine,
Make it Thy quiet dwelling-place,
Thy inner confecrated fhrine!
Forgive that oft my fpirit wears
Her time and ftrength in trivial cares,
Enfold her in Thy changelefs peace,
So fhe from all but Thee may ceafe!

3

O God the Son! Thy wifdom's light
Now on my darken'd reafon pour;
Forgive that things of fenfe and fight
Have been her only joy of yore;
Henceforth let every thought and deed
On Thee be fix'd, from Thee proceed;
Draw me to Thee, for I would rife
Above thefe earthly vanities!

4

O Holy Ghoft! Thou fire of love!
Enkindle with Thy flame my will;
Come with Thy ftrength, Lord, from above
Help me Thy bidding to fulfil:
Forgive that I fo oft have done
What I as finful ought to fhun;
Let me with pure and quenchlefs fire
Thy favour and Thyfelf defire.

5

Moft High and Holy Trinity!
O draw me now away far hence,
And fix upon eternity
All powers alike of foul and fenfe!
Make me at one within; at one
With Thee on earth; when life is done
Take me to dwell in light with Thee,
Moft High and Holy Trinity!

(Index of Tunes, xcviii.) SAINTS' DAYS.

77.
Tune.—"Open now Thy gates of beauty."

Who are thofe that, far be—fore me, Round the
Shin—ing as the ftars in glo—ry, Crown'd with

throne of God I fee, Hal—le—lu—jahs,
light and pu—ri—ty?

hark! they fing, So—lemn praife to God they bring.

4

They are thofe who, daily ferving
Here as priefts before their Lord,
Offer'd up with faith unfwerving
Soul and body at His word;
Now within the Holy place
They behold Him face to face.

5

As the hunted hart hath panted
For the river frefh and clear,
So their hearts with longing fainted
For the Living Fountain here.
Now their thirft is quench'd, they dwell
With the Lord they loved fo well.

6

I too ftretch my hands with longing
Thither, Jefus, day by day,
While my foes are round me thronging,
In Thy houfe on earth I pray,—
Let me fink not in the war,
Drive for me my foes afar.

7

Thus, O Lord, in earth and heaven
With Thy fervants caft my lot,
Let my fins be all forgiven,
In my need forfake me not;
Near the throne where Thou doft fhine
May a place at laft be mine!

2

Who are thofe array'd in brightnefs,
Clothed in righteoufnefs divine,
Wearing robes of dazzling whitenefs,
That unftain'd fhall ever fhine,
And can never more decay,—
Whence came all this fair array?

3

They are thofe whofe hearts were riven
Here with forrow, grief, and care,
Who by day and night have ftriven
With the mighty God in prayer;
Now their warfare finds its clofe,
God hath ended all their woes.

(Index of Tunes, LXIII.)

78.

Tune.—" Deal with me, God, in mercy now."

Rife, fol-low Me! our Mas-ter faith, All ye who make My yoke your choice; For-fake the world, nor count it
De-ny your-felves, be true to death, Fol-low wher-e'er ye hear My voice;

lofs, Tread in My fteps, and bear My crofs.

1 Though heavy it may feem, yet think
I went before, I ftill am near,
I fought the fight, and did not fhrink,
I trod the path of fuffering here;
My banner ftill is in the field,
Would ye, faint hearts, then fly or yield?

3 For he who feeks to fave his life
Shall find his care without Me vain
Who feems to lofe it in the ftrife
Shall find it in his God again;
Who follows not My crofs through all
He is not worthy of My call.

4 Then let us follow Thee, dear Lord,
As Thy true fervants did of old,
Forfaking all things at Thy word,
In fuffering calm, in danger bold;
'Tis only he who wins the fight
May hope to wear their crown of light.

(Index of Tunes, XC.)

79.

Tune.—" Ye fervants of the Lord, who ftand."

True Shep-herd, who in love moft deep Didft

watch and fuf-fer for Thy fheep, And didft ap-point Thy faints of old To teach and rule and ferve Thy fold;

2	3	4	5
We thank Thee for that gracious care,	Yea, all who own Thee for their Head,	No better trophy hath this day	Nor for ourfelves we pray alone,
And pray that now and everywhere	Oh let them in Thy footfteps tread,	Than hearts new-kindled to obey	In Thee Thy Church is ever one.
Thy fervants call'd to preach Thy Word	Owning and loving more Thy crofs	The call, for Thee that bids them live,	Unite us here in faith and love
Be faithful fhepherds, like their Lord.	Through perfecution, fhame, or lofs.	And gladly yield all earth can give.	Until we worfhip Thee above.

PRESENTATION IN THE TEMPLE.

(Index of Tunes, XCIX.)

80.

Tune.—" Farewell I gladly bid Thee."

Light of the Gen-tile na-tions, Thy peo-ple's joy and love, Thy
Drawn by Thy Spi-rit hi-ther, We glad-ly come to prove

pre-fence in Thy tem-ple, And wait with earn-eft mind, As Sim-eon once had waited His Saviour God to find.

2 Yes, Lord, Thy servants meet Thee,
   Ev'n now, in ev'ry place,
Where Thy true word hath promised
   That they should see Thy face.
Thou yet wilt gently grant us,
   Who gather round Thee here,
In faith's strong arms to bear Thee,
   As once that aged seer.

3 Be Thou our joy, our brightness,
   That shines 'mid pain and loss,
Our Sun in times of terror,
   The glory round our cross;
A glow in sinking spirits,
   A sunbeam in distress,
Physician, friend in sickness,
   In death our happiness.

4 Let us, O Lord, be faithful
   With Simeon to the end,
That so his dying song may
   From all our hearts ascend:
" O Lord, now let Thy servant
   Depart in peace for aye,
Since I have seen my Saviour,
   Have here beheld His day."

5 My Saviour, I behold Thee
   Now with the eye of faith;
No foe of Thee can rob me,
   Though bitter words he saith;
Within Thy heart abiding,
   As Thou dost dwell in me,
No pain, no death has terrors
   To part my soul from Thee !

(LXVIII.—„Mit Fried und Freud fahr ich dahin.")
81.
Original Tune.

In peace and joy I now de - part,

Ac - cord - ing to God's will, For full of com - fort is my heart, So calm and

sweet and still; So doth God His pro - mise keep, And death to me is but a sleep.

2

'T is Christ hath wrought this work for me,
   Thy dear and only Son,
Whom Thou hast suffer'd me to see,
   And made Him surely known
As my Help when trouble 's rife,
   And even in death itself my Life.

3

For Thou in mercy unto all
   Hast set this Saviour forth ;
And to His kingdom Thou dost call
   The nations of the earth
Through His blessed wholesome Word,
   That now in every place is heard.

4

He is the heathens' saving Light,
   And He will gently lead
Those who now know Thee not aright,
   And in His pastures feed ;
While His people's joy He is,
   Their Sun, their glory, and their bliss.

ANNUNCIATION.

(xxv.—„Du keufche Seele bu.")

82.
Original Tune.

Thou vir-gin foul! O thou The crown of wo-man's fto-ry, Thy Jo-feph's bliß and glo-ry, Thy kins-wo-man thou feek-eft now, There thy faith to cheer and ftir Through what God hath wrought for her.

2

My faith, alas! is weak,
And where it fees not plainly
It ftrives to grafp but vainly,
And fcarcely cares new ftrength to feek;
Seeing now what God can do,
May my faith grow ftronger too!

3

Thou Pearl of women, here
Haft to His will refign'd thee,
Thou wilt not look behind thee;
Thy tender heart, towards one fo dear
To thy friends, doth warmly glow,
Loving fervice fain would fhow.

4

God! I lament to Thee,
My will towards good is idle,
And yet I fcarce can bridle
Its finful impulfes in me;
May my courfe hereafter prove
Rich in good works and in love!

5

At laft thou goeft forth,
Moft loving foul and faireft,
With thee thy Lord thou beareft,
The Father's Word come down to earth.
Happy thou! that He will be
Thus companion unto thee.

6

The world is fuch a place,
Where we are pilgrims only,
And we muft fear, if lonely
We meet the end that comes apace.
Jefus! let me then by faith
Walk with Thee through life and death!

ST. JOHN THE BAPTIST.

(Index of Tunes, LXXXIX.)

83.
Tune.—"When the Lord recalls the banifhed."

Com-fort, com-fort ye my peo-ple, Speak ye
Com-fort thofe who fit in dark-nefs, Mourn-ing
peace, thus faith our God; Speak ye to Je-
'neath their for-rows' load;
ru-fa-lem Of the peace that waits for them,

Tell her that her fins I cov - - er,

And her war - fare now is o - - ver.

2

Yea, her fins our God will pardon,
  Blotting out each dark mifdeed ;
All that well deferved His anger
  He will no more fee nor heed.
She hath fuffer'd many a day,
Now her griefs have paffed away,
God will change her pining fadnefs
Into ever-fpringing gladnefs.

3

For Elijah's voice is crying
  In the defert far and near,
Bidding all men to repentance,
  Since the kingdom now is here.
Oh that warning cry obey,
Now prepare for God a way ;
Let the valleys rife to meet Him,
And the hills bow down to greet Him.

4

Make ye ftraight what long was crooked,
  Make the rougher places plain,
Let your hearts be true and humble,
  As befits His holy reign ;
For the glory of the Lord
Now o'er earth is fhed abroad,
And all flefh fhall fee the token
That His Word is never broken.

(Index of Tunes, CII.)

84.

Tune.—" From God fha)l nought divide me."

Ye fons of men, in earn - eft Pre-
The won - 'drous Con - qu'ror com - eth, Whofe

pare your hearts with - in, Whom God in grace a - lone
power can fave from fin,

Hath pro - mifed long to fend us, To light - en and be-

friend us, And make His mer - cy known.

2

Oh fet your ways in order
  When fuch a gueft is nigh ;
Make plain the paths before Him
  That now deferted lie.
Forfake what He doth hate,
Exalt the lowly valleys,
Bring down all pride and malice,
  And make the crooked ftraight.

3

The heart that's meek and lowly
  Is higheft with our God ;
The heart now proud and lofty
  He humbles with His rod ;
The heart that's unenticed
By fin, and fears to grieve Him,
Is ready to receive Him,
  To fuch comes Jefus Chrift.

4

'Twas thus St. John hath taught us,
  'Twas thus he preach'd of yore ;
And they will feel God's anger
  Who lift not to his lore.
Ah God ! now let his voice
To Thy true fervice win us,
That Chrift may come within us,
  And we in Him rejoice !

ST. MICHAEL AND ALL ANGELS.

85.

Tune.—"Shall I not fing praife to Thee."

Praife and thanks to Thee be sung, Migh-ty God, in
Lo! from ev'-ry land and tongue Na-tions ga-ther

fweet-eft tone! Praif-ing Thee that Thou doft fend,
round Thy throne,

Dai-ly from Thy heav'n a-bove, An-gel-mef-fen-

gers of love, Who Thy threat-en'd Church de-fend. Who can of-fer wor-thi-ly, Lord of an-gels, praife to Thee!

2

'T is your office, Spirits bright,
  Still to guard us night and day,
And before your heavenly might
  Powers of darknefs flee away;
Ever doth your unfeen hoft
  Camp around us, and avert
  All that feeks to do us hurt,
Curbing Satan's malice moft.
Lord, who then can worthily
For fuch goodnefs honour Thee!

3

And ye come on ready wing,
  When we drift toward fheer defpair,
Seeing nought where we might cling,
  Suddenly, lo, ye are there!
And the wearied heart grows ftrong,
  As an angel ftrengthen'd Him,
  Fainting in the garden dim
Neath the world's vaft woe and wrong.
Lord, who then can worthily
For fuch mercy honour Thee!

4

Right and feemly is it then
  We fhould glory, that our God
Hath fuch honour put on men,
  That He fends o'er earth abroad
Princes of the realm above,
  Champions, who by day and night
  Shield us with His holy might;
Come, behold how great His love!
Lord, who then can worthily
For fuch favour honour Thee!

5

Praife and thanks to Thee be fung,
  Mighty God, in fweeteft tone!
Lo! from ev'ry land and tongue
  Nations gather round Thy throne,
Praifing Thee that Thou doft fend,
  Hourly from Thy glorious fphere,
  Angels down to help us here,
And Thy threaten'd Church defend.
Let us henceforth worthily,
Lord of angels, honour Thee.

EMBER WEEKS.

86.
Original Tune.

Come, Ho-ly Ghoft, Cre-a-tor, come, And vi-fit all the fouls of Thine:

Thou haft in-fpired our hearts with life; In-fpire them now with life di-vine.

Thou art the Comforter, the gift
  Of God moft high; the fire of love,
The everlafting fpring of joy,
  And holy unction from above.

Thy gifts are manifold; Thou writ'ft
  God's laws in every faithful heart;
The promife of the Father, Thou
  Doft heavenly eloquence impart.

Enlighten our dark fouls, till they
  Thy love, Thy heavenly love embrace;
And fince we are by nature frail
  Affift us with Thy faving grace.

Drive far from us the mortal foe,
  And grant us to have peace within;
That, with Thy light and guidance bleft,
  We may efcape the fnares of fin.

6

Teach us the Father to confefs,
 And Son, who from the grave revived;
And, with the Father and the Son,
 Thee, Holy Ghoft, from both derived.

(Index of Tunes, XXIII.)

7

With Thee, O Father, therefore may
 The Son, who was from death reftor'd,
And facred Comforter, One God,
 To endlefs ages be adored!

87.

Tune.—"Jehovah, let me now adore Thee."

Wake, Spi-rit, who in times now old-en
And a-gainft ev-'ry foe em-bold-en,

Didft fire the watch-men of the Church-'s youth,
To wit-nefs day and night th'e-ter-nal truth,

Whofe voi-ces through the world are ring-ing ftill,

And bring-ing hofts to know and do Thy will:

2

Soon may that fire from heaven be lent us,
That fwift from land to land its flame may leap!
Soon, Lord, that pricelefs boon be fent us
Of faithful fervants, fit for Thee to reap
The harveft of the foul,—look down and view
How great the harveft, but the labourers few.

3

Lord, to our earneft prayer now hearken,
The prayer we offer at Thy Son's command;
For, lo! while ftorms around us darken,
Thy children's hearts are ftirr'd in every land,
To cry for help, with fervent foul, to Thee;
O hear us, Lord, and fpeak: "Thus let it be!"

4

Oh fpeedily that help be granted!
Send forth evangelifts, in fpirit ftrong,
 Arm'd with Thy Word, a hoft undaunted,
Bold to attack the rule of ancient wrong,
And let them all the earth for Thee reclaim,
To be Thy kingdom and to know Thy name!

5

Grant that for which Thy people calleth!
Send down Thy promifed Spirit, Lord, in might,
Before whom every barrier falleth,
And let it thus at evening-time be light;
Oh rend the heavens, and make Thy prefence felt,
The chains that bind us at Thy touch would melt.

6

Let Zion's paths lie wafte no longer,
Remove the hindrances that there have lain,
 And let Thy Word go forth to conquer;
Deftroy falfe doctrine, root out notions vain,
Set free from hirelings, let the Church and fchool
Bloom as a garden 'neath thy profpering rule.

(xc.—Pfalm 134, Goudimel.)

88.

Original Tune.

Ye ferv-ants of the Lord, who ftand With-in His tem-ple night and day, To wait and watch for

His com-mand, Oh praife the Lord whom ye o-bey.

2

Lift up your hands in praife and prayer,
 And thank Him in His holy place;
Let heart and voice alike declare
 His wondrous glory and His grace.

3

And God who earth and heaven hath made,
 And holds in being by His power,
Be now from Zion your conftant aid,
 And richeft bleffings o'er you fhower!

BAPTISM.

(Index of Tunes, CIII.)

89.

Tune.—"O enter, Lord, Thy temple."

Thy pa-rents' arms now yield thee, With love all glow-ing warm,
To Him who beſt can ſhield thee, To that E-ter-nal Arm

That bids the dead a-riſe, And earth and heav'n up-hold-eth, That ten-der babes en-fold-eth, And leads them to the ſkies.

2

Waſh'd in the blood that guſhes
From out His wounded heart,
Wrapp'd in the peace that huſhes
All earthly woe and ſmart,
Begin thy pilgrimage,
And ſeek, as more thou learneſt,
With wiſdom glad yet earneſt,
Thy proper heritage.

3

Oh ſweet ſhall ſound the voices
That hail thee from above,
Where heaven's bright hoſt rejoices
Before the Eternal Love:
"Now paſt is all thy ſtrife,
And thou canſt wander never,
Then bleſs the hour for ever
That call'd thee into life!"

(Index of Tunes, LXI.)

90.

Tune.—"Bleſſed Jeſus, at Thy word."

Bleſſ-ed Je-ſus, here we ſtand,
And this child at Thy com-mand

Met to do as Thou haſt ſpo--ken,
Now we bring to Thee, in to--ken

That to Chriſt it here is giv--en,

For of ſuch ſhall be His Hea--ven.

2

Yes, Thy warning voice is plain,
And we fain would keep it duly,
"He who is not born again,
Heart and life renewing truly,
Born of water and the Spirit,
Will My kingdom ne'er inherit."

3

Therefore haſten we to Thee,
Take the pledge we bring, oh take it!
Let us here Thy glory ſee,
And in tender pity make it
Now Thy child, and leave it never—
Thine on earth, and Thine for ever.

4

Turn the darkneſs into light,
To Thy grace receive and ſave it;
Heal the ſerpent's venom'd bite,
In the font where now we lave it;
Let Thy Spirit pure and lowly
Baniſh thought or taint unholy.

5

Make it, Head, Thy member now,
Shepherd, take Thy lamb and feed it,
Prince of Peace, its peace be Thou,
Way of life, to Heaven oh lead it,
Vine, this branch may nothing ſever,
Grafted firm in Thee for ever.

6

Now upon Thy heart it lies,
What our hearts ſo dearly treaſure,
Heavenward lead our burden'd ſighs,
Pour Thy bleſſing without meaſure,
Write the name we now have given,
Write it in the book of Heaven.

(Index of Tunes, XCV.)

91.   CONFIRMATION.

Tune.—"Jeſu, day by day."

From Thy heav'n-ly throne, Son of God, make known Now Thy pow'r, Thy Spi-rit ſend us,

Strength for this great work to lend us, That we all may be Whol-ly giv'n to Thee.

2	3	4	5
Thou our hearts prepare,	Draw our hearts above,	And as we draw near	Let Thy Spirit, Lord,
Shed Thy gladnefs there,	Fill them with Thy love,	For Thy bleffing here,	Promifed in Thy Word,
That we boldly may confefs Thee	So to keep the vows we offer,	May Thy grace in heavenly fhowers	Keep us fteadfaftly in union
As our only Lord, and blefs Thee	Scorning all that earth can proffer,	Quicken all our inner powers,	With Thy faithful faints' communion,
Whofe moft precious blood	Truly day by day	And Thy light and peace	Till in yon bleft place
Flow'd to work our good.	Walking in Thy way.	In our hearts increafe.	We behold Thy face !

92.

Tune.—"If thou but fuffer God to guide thee."

Bap-tized in-to Thy name moft ho-ly,
I claim a place, though weak and low-ly,

O Fa-ther, Son, and Ho-ly Ghost,
A-mong Thy feed, Thy cho-fen hoft;

Bu-ried with Chrift, and dead to fin,

Thy Spi-rit now fhall live with-in.

2

My loving Father here doth take me
　To be henceforth His child and heir;
My faithful Saviour now doth make me
　The fruit of all His forrows fhare;
My Comforter will comfort me
When darkeft clouds around I fee.

3

And I have vowed to fear and love Thee,
　And to obey Thee, Lord, alone;
I felt Thy Spirit inly move me,
　And dared to pledge myfelf Thy own,
Renouncing fin to keep the faith,
And war with evil to the death.

4

My faithful God, Thou faileft never,
　Thy covenant furely will abide;
Oh caft me not away for ever,
　Should I tranfgrefs it on my fide,
If I have fore my foul defiled,
Yet ftill forgive, reftore Thy child.

5

Yea, all I am and love moft dearly
　To Thee I offer now the whole;
Oh let me make my vows fincerely,
　Take full poffeffion of my foul,
Let nought within me, nought I own,
Serve any will but Thine alone.

6

And never let my purpofe falter,
　O Father, Son, and Holy Ghoft,
But keep me faithful to Thine altar,
　Till Thou fhalt call me from my poft;
So unto Thee I live and die,
And praife Thee evermore on high.

(xciv.—„Schmücke dich, o liebe Seele.")
93.
Original Tune.

HOLY COMMUNION.

Deck thy-self, my soul, with glad-ness, Leave the
Come in-to the day-light's splen-dour, There with

gloo-my haunts of sad-ness,
joy thy prais-es ren-der   Un-to Him whose grace un-bound-ed

Hath this won-drous ban-quet found-ed, High o'er all the heav'ns He

reign-eth, Yet to dwell with thee He deign-eth.

(Index of Tunes, LXXIV.)

2 Hasten as a Bride to meet Him,
And with loving reverence greet Him,
For with words of life immortal
Now He knocketh at thy portal;
Haste to ope the gates before Him,
Saying, while thou dost adore Him,
"Suffer, Lord, that I receive Thee,
And I never more will leave Thee."

3 Ah how hungers all my spirit
For the love I do not merit!
Oft have I, with sighs fast thronging,
Thought upon this food with longing,
In the battle well-nigh worsted,
For this cup of life have thirsted,
For the Friend, who here invites us,
And to God Himself unites us.

4 Now I sink before Thee lowly,
Fill'd with joy most deep and holy,
As with trembling awe and wonder
On Thy mighty works I ponder,
How, by mystery surrounded,
Depths no man hath ever sounded,
None may dare to pierce unbidden
Secrets that with Thee are hidden.

5 Sun, who all my life dost brighten,
Light, who dost my soul enlighten,
Joy, the sweetest man e'er knoweth,
Fount, whence all my being floweth,
At Thy feet I cry, my Maker,
Let me be a fit partaker
Of this blessed food from heaven,
For our good, Thy glory, given.

6 Jesus, Bread of Life, I pray Thee,
Let me gladly here obey Thee,
Never to my hurt invited,
Be Thy love with love requited;
From this banquet let me measure,
Lord, how vast and deep its treasure;
Through the gifts Thou here dost give me
As Thy guest in heaven receive me.

94.
Tune.—" My soul, now praise thy Maker."

O Liv-ing Bread from hea - ven, How rich-ly hast Thou fed Thy guest!
The gifts Thou now hast giv - en Have fill'd my heart with joy and rest.

O won-drous food of bless - ing, O cup that heals our woes,

My heart this gift pos-sess - - ing In thank-ful songs o'er - flows;

For while the life and ftrength in me Were quicken'd by this food,

My foul hath gaz'd a-while on Thee, My high-eft, on - - - ly Good!

2
My God, Thou here haft led me
Within Thy temple's holieft place,
And there Thyfelf haft fed me
With all the treafures of Thy grace;
Oh boundlefs is Thy kindnefs,
And righteous is Thy power,
While I in finful blindnefs
Am erring hour by hour;
And yet Thou comeft, doft not fpurn
A finner, Lord, like me!
Ah how can I Thy love return,
What gift have I for Thee?

3
A heart that hath repented,
And mourns for fin with bitter fighs,—
Thou, Lord, art well-contented
With this my only facrifice.
I know that in my weaknefs
Thou wilt defpife me not,
But grant me in Thy meeknefs
The favour I have fou3ht;
Yes, Thou wilt deign in grace to heed
The fong that now I raife,
For meet and right is it indee.l
That I fhould fing Thy piaife.

4
Grant what I have partaken
May through Thy grace fo work in me,
That fin be all forfaken,
And I may cleave alone to Thee,
And all my foul be heedful
How fhe Thy love may know,
For this alone is needful,
Thy love fhould in me glow;
Then let no beauty pleafe mine eyes,
No joy allure my heart,
But what in Thee, my Saviour, lies,
What Thou doft here impart.

5
O well for me that, ftrengthen'd
With heavenly food and comfort here,
Howe'er my courfe be lengthen'd,
I now may ferve Thee free from fear.
Away then earthly pleafure,
All earthly gifts are vain,
I feek a heavenly treafure,
My home I long to gain,
Where I fhall live and praife my God,
And none my peace deftroy,
Where all the foul is overflow'd
With pure eternal joy.

(Index of Tunes, XCIX.)

95.

Tune.—"Farewell I gladly bid Thee."

Oh how could I for-get Him, Who ne'er for-get-teth me?
Or tell the love that let Him De-fcend to fet me free? Have

I not feen Him dy-ing For us on

yon-der tree? Have I not heard Him

cry-ing, A-rife and fol-low Me!

2
For ever will I love Him
Who faw my hopelefs plight,
Who felt my forrows move Him,
And brought me life and light;
Whofe arm fhall be around me
When my laft hour is come,
And fuffer none to wound me,
Though dark the paffage home.

3
He gives me pledges holy,
His body and His blood,
He lifts the fcorn'd, the lowly,
He makes my courage good,
For He will reign within me,
And fhed His graces there;
The heaven He died to win me
Can I then fail to fhare?

4
In joy and forrow ever
Shine through me, Bleffed Heart,
Who bleeding for us, never
Didft fhrink from foreft fmart!
Whate'er I've lov'd, or ftriven,
Or borne, I bring to Thee,
Now let Thy heart and heaven
Stand open, Lord, to me.

(LXXIII.—„ Nun laſſ't uns den Leib begraben.")

96.

Original Tune.

BURIAL OF THE DEAD.

Now lay we calm - ly in the grave This form, where - of no doubt we have

That it ſhall riſe a - gain that day, In glo - rious tri - umph o'er de - cay.

2
And ſo to earth again we truſt
What came from duſt, and turns to duſt,
And from the duſt ſhall ſurely riſe
When the laſt trumpet fills the ſkies.

3
His ſoul is living now in God
Whoſe grace his pardon hath beſtow'd,
Who through His Son redeem'd him here
From bondage unto ſin and fear.

4
His trials and his griefs are paſt,
A bleſſed end is his at laſt ;
He bore Chriſt's yoke, and did His will,
And though he died he liveth ſtill.

5
He lives where none can mourn and weep,
And calmly ſhall this body ſleep
Till God ſhall Death himſelf deſtroy
And raiſe it into glorious joy.

6
He ſuffer'd pain and grief below,
Chriſt heals him now from all his woe ;
For him hath endleſs joy begun ;
He ſhines in glory like the ſun.

7
Then let us leave him to his reſt,
And homeward turn, for he is bleſt,
And we muſt well our ſouls prepare,
When death ſhall come, to meet him there.

8
So help us, Chriſt, our Hope in loſs !
Thou haſt redeem'd us by Thy croſs
From endleſs death and miſery ;
We praiſe, we bleſs, we worſhip Thee !

(Index of Tunes, LXXIII.)

97.

Tune.—" Now lay we calmly in the grave."

Now huſh your cries, and ſhed no tear, On ſuch death none ſhould look with fear ;

He died a faith - ful Chriſ - tian man, And with his death true life be - gan.

2 Coffin and grave we deck with care,
His body reverently we bear,
It is not dead but reſts in God,
And ſoftly ſleeps beneath the ſod.

3 It ſeems as all were over now,—
The heavy limbs, the ſoulleſs brow,—
Yet through theſe rigid limbs once more
A nobler life, ere long, ſhall pour.

4 Theſe dead dry bones again ſhall feel
New warmth and vigour through them ſteal,
Reknit and living they ſhall ſoar
On high where Chriſt lives evermore.

5 This body, lying ſtiff and ſtark,
Shall riſe unharm'd from out the dark,
And ſwiftly mount up through the ſkies,
Even as the ſpirit heavenwards flies.

6 The buried grain of wheat muſt die,
Wither'd and worthleſs long muſt lie,
Yet ſprings to light all ſweet and fair,
And proper fruits ſhall richly bear :

7 Even ſo this body made of duſt,
To earth we once again entruſt,
And painleſs it ſhall ſlumber here,
Until the Laſt Great Day appear.

8 God breathed into this houſe of clay
The ſpirit that hath paſs'd away,
Chriſt gave the true courageous mind,
The noble heart, ye no more find.

9 Now earth has hid it from our eyes,
Till God ſhall bid it wake and riſe,
Who ne'er the creature will forget,
On whom His image He hath ſet.

10 Ah would that promiſed Day were here,
When Chriſt ſhall once again appear ;
When He ſhall call, nor one be loſt,
To endleſs life earth's buried hoſt !

(Index of Tunes, xl.)

98.

Tune.—" Ah wounded Head ! "

The pre - cious feed of weep - ing
The form of one now fleep - ing,

To - day we fow once more,
Whofe pil - grim - age is o'er. Ah!

death but fafe - ly lands him Where

we too would at - tain; Our Fa - ther's voice de -

mands him, And death to him is gain.

2

He has what we are wanting,

He fees what we believe,

The fins on earth fo haunting

Have there no power to grieve ;

Safe in His Saviour's keeping,

Who fent him calm releafe,—

'Tis only we are weeping,

He dwells in perfect peace.

3

The crown of life he weareth,

He bears the fhining palm,

The " Holy, holy," fhareth,

And joins the angels' pfalm ;

But we poor pilgrims wander

Still through this land of woe,

Till we fhall meet him yonder,

And all his joy fhall know.

(LXXII.—,, Nun komm, der Heiden Heiland.")

99.

Chrift will ga - ther in His own To the place where He is gone,

Where their heart and trea - fure lie, Where our life is hid on high.

2 Day by day the voice faith, " Come,
Enter thine eternal home ; "
Afking not if we can fpare
This dear foul it fummons there.

3 Had he afk'd us, well we know
We fhould cry, oh fpare this blow !
Yes, with ftreaming tears fhould pray,
" Lord, we love him, let him ftay ! "

4 But the Lord doth nought amifs,
And fince He hath order'd this,
We have nought to do but ftill
Reft in filence on His will.

5 Many a heart no longer here,
Ah ! was all too inly dear ;
Yet, O Love, 't is Thou doft call,
Thou wilt be our All in all.

(Index of Tunes, LXXXII.)

100.
Tune.—" Lord Jesus Christ, my Life, my Light."

WORD OF GOD.

O Christ, our true and on-ly Light, Il - lu - mine those who sit in night; Let those a - far now hear Thy voice, And in Thy fold with us re - joice.

2
Fill with the radiance of Thy grace
The souls now lost in error's maze,
And all whom in their secret minds
Some dark delusion hurts and blinds.

3
And all who else have stray'd from Thee,
Oh gently seek! Thy healing be
To every wounded conscience given,
And let them also share Thy heaven.

4
Oh make the deaf to hear Thy word,
And teach the dumb to speak, dear Lord,
Who dare not yet the faith avow,
Though secretly they hold it now.

5
Shine on the darken'd and the cold,
Recall the wand'rers from Thy fold,
Unite those now who walk apart,
Confirm the weak and doubting heart.

6
So they with us may evermore
Such grace with wondering thanks adore,
And endless praise to Thee be given
By all Thy Church in earth and heaven.

(LXXI.—,, Nun freut euch lieben Christeng'mein.")
101.

Ah God, from heav'n look down and see,
How few, a - las! Thy ser - vants be,
And let com - pas - sion move Thee,
How help - less those who love Thee. Thy
Word is suf - fer'd not to stand, And Faith seems quench'd on
ev' - ry hand In this dark time of trou - ble.

2
False teachings now men spread abroad,
Mere schemes of men's invention,
Not grounded on God's own true Word,
And so they breed dissension;
Their outward seeming may be fair,
But one goes here, another there,
And rends the Church asunder.

3
Therefore, saith God, I will arise,
These men my poor are wronging,
I hear my people's bitter sighs,
And I will grant their longing;
My saving Word shall take the field,
Shall be the poor man's strength and shield,
And all my foes shall conquer.

4
As silver that through fire hath passed
Is pure from all its drosses,
So shall God's Word shine forth at last
The brighter for these crosses;
Through trial is its power made known,
Till all men far and near shall own
How pure and strong its glory.

5
Therefore, O God, preserve it pure
From all that would abuse it,
And in the Faith our hearts secure,
That we may never lose it;
For trouble and rebuke shall be
Among the people,—when we see
Ungodly men exalted.

(Index of Tunes, CIX.)

102.
Tune.—" Whate'er my God ordains is right."

Thy Word, O Lord, is gen - tle dew,
O shed that heav'n - ly balm a - new,
To suf - fring hearts that want it;
To all Thy gar - den grant it.
Re - fresh'd by Thee, May ev - 'ry tree Bud forth and blos - som to Thy praise,

2

Thy Word is like a flaming fword,
A fharp and mighty arrow,
A wedge that cleaves the rock, that Word
Can pierce through heart and marrow;
O fend it forth
O'er all the earth,
The darken'd heart to cleanfe and win,
And fhatter all the might of fin.

3

Thy Word, a wondrous Star, fupplies
True guidance when we need it,
It points to Chrift, it maketh wife
All fimple hearts that heed it;
Let not its light
E'er fink in night,
But ftill in every fpirit fhine,
That none may mifs that light divine.

(xxvii.—„ Erhalt uns Herr bei Deinem Wort.")
103.
Original Tune.

Lord, keep us stead-faft in Thy word; Curb
thofe who fain by craft or fword Would wreft the king-dom
from Thy Son, And fet at nought all He hath done.

2

Lord Jefu Chrift, Thy power make known,
For Thou art Lord of lords alone;
Defend Thy Chriftendom, that we
May evermore fing praife to Thee.

3

O Comforter, of pricelefs worth,
Send peace and unity on earth,
Support us in our final ftrife,
And lead us out of death to life.

(Index of Tunes, XCIII.) **THE CHURCH ON EARTH.**
104.
Tune.—" Strive aright when God doth call thee."

Hark! the Church pro-claims her hon-our, And her
strength is on-ly this: God hath laid His choice upon her, And the work fhe doth is His.

2

He His Church hath firmly founded,
He will guard what He began;
We, by fin and foes furrounded,
Build her bulwarks as we can.

3

Frail and fleeting are our powers,
Short our days, our forefight dim,
And we own the choice not ours,
We were chofen firft by Him.

4

Onward then! for nought defpairing,
Calm we follow at His word,
Thus through joy and forrow bearing
Faithful witnefs to our Lord.

5

Though we here muft ftrive with weaknefs,
Though in tears we often bend,
What His might began in meeknefs
Shall achieve a glorious end.

(LXXX.—„O gesegnetes Regieren.")

105.

Heart and heart to-ge-ther bound, Seek in God your true re-pose, We the mem-bers, He the Head,
In your love the price be found Of your Sa-viour's love and woes;

We the rays and He the Sun, Breth-ren by our Maf-ter led, In our Lord we all are one.

2 Children of His realm, draw near,
   Make your covenant ftronger ftill,
From your hearts allegiance fwear
   Unto Him who conquer'd ill.
If your bonds are yet too weak,
If but fragile yet they prove,
Help from His good Spirit feek
   Who can fteel the chains of love.

3 Only fuch love will fuffice,
   As the love that dwells in Him,
Love that from the crofs ne'er flies,
   Love that fpares not life or limb :
'T was for finners He was flain,
'T was for foes He fhed His blood,
That His death for all might gain
   Endlefs life,—the Higheft Good.

4 Thus, O trueft Friend, unite
   All Thy confecrated band,
That their hearts be fet aright
   To fulfil Thy laft command.
Each muft onward urge his friend,
   Helping him in word and deed,
Love's bleft pathway to afcend,
   Following where Thou doft lead.

5 Thou who doft command that all
   Practife love who bear Thy name,
Wake the dead, new followers call,
   Touch the flothful with Thy flame.
Let us live, O Lord, at one,
   As Thou with the Father art,
That through all the world be none
   Of Thy members left apart.

6 Then were given what Thou haft fought,
   In the Son were all men freed,
And the world at laft were taught
   That Thy rule is bleft indeed.
Father of all fouls, we praife
   Thee who fhineft in the Son ;
Lord, to Thee our hymns we raife,
   Who haft all men to Thee drawn !

(Index of Tunes, IV.)

106.

Tune.—" What fhall I, a finner, do ? "

Je-fus, whom Thy Church doth own As her Head and King a-lone, Blefs me Thy poor mem-ber too ;

And Thy Spi-rit's in-fluence give That to Thee hence-forth I live, Dai-ly Thou my ftrength re-new.

2
Let Thy living Spirit flow
Through Thy members all below,
   With its warmth and power divine ;
Scatter'd far apart they dwell,
Yet in every land, full well,
   Lord, Thou knoweft who is Thine.

3
Thofe who ferve Thee I would ferve,
Never from their union fwerve,
   Here I cry before Thy face,—
   Zion, God give thee good fpeed,
Chrift thy footfteps ever lead,
   Make thee fteadfaft in His ways ! "

4
Thofe o'er whom Thy billows roll
Strengthen Thou to leave their foul
   In Thy hands, for Thou art Love ;
Make them through their bitter pain
Pure from pride and finful ftain,
   Fix their hopes and hearts above.

5
And from thofe I love, I pray,
Turn not, Lord, Thy face away,
   Hear me while for them I plead ;
Be Thou their Eternal Friend,
Unto each due blefling fend,
   For Thou knoweft all they need.

6
Ah Lord, at this gracious hour
Vifit all our fouls with power ;
   Let Thy gladnefs in them fhine ;
Draw them with Thy love away,
From vain pleafures of a day,
   Make them wholly ever Thine.

7
Dearly were we purchafed, Lord,
When Thy blood for us was pour'd ;
   Think, O Chrift, we are Thine own !
Hold me, guide me, as a child,
Through the battle, through the wild,
   Leave me never more alone,

8
Till at laft I meet on high
With the faithful hoft who cry
   Hallelujah night and day ;
Pure from ftain we there fhall fee
Thee in us, and us in Thee,
   And be one in Thee for aye.

II. THE CHRISTIAN LIFE.

(II.—„Ach Gott und Herr.")

107.
Original Tune.

PENITENCE.

A-las! my God! my sins are great, My con-science doth up-braid me;
And now I find that at my strait No man hath pow'r to aid me.

2
And fled I hence, in my despair,
In some lone spot to hide me,
My griefs would still be with me there,
Thy hand still hold and guide me.

3
Nay, Thee I seek;—I merit nought,
Yet pity and restore me;
Be not Thy wrath, just God, my lot,
Thy Son hath suffer'd for me.

4
If pain and woe must follow sin,
Then be my path still rougher,
Here spare me not; if heaven I win,
On earth I gladly suffer.

5
But curb my heart, forgive my guilt,
Make Thou my patience firmer,
For they must miss the good Thou wilt,
Who at Thy teachings murmur.

6
Then deal with me as seems Thee best,
Thy grace will help me bear it,
If but at last I see Thy rest,
And with my Saviour share it.

(Index of Tunes, XL.)

108.
Tune.—"Ah wounded Head!"

My God, be-hold me ly-ing Be-fore Thee in the dust; Bright hours I spent glad-
Where are my hopes un-dy-ing? Where is my joy-ous trust?
heart-ed Ere of Thy light be-reft; Ah, all hath now de-part-ed, My pain a-lone is left.

2
I see the threatening danger,
And shrink in sore alarm,
As were I yet a stranger
To Thy protecting arm;
As though the woes that grieve me
To Thee were all unknown;
Nor Thou wouldst then relieve me
When other aid is gone.

3
O Father, look upon me,
So tried within, without;
With pitying grace look on me,
Forgive my faithless doubt;
My heart for grief doth languish,
Thou seest it, my God!
O soothe my conscience' anguish,
Lift off my sorrows' load.

4
I know Thy thoughts are ever
Of peace and love towards me,
Thy purpose changes never,
Could I but build on Thee!
That Thou fulfillest surely
Thy promises, dear Lord,
Here I can stand securely,
My life is in Thy Word

5
Then let thy faith be stronger,
My soul, shake off thy fears;
Thou soon shalt weep no longer,
Though bitter now thy tears;
Thy Saviour's love hath found thee,
He comes, He comes at last;
His light is breaking round thee,
The clouds and storms are past!

109.

Tune.—" Come, my foul, awake, 'tis morning."

Je-fus, pity-ing Saviour, hear me, Draw Thou near me, Turn Thee, Lord, in grace to me; For Thou know-eft all my

for-row, Night and mor-row Doth my cry go up to Thee.

6

Blefs my trials thus to fever
    Me for ever
From the love of felf and fin ;
Let me through them fee Thee clearer,
    Find Thee nearer,
Grow more like to Thee within.

2

Sin of courage hath bereft me,
    And hath left me
Scarce a fpark of faith or hope ;
Bitter tears my heart oft fheddeth
    As it dreadeth
I am paft Thy mercy's fcope.

3

Peace I cannot find, oh take me,
    Lord, and make me
From the yoke of evil free ;
Calm this longing never-fleeping,
    Still my weeping,
Grant me hope once more in Thee.

4

Lord, wilt Thou be wroth for ever ?
    Oh deliver
Me from all I moft deferved ;
'Tis Thyfelf, dear Lord, haft fought me,
    Thou haft taught me
Thee to feek from whom I fwerved.

5

Thou, my God and King, haft known me,
    Yet haft fhown me
True and loving is Thy will ;
Though my heart from Thee oft ranges,
    Through its changes,
Lord, Thy love is faithful ftill.

7

In the patience that Thou lendeft
    All Thou fendeft
I embrace, I will be ftill ;
Bend this ftubborn heart, I pray Thee,
    To obey Thee,
Calmly waiting on Thy will.

8

Here I bring my will, oh take it,
    Thine, Lord, make it,
Calm this troubled heart of mine ;
In Thy ftrength I too may conquer,
    Wait no longer,
Show in me Thy grace Divine.

110.

Original Tune.

What fhall I, a fin-ner, do? Whi-ther fhall I turn for aid? Con-fcience wak-ing brings to view

Sins that make me fore a-fraid. This my con-fi-dence fhall be, Je-fus, I will cleave to Thee.

2

True, I have tranfgreff'd Thy will,
    Oft have grieved Thee by my fin,
Yet I know Thou lov'ft me ftill,
    For I hear Thy voice within ;
Then, though fin accufes me,
Jefus, I will cleave to Thee.

3

Here the Chriftians oft muft bear
    Many a crofs and bitter fmart ;
If their lot in this I fhare,
    Shall I waver or depart ?
Loyal ftill my heart fhall be,
Jefus, ftill I cleave to Thee.

4

Well I know this life of ours
    Is but as a fleeting dream ;
Round us darknefs ever lowers,
    Death is nearer than we deem ;
Who knows what to-day may fee ?
Jefus, I will cleave to Thee.

5

If I die, I do but ceafe
    Sooner from this toil and care,
And I reft in perfect peace
    In the grave, fince Thou wert there ;
There Thy light fhall comfort me,
There too I will cleave to Thee.

6

Then, Lord Jefu, Thou art mine,
    Till Thou bring me to that place
Where I fhall for ever fhine
    In Thy light, and fee Thy face :
Bleffed will that haven be !
Jefus, I will cleave to Thee.

III.

Tune.—" Heart and heart together bound."

Thou who break-eft ev'-ry chain, Thou who ftill art ev-er near,
Thou with whom dif-grace and pain Turn to joy and heav'n e'en here;

Let Thy fur-ther judg-ments fall On the A-dam ftrong with-in,

Till Thy grace hath freed us all From the pri-fon-houfe of fin.

4 Lord, we do not afk for reft
　　For the flefh, we only pray
　　Thou wouldft do as feems Thee beft,
　　　Ere yet comes our parting day ;
　　But our fpirit clings to Thee,
　　　Will not, dare not, let Thee go,
　　Until Thou have fet her free
　　　From the bonds that caufe her woe.

2 'Tis Thy Father's will towards us
　　Thou fhouldft end Thy work at length ;
　Hence in Thee are centred thus
　Perfect wifdom, love, and ftrength,
　That Thou none fhouldft lofe of thofe
　　Whom He gave Thee, though they roam
　'Wilder'd here amid their foes,
　　Thou fhouldft bring them fafely home.

3 Look upon our bonds, and fee
　　How doth all creation groan
　'Neath the yoke of vanity,
　　Make Thy full redemption known.
　Still we wreftle, cry, and pray,
　　Held in bitter bondage faft,
　Though the foul would break away
　　Into higher things at laft.

5 Ours the fault it is, we own,
　　We are flaves to felf and floth,
　Yet oh leave us not alone
　In the living death we loathe !
　Crufh'd beneath our burden's weight,
　　Crying at Thy feet we fall,
　Point the path, though fteep and ftrait,
　　Thou didft open once for all.

6 Ah how dearly were we bought
　　Not to ferve the world or fin ;
　By the work that Thou haft wrought
　Muft Thou make us pure within,
　Wholly pure and free,—in us
　　Be Thine image now reftored :
　Fill'd from out Thy fulnefs thus
　　Grace for grace on us is pour'd.

7 Draw us to Thy crofs, O Love,
　　Crucify with Thee whate'er
　Cannot dwell with Thee above ;
　Lead us to thofe regions fair !
　Courage ! long the time may feem,
　　Yet His day is coming faft ;
　We fhall be like them that dream
　　When our freedom dawns at laft.

(VI.—„ Allein zu Dir, Herr Jefu Chrift.")

112.

Original Tune.

Lord Je-fu Chrift, in Thee a-lone My on-ly hope on
For o-ther com-fort-er is none, No help have I but

earth I place,
in Thy grace.　There is no man nor crea-ture here, No

an-gel in the heav'n-ly fphere, Who at my need can fuc-cour me;

I cry to Thee, For Thou canft end my mi-fe-ry.

2

My fin is very fore and great,
　I weep and mourn its load beneath ;
O free me from this heavy weight,
　My Saviour, through Thy precious death ;
And with my Father for me plead
That Thou haft fuffer'd in my ftead ;
From me the burden then is roll'd,
　　And I lay hold
On Thy dear promifes of old.

3

And of Thy mercy now beftow
　True Chriftian faith on me, O Lord !
That all the fweetnefs I may know
　That in Thy holy crofs is ftored ;
Love Thee o'er earthly pride or pelf,
And love my neighbour as myfelf ;
And when at laft is come my end,
　　Be Thou my Friend,
From all affaults my foul defend.

4

Glory to God in higheft heaven,
　The Father of eternal love ;
To His dear Son, for finners given,
　Whofe watchful grace we daily prove ;
To God the Holy Ghoft on high ;
Oh ever be His comfort nigh,
And teach us, free from fin and fear,
　　To pleafe Him here,
And ferve Him in the finlefs fphere !

(Index of Tunes, LXV.)

113.

Tune.—" My Jefus, if the Seraphim."

Pure Ef-fence! Spot-lefs Fount of Light, That fad-eth
O Thou, whofe eyes, more clear and bright Than noon-day

nev-er in-to dark! Our fins; lo, bare be-fore Thy face
fun, are quick to mark

Lies all the de-fert of-my heart, My once fair foul in

ev-'ry part Now ftain'd with e-vil foul and bafe.

2

Since but the pure in heart are bleft
  With promifed vifion of their God,
Sore fear and anguifh fill my breaft,
  Remem'ring all the ways I trod ;
Mourning I fee my loft eftate,
  And yet in faith I dare to cry,
  Oh let my evil nature die,
Another heart in me create !

3

Enough, Lord, that my foe too well
  Hath lured me once away from Thee ;
Henceforth I know his craft how fell,
  And all his deep-laid fnares I flee.
Lord, through the Spirit whom Thy Son
  Hath bidden us in prayer to afk,
  Arm us with might that every tafk,
Whate'er we do, in Thee be done.

4

Unworthy am I of Thy grace,
  So deep are my tranfgreffions, Lord,
And yet once more I feek Thy face ;
  My God, have mercy, nor reward
My fins and follies, dark and vain ;
  Reject, reject me not in wrath,
  But let Thy funfhine now beam forth,
And quicken me with hope again.

5

The Holy Spirit Thou haft given,
  The wondrous pledge of love divine,
Who fills our hearts with joys of heaven,
  And bids us earthly toys refign ;
Oh let His feal be on my heart,
  Oh take Him nevermore away,
  Until this flefhly houfe decay,
And Thou fhalt bid me hence depart.

6

But ah ! my coward fpirit droops,
  Sick with the fear that enters in
Whene'er a foul to bondage ftoops,
  And wears the fhameful yoke of fin ;
Oh quicken with the ftrength that flows
  From out the Eternal Fount of Life,
  My foul half-fainting in the ftrife,
And make an end of all my woes.

7

I cling unto Thy grace alone,
  Thy fteadfaft oath my only reft ;
To Thee, Heart-fearcher, all is known
  That lieth hidden in my breaft ;
Thy joy, O Spirit, on me pour,
  Thy fervent will my floth infpire,
  So fhall I have my heart's defire,
And ferve and praife Thee evermore.

(c.—„ Vater unfer im Himmelreich.")

114.   PRAYER.

Our Fa-ther, Thou in heav'n a-bove, Who bid-deft us to dwell in love, As bre-thren of one fa-mi-ly,

And cry for all we need to Thee; Teach us to mean the words we fay, And from the in-moft heart to pray.

2

All hallow'd be Thy name, O Lord !
Oh let us firmly keep Thy Word,
And lead, according to Thy name,
A holy life, untouch'd by blame ;
Let no falfe teachings do us hurt—
All poor deluded fouls convert.

3

Thy kingdom come ! Thine let it be
In time, and through eternity !
Oh let Thy Holy Spirit dwell
With us, to rule and guide us well ;
From Satan's mighty power and rage
Preferve Thy Church from age to age.

4

Thy will be done on earth, O Lord,
As where in heaven Thou art adored !
Patience in time of grief beftow,
Obedience true through weal and woe ;
Strength, tempting wifhes to control
That thwart Thy will within the foul.

5

Give us to-day our daily bread,
Let us be duly clothed and fed,
And keep Thou from our homes afar
Famine and peftilence and war,
That we may live in godly peace,
Unvex'd by cares and avarice.

6

Forgive our fins, that they no more
May grieve and haunt us as before,
As we forgive their trefpaffes
Who unto us have done amifs ;
Thus let us dwell in charity,
And ferve each other willingly.

7

Into temptation lead us not,
And when the foe doth war and plot
Againft our fouls on every hand,
Then, arm'd with faith, oh may we ftand
Againft him as a valiant hoft,
Through comfort of the Holy Ghoft.

8

Deliver us from evil, Lord,
The days are dark and foes abroad ;
Redeem us from the fecond death,
And when we yield our dying breath,
Confole us, grant us calm releafe,
And take our fouls to Thee in peace.

9

Amen ! that is, fo let it be !
Strengthen our faith and truft in Thee,
That we may doubt not, but believe
That what we afk we fhall receive ;
Thus in Thy name and at Thy word
We fay Amen, now hear us, Lord !

(LXXXI.—„ O Gott bu frommer Gott.")

115.

Original Tune.

O God, Thou faith-ful God, Thou All
With -out whom no -thing is,

Foun-tain ev - er flow - ing, A pure and healthy frame
per -feft gifts be -ftow -ing ;

O give me, and with -in A con -fcience free from

blame, A foul un -hurt by fin.

2

And grant me, Lord, to do,
With ready heart and willing,
Whate'er Thou fhalt command,
My calling here fulfilling,
And do it when I ought,
With all my ftrength, and blefs
The work I thus have wrought,
For Thou muft give fuccefs.

3

And let me promife nought
But I can keep it truly,
Abftain from idle words,
And guard my lips ftill duly ;
And grant, when in my place
I muft and ought to fpeak,
My words due power and grace,
Nor let me wound the weak.

4

If dangers gather round,
Still keep me calm and fearlefs ;
Help me to bear the crofs
When life is dark and cheerlefs ;
To overcome my foe
With words and actions kind ;
When counfel I would know,
Good counfel let me find.

5

And let me be with all
In peace and friendfhip living,
As far as Chriftians may.
And if Thou aught art giving
Of wealth and honours fair,
Oh this refufe me not,
That nought be mingled there
Of goods unjuftly got.

6

And if a longer life
Be here on earth decreed me,
And Thou through many a ftrife
To age at laft wilt lead me,
Thy patience in me fhed,
Avert all fin and fhame,
And crown my hoary head
With pure untarnifh'd fame.

7

Let nothing that may chance,
Me from my Saviour fever ;
And dying with Him, take
My foul to Thee for ever ;
And let my body have
A little fpace to fleep
Befide my fathers' grave,
And friends that o'er it weep.

8

And when the Day is come,
And all the dead are waking,
Oh reach me down Thy hand,
Thyfelf my flumbers breaking ;
Then let me hear Thy voice,
And change this earthly frame,
And bid me aye rejoice
With thofe who love Thy name.

(XLVI.—„Ich ruf' zu Dir Herr Jesu Chrift.")

116.
Original Tune.

Lord, hear the voice of my com-plaint, To
Let not my heart and my hope grow faint, But

Thee I now com-mend me, 'True faith from Thee, my God, I feek,
deign Thy grace to fend me;

The faith that loves Thee fole-ly, Keeps me low-ly, And

prompt to aid the weak, And mark each word that Thou doft speak.

2
Yet more from Thee I dare to claim,
  Whose goodnefs is unbounded;
Oh let me ne'er be put to fhame,
  My hope be ne'er confounded;
But e'en in death ftill find Thee true,
  And in that hour, elfe lonely,
    Truft Thee only,
  Not aught that I can do,
For fuch falfe truft I fore fhould rue.

3
Oh grant that from my very heart
  My foes be all forgiven,
Forgive my fins and heal their fmart,
  And grant new life from heaven;
Thy word, that bleffed food, beftow,
  Which beft the foul canft nourifh;
    Make it flourifh
  Through all the ftorms of woe
That elfe my faith might overthrow.

4
Then be the world my foe or friend,
  Keep me to her a ftranger,
Thy fteadfaft foldier to the end,
  Through pleafure and through danger;
From Thee alone comes fuch high grace,
  No works of ours obtain it,
    Or can gain it;
  Our pride hath here no place,
'Tis Thy free promife we embrace.

5
Help me, for I am weak; I fight,
  Yet fcarce can battle longer;
I cling but to Thy grace and might,
  'Tis Thou muft make me ftronger;
When fore temptations are my lot,
  And tempefts round me lower,
    Break their power.
So, through deliverance wrought,
I know that Thou forfak'ft me not!

(XXIII.—„Dir bir Jehovah will ich fingen.")

117.
Original Tune.

Je-ho-vah, let me now a-dore Thee, For where is there a God fuch, Lord, as Thou?
With fongs I fain would come be-fore Thee; Oh let Thy Spi-rit deign to teach me now

To praife Thee in His name, through whom a-lone
Our fongs can pleafe Thee, through Thy bleff-ed Son.

2 Yes, draw me to the Son, O Father,
That fo the Son may draw me up to Thee.
Let every power within me gather,
To own Thy fway, O Spirit,—rule in me,
That fo the peace of God may in me dwell,
And I may fing for joy and praife Thee well.

3 Grant me Thy Spirit; then my praifes
Will found aright, no jarring tone or word;
Sweet are the fongs the heart then raifes,
Then I can pray in truth and fpirit, Lord;
Thy Spirit bears mine up on eagles' wing,
To join the pfalms the heavenly choirs now fing.

4 For He can plead for me with fighings
That are unutterable to lips like mine;
He bids me pray with earneft cryings,
Bears witnefs with my foul that I am Thine,
Co-heir with Chrift, and thus may dare to fay,
O Abba, Father, hear me when I pray.

5   When thus Thy Spirit in me burneth,
  And makes this cry to break from out my heart,
    Thy heart, O Father, toward me yearneth,
  And longs all precious blessings to impart,
  Thy ready love rejoiceth to fulfil
  The prayer breathed out according to Thy will.

6   And what Thy Spirit thus hath taught me
  To seek from Thee, must needs be such a prayer
    As Thou wilt grant, through Him who bought me,
  And raised me up to be Thy child and heir;
  In Jesu's name fearless I seek Thy face,
  And take from Thee, my Father, grace for grace.

7   O joy! our hope and trust are founded
  On His sure Word, and witness in the heart;
    I know Thy mercies are unbounded,
  And all good gifts Thou freely wilt impart,
  Nay, more is lavish'd by Thy bounteous hand,
  Than we can ask or seek or understand.

8   O joy! In His name we draw near Thee,
  Who ever pleadeth for the sons of men;
    I ask in faith and Thou wilt hear me,
  In Him Thy promises are all Amen.
  O joy for me! and praise be ever Thine,
  Whose wondrous love has made such blessings mine!

(Index of Tunes, XXXVII.)

118.

Tune.—" Lord Jesus Christ, be present now."

O God, I long Thy Light to see, My God, I
hour-ly think on Thee; Oh draw me up, nor hide Thy
face, But help me from Thy ho-ly place.

2
As toward her sun the sunflower turns,
Towards Thee, my Sun, my spirit yearns;
Oh would that free from sin I might
Thus follow evermore Thy Light!

3
But sin hath so within me wrought,
Such deadly sickness on me brought,
My languid soul sits drooping here
And cannot reach the heavenly sphere.

4
Ah how shall I my freedom win?
How break this heavy yoke of sin?
My fainting spirit thirsts for Thee,
Come, Lord, to help and set me free.

5
My heart is set to do Thy will,
But all my deeds are faulty still;
My best attempts are nothing worth,
But foil'd with cleaving taint of earth.

6
Remember that I am Thy child,
Forgive whate'er my soul defiled,
Blot out my sins, that I may rise
Freely to Thee beyond the skies.

7
Help me to love the world no more,
Be Master of my house and store,
The shield of faith around me throw,
And break the arrows of my foe.

8
Fain would my heart henceforward be
Fix'd, O my God, alone on Thee,
That heart and soul, by Thee possest,
May find in Thee their perfect rest.

9
Begone, ye pleasures false and vain,
Untasted, undesired remain!
In heaven alone those joys abound,
Where all my true delight is found.

10
Oh take away whate'er has stood
Between me and the Highest Good;
I ask no better boon than this,
To find in God my only bliss.

(XXXIX.—„Herzlich lieb hab' ich Dich.")

119.
Original Tune.

Lord, all my heart is fix'd on Thee, I pray Thee, be not far from me, With ten-der grace up-hold me. Yea,
The whole wide world de-lights me not, Of heaven or earth, Lord, ask I not, If but Thy love en-fold me.

though my heart be like to break, Thou art my trust that nought can shake, My por-tion and my hid-den joy, Whose cross could

all my bonds de-stroy; Lord Je-sus Christ! My God and

Lord! My God and Lord! For-sake me not who trust Thy word!

2

Rich are Thy gifts! 'Twas God that gave
Body and soul, and all I have
In this poor life of labour;
Oh grant that I may through Thy grace
Use all my powers to show Thy praise,
And serve and help my neighbour;
From all false doctrine keep me, Lord;
All lies and malice from me ward;
In every cross uphold Thou me,
That I may bear it patiently;
Lord Jesus Christ!
My God and Lord! My God and Lord!
In death Thy comfort still afford.

3

Ah Lord, let Thy dear angels come
At my last end, to bear me home,
That I may die unfearing;
And in its narrow chamber keep
My body safe in painless sleep
Until my Lord's appearing;
And then from death awaken me,
That these mine eyes with joy may see,
O Son of God, Thy glorious face,
My Saviour, and my Fount of Grace!
Lord Jesus Christ!
Receive my prayer, receive my prayer,
Thy love will I for aye declare.

(XLIX.—„In Dich hab' ich gehoffet, Herr.")

120.
Original Tune.

In Thee, Lord, have I put my trust, Leave me not help-less in the dust, Let

not my hope be brought to shame, But still sus-tain, Through want and pain, My faith that Thou art aye the same.

Incline a gracious ear to me,
And hear the prayers I raise to Thee,
Show forth Thy power and haste to save!
For woes and fear
Surround me here,
Oh swiftly send the help I crave!

3
My God and Shield, now let Thy power
Be unto me a mighty tower,
Whence I may freely, bravely, fight
Against the foes
That round me close,
For fierce are they and great their might.

Thy Word hath said, Thou art my Rock,
The Stronghold that can fear no shock,
My help, my safety, and my life,
Howe'er distress
And dangers press;
What then shall daunt me in the strife?

5
The world for me hath falsely set
Full many a secret snare and net,
Dark lies, delusions sweet and vain;
Lord, hear my prayers,
And break these snares,
And make my path before me plain.

6
With Thee, Lord, would I cast my lot;
My God, my God, forsake me not,
O faithful God, for I commend
My soul to Thee;
Deliver me
Both now, and when this life must end.

121.

Tune.—" When on the croſs the Saviour hung."

I know, my God, and I re - joice That on Thy right - eous will and choice All hu - man works and ſchemes muſt reſt : Suc - ceſs and bleſſ - ing are of Thee, What Thou ſhalt ſend is ſure - ly beſt !

It ſtands not in the power of man
To bring to paſs the wiſeſt plan
 So ſurely that it cannot fail ;
Thy counſel, Higheſt, muſt enſure
That our poor wiſdom ſhall avail.

A man oft thinks within his breaſt,
That lot for him were ſurely beſt,
 This, that his Father may ordain,
Were hurtful ;—yet, behold, it proves
This is his bleſſing, that his bane.

Then, O my Father, hear my cry,
Grant me true judgment from on high,
 On my own will I would not build ;
Be Thou my Friend and Counſellor,
So what is beſt ſhall be fulfilled.

And if this work be Thine, oh bleſs
Our poor weak efforts with ſucceſs ;
 If not, deny it, change our mind,—
Whate'er Thou workeſt not will ſoon
Diſperſe like ſand before the wind.

6 Grant us what is our trueſt good,
 And not what pleaſes fleſh and blood ;
 Our inmoſt ſpirits do Thou prove,
 Our higheſt aim, our beſt delight,
 Shall be Thy glory and Thy love.

122.

Original Tune.

Here be - hold me, as I caſt me At Thy throne, O glo - rious King !

Tears faſt throng - ing, child-like long - ing, Son of Man, to Thee I bring.

Let me find Thee— let me find Thee ! Me poor and worthleſs thing.

2 Look upon me, Lord, I pray Thee,
 Let Thy Spirit dwell in mine ;
 Thou haſt ſought me, Thou haſt bought me,
 Only Thee to know I pine ;
 Let me find Thee—let me find Thee !
 Take my heart and grant me Thine.

3 Nought I aſk for, nought I ſtrive for,
 But Thy grace ſo rich and free,
 That Thou giveſt whom Thou loveſt,
 And who truly cleave to Thee ;
 Let me find Thee—let me find Thee !
 He hath all things who hath Thee.

4 Earthly treaſure, mirth and pleaſure,
 Glorious name, or richeſt hoard,
 Are but weary, void and dreary,
 To the heart that longs for God ;
 Let me find Thee—let me find Thee !
 I am ready, mighty Lord.

CHRISTIAN FAITH AND RESOLVE.

(Index of Tunes, XXVII.)

123.

Tune.—" Lord, keep us steadfast in Thy Word."

Faith is a liv-ing power from heav'n That grasps the prom-ise God hath given, A trust that can-not be o'er-thrown, Fix'd heart-i-ly on Christ a-lone.

2 Faith finds in Christ whate'er we need
To save or strengthen us indeed,
Receives the grace He sends us down,
And makes us share His cross and crown.

3 Faith in the conscience worketh peace,
And bids the mourner's weeping cease ;
By Faith the children's place we claim,
And give all honour to One Name.

4 Faith feels the Spirit's kindling breath
In love and hope that conquer death ;
Faith worketh hourly joy in God,
And trusts and blesses e'en the rod.

5 We thank Thee then, O God of heaven,
That Thou to us this faith hast given
In Jesus Christ Thy Son, who is
Our only Fount and Source of bliss

6 Now from His fulness grant each soul
The rightful faith's true end and goal,
The blessedness no foes destroy,
Eternal love and light and joy.

(XXVI.—„ Ein' feste Burg ist unser Gott.")

124.

Original Tune.

A sure strong-hold our God is He, A trusty shield and wea-pon; That old ma-li-cious foe Means us dead-ly woe; Arm'd with might from hell And deep-est craft as well, On earth is not his fel-low.

Our help He'll be and set us free From ev'-ry ill can hap-pen.

Through our own force we nothing can,
Straight were we lost for ever ;
But for us fights the proper Man,
By God sent to deliver.
Ask ye who this may be ?
Jesus Christ is He,
Of Sabaoth Lord,
Sole God to be adored—
'T is He must win the battle.

3

And were the world with devils fill'd,
All eager to devour us,
Our souls to fear should little yield,
They cannot overpower us.
Their dreaded Prince no more
Harms us as of yore ;
Look grim as he may,
Doom'd is his ancient sway,
A word can overthrow him.

4

Still shall they leave that Word His might
And yet no thanks shall merit ;
Still is He with us in the fight,
By His good gifts and Spirit.
E'en should they take our life,
Wealth, name, child, or wife—
Though all these be gone,
Yet nothing have they won,
God's kingdom ours abideth !

125.

Tune.—" Not in anger, Mighty God."

Rise, my soul, to watch and pray, From thy sleep a-wake thee,
Lest at last the e - vil day Sud - den - ly o'er-take thee;
For the foe, Well we know, Oft his har - vest reap - eth While the Chris - tian sleep - eth.

2
Wake and watch, or else thy night
Christ can ne'er enlighten;
Far off still will seem the light
That thy path should brighten;
God demands
Willing hands,
Hearts His love confessing,—
Such He fills with blessing.

3
Watch against the world that frowns
Darkly to dismay thee;
Watch, when she thy wishes crowns,
Smiling to betray thee;
Watch and see
Thou art free
From false friends that charm thee,
While they seek to harm thee.

4
Watch against thyself, my soul,
See thou do not stifle
Grace that should thy thoughts control,
Nor with mercy trifle;

(4) Pride and sin
Lurk within,
All thy hopes to scatter;
Lift not, when they flatter.

5
But while watching, also see
That thou pray unceasing,
For the Lord must make thee free,
Strength and faith increasing,
So to do
Service true;
Let not sloth enslave thee,
Pray, and He will save thee.

6
Courage then, for He will give
All that we are needing,
Through the Son, in whom we live,
Who for us is pleading.
Day by day
Watch and pray,
While the tempests lower,
Till He comes with power.

126.

Tune.—" Ere yet the dawn hath fill'd the skies."

Cour - age, my sore - ly - tempt - ed heart! Break through thy woes, for - get their smart; Come forth and

Bridegroom

on thy Bride - groom gaze, The Lamb of God, the Fount of grace; Here is thy place!

2
His arms are open, thither flee!
There rest and peace are waiting thee,
The deathless crown of righteousness,
The entrance to eternal bliss;
He gives thee this!

3
Then combat well, of nought afraid,
For thus His follower thou art made,
Each battle teaches thee to fight,
Each foe to be a braver knight,
Arm'd with His might.

4
If storms of fierce temptation rise,
Unmoved I'll face the frowning skies;
If but the heart is true indeed,
Christ will be with me in my need,—
His own could bleed.

5
I flee away to Thy dear cross,
For hope is there for every loss,
Healing for every wound and woe,
There all the strength of love I know,
And feel its glow.

6
Before the Holy One I fall,
The Eternal Sacrifice for all;
His death has freed us from our load,
Peace on the anguish'd soul bestow'd,
Brought us to God.

7
How then should I go mourning on?
I look to Thee,—my fears are gone,
With Thee is rest that cannot cease,
For Thou hast wrought us full release,
And made our peace.

8
Thy word hath still its glorious powers,
The noblest chivalry is ours;
O Thou, for whom to die is gain,
I bring Thee here my all, oh deign
T'accept and reign!

(XLV.—„ Ich hab' mein' Sach' Gott heimgestellt.")
127.
Original Tune.

My caufe is God's, and I am ftill, Let Him do with me as He will;

Whe-ther for me the race is run, Or fcarce be-gun, I afk no more— His will be done!

My fins are more than I can bear,
Yet not for this will I defpair,
I know to death and to the grave
    The Father gave
His deareft Son, that He might fave.

To Him I live and die alone,
Death cannot part Him from His own;
Living or dying, I am His
    Who only is
Our comfort, and our gate of blifs.

This is my folace, day by day,
When fnares and death befet my way,
I know that at the morn of doom
    From out the tomb
With joy to meet Him I fhall come.

Then I fhall fee God face to face,
I doubt it not, through Jefu's grace,
Amid the joys prepared for me !
    Thanks be to Thee
Who giveft us the victory !
      6

(XCHI.—„ Ringe recht wenn Gottes Gnade.")
128.
Original Tune.

Strive a-right when God doth call thee, When He

draws thee by His grace, Caft off all that would en-

thrall thee, And de-ter thee from the race.

Amen, dear God ! now fend us faith,
And at the laft a happy death ;
And grant us all ere long to be
    In heaven with Thee,
To praife Thee there eternally.

2 Wreftle, till thy zeal is burning
    And thy love is glowing warm,
All that earth can give thee fpurning :—
    Half love will not bide the ftorm.

3 Combat, though thy life thou giveft,
    Storm the kingdom, but prevail ;
Let not him with whom thou ftriveft
    Ever make thee faint or quail.

4 Perfect truth will never waver,
    Wars with evil day and night,
Changes not for fear or favour,
    Only cares to win the fight.

5 Perfect truth will love to follow
    Watchfully our Mafter's ways ;
Seeks not comfort poor and hollow,
    Looks not for reward or praife.

6 Perfect truth from worldly pleafure,
    Worldly turmoil, ftands apart ;
For in heaven is hid our treafure,
    There muft alfo be the heart.

7 Soldiers of the Crofs, take courage !
    Watch and war 'mid fear and pain ;
Daily conquering fin and forrow,
    Till our King o'er earth fhall reign.

(XLIII.—„ Höchfter Priefter, der Du Dich.")
129.
Original Tune.

Great High-prieft, who deign'dft to be Once the

fa-cri-fice for me, Take this liv-ing heart of mine, Lay it on Thy ho-ly fhrine.

2
Love I know accepteth nought,
Save what Thou, O Love, haſt wrought;
Offer Thou my ſacrifice,
Elſe to God it cannot riſe.

3
Slay in me the wayward will,
Earthly ſenſe and paſſion kill,
Tear ſelf-love from out my heart,
Though it coſt me bitter ſmart.

4
Kindle, Mighty Love, the pyre,
Quick conſume me in Thy fire,
Fain were I of ſelf bereft,
Nought but Thee within me left.

5
So may God, the Righteous, brook
On my ſacrifice to look,
In whoſe ſight no gift has worth
Save a Chriſt-like life on earth.

(VIII.—„Alles ist an Gottes Segen.")

130.
Original Tune.

All things hang on our poſ-ſeſſ-ing God's free love and grace and bleſſ-ing, Though all earth-ly wealth de-part;

He who God for his hath tak-en, 'Mid the chang-ing world un-ſha-ken Keeps a free he-ro-ic heart.

2
He who hitherto hath fed me,
And to many a joy hath led me,
Is and ſhall be ever mine;
He who did ſo gently ſchool me,
He who ſtill doth guide and rule me,
Will not leave me now to pine.

3
Shall I weary me with fretting
O'er vain trifles, and regretting
Things that never can remain?
I will ſtrive but that to win me
That can ſhed true reſt within me,
Reſt the world muſt ſeek in vain.

4
When my heart with longing ſickens,
Hope again my courage quickens,
For my wiſh ſhall be fulfill'd,
If it pleaſe His love moſt tender;
Life and ſoul I all ſurrender
Unto Him on whom I build.

5
Well He knows how beſt to grant me
All the longing hopes that haunt me;
All things have their proper day;
I would dictate to Him never,
As God wills ſo be it ever,
When He wills I will obey.

6
If on earth He bids me linger,
He will guide me with His finger
Through the years that now look dim;
All that earth has fleets and changes
As a river onward ranges,
But I reſt in peace on Him.

(Index of Tunes, IV.)

131.
Tune.—"What ſhall I, a ſinner, do?"

Now at laſt I end this ſtrife, To my God I give my life Whol-ly, with a ſtead-faſt mind;

Sin I will not heark-en more, World, I turn from thee, 'tis o'er; Not a look I'll caſt be-hind.

2
Hath my heart been wavering long,
Have I dallied oft with wrong,
Now at laſt I firmly ſay,—
All my will to this I give,
Only to my God to live,
And to ſerve Him night and day.

3
Lord, I offer at Thy feet
All I have moſt dear and ſweet,
Lo! I keep no ſecret hoard:
Try my heart, and lurks there aught
Falſe within its inmoſt thought,
Take it hence this moment, Lord!

4
I will ſhun no toil or wo,
Where Thou leadeſt I will go,
Be my pathway plain or rough;
If but every hour may be
Spent in work that pleaſes Thee,
Ah, dear Lord, it is enough!

5
Thee I make my choice alone,
Make for ever, Lord, Thine own
All my powers of ſoul and mind;
Here I give myſelf away,
Let the cov'nant ſtand for aye
That my hand to-day hath ſign'd.

(LXXIX.—„ O ber Alles hätt' verloren.")

132.
Original Tune.

Well for him who all things lof-ing, E'en him-felf doth count as nought,

Still the one thing need-ful choof-ing, That with all true blifs is fraught!

2
Well for him who nothing knoweth
But his God, whofe boundlefs love
Makes the heart wherein it gloweth
Calm and pure as faints above!

3
Well for him who all forfaking
Walketh not in fhadows vain,
But the path of peace is taking
Through this vale of tears and pain!

4
Oh that we our hearts might fever
From earth's tempting vanities,
Fixing them on Him for ever
In whom all our fulnefs lies!

5
Oh that ne'er our eyes might wander
From our God, fo might we ceafe
Ever o'er our fins to ponder,
And our confcience be at peace!

6
Thou abyfs of love and goodnefs,
Draw us by Thy crofs to Thee,
That our fenfes, foul, and fpirit,
Ever one with Chrift may be!

(Index of Tunes, LXIII.)

SONGS OF THE CROSS AND CONSOLATION.

133.

Tune.—" Deal with me, God, in mercy now."

My God, in Thee all ful-nefs lies, All want in me, from Thee a-part; Poor as the poor-eft here I
In Thee my foul hath end-lefs joys, In me is but an ach-ing heart;

pine, In Thee a heav'n-ly king-dom's mine.

2 Thou feeft whatfoe'er I need,
Thou feeft it, and pitieft me;
Thy fwift compaffions hither fpeed,
Ere yet my woes are told to Thee;
Thou heareft, Father, ere we cry,
Shall I not ftill before Thee lie?

3 I leave to Thee whate'er is mine,
And in Thy will I calmly reft;
I know that richeft gifts are Thine,
Thou canft and Thou wilt make me bleft,
For Thou haft promifed, and our Lord
Will never break His promifed word.

4 Thou lov'ft me, Father, with the love
Wherewith Thou lovedft Chrift Thy Son,
And fo a brightnefs from above
Still glads me though my tears may run,
For in Thy love I find and know
What all the world could ne'er beftow.

5 Then I can let the world go by,
And yet be ftill and reft in Thee,
I fit, I walk, I ftand, I lie,
Thou ever watcheft over me,
And when the yoke is preffing fore
I think, my God lives evermore!

(oxv.—„ Wer nur ben lieben Gott läßt walten.")

134.
Original Tune.

If thou but fuf-fer God to guide thee, And hope in Him through all thy ways,
He'll give thee ftrength what-e'er be-tide thee, And bear thee through the e-vil days.

Who truft in God's un-chang-ing love Builds on the rock that nought can move.

2

What can thefe anxious cares avail thee,
 Thefe never-ceafing moans and fighs ?
What can it help, if thou bewail thee
 O'er each dark moment as it flies ?
Our crofs and trials do but prefs
The heavier for our bitternefs.

3

Only be ftill and wait His leifure
 In cheerful hope, with heart content
To take whate'er thy Father's pleafure
 And all-deferving love hath fent,
Nor doubt our inmoft wants are known
To Him who chofe us for His own.

4

He knows the time for joy, and truly
 Will fend it when He fees it meet,
When He has tried and purged thee throughly
 And finds thee free from all deceit,
He comes to thee all unaware
And makes thee own His loving care.

5

Nor think amid the heat of trial
 That God hath caft thee off unheard,
That he whofe hopes meet no denial
 Muft furely be of God preferred ;
Time paffes and much change doth bring,
And fets a bound to everything.

6

All are alike before the Higheft.
 'Tis eafy to our God, we know,
To raife thee up though low thou lieft,
 To make the rich man poor and low ;
True wonders ftill by Him are wrought
Who fetteth up and brings to nought.

7

Sing, pray, and keep His ways unfwerving,
 So do thine own part faithfully,
And truft His Word, though undeferving,
 Thou yet fhalt find it true for thee ;
God never yet forfook at need
The foul that trufted Him indeed.

(cix.—„Was Gott thut das ift wohlgethan.")

135.
Original Tune.

What - e'er my God or - dains is right,
I will be ftill what - e'er He doth,

Ho - ly His will a - bid - eth ;
And fol - low where He guid - eth.

He is my God, Though dark my road,

He holds me that I fhall not fall,

Where - fore to Him I leave it all.

2 Whate'er my God ordains is right,
 He never will deceive me ;
He leads me by the proper path,
 I know He will not leave me,
  And take content
  What He hath fent ;
His hand can turn my griefs away,
And patiently I wait His day.

3 Whate'er my God ordains is right,
 His loving thought attends me ;
No poifon'd draught the cup can be
 That my Phyfician fends me,
  But medicine due ;
  For God is true,
And on that changelefs truth I build,
And all my heart with hope is fill'd.

4 Whate'er my God ordains is right,
 Though now this cup in drinking
May bitter feem to my faint heart,
 I take it all unfhrinking ;
  Tears pafs away
  With dawn of day,
Sweet comfort yet fhall fill my heart,
And pain and forrow fhall depart.

5 Whate'er my God ordains is right,
 Here fhall my ftand be taken ;
Though forrow, need, or death be mine,
 Yet am I not forfaken,
  My Father's care
  Is around me there,
He holds me that I fhall not fall,
And fo to Him I leave it all.

(Index of Tunes, c.)

136.

Tune.—" Our Father, Thou in heaven above."

Ah God, my days are dark in-deed, How oft this ach-ing heart muft bleed; The nar-row way, how fill'd with pain, That I muft paſs ere heav'n I gain! How hard to teach this fleſh and blood To ſeek a-lone th'E-ter-nal Good!

2 Ah whither now for comfort turn ?
For Thee, my Jeſus, do I yearn,·
In Thee have I, howe'er diſtreſt,
Found ever counſel, aid, and reſt ;
I cannot all forſaken be
While ſtill my heart can truſt in Thee.

3 Jeſus, my only God and Lord,
What ſweetneſs in Thy name is ſtored !
So dark and hopeleſs is no grief
But Thy ſweet Name can bring relief,
So keen no ſorrows' rankling dart
But Thy ſweet Name can heal my heart.

4 The world can ſhow no truth like Thine,
And therefore will I not repine ;
I know Thou wilt forſake me not,
Thy truth is fix'd, though dark my lot ;
Thou art my Shepherd, and Thy ſheep
From every real harm Thou wilt keep.

5 Jeſus, my boaſt, my light, my joy,
The treaſure nought can e'er deſtroy,
No words, no ſong that I can frame
Speak half the ſweetneſs of Thy name ;
They only all its power ſhall prove
Whoſe hearts have learnt Thy faith and love.

6 How many a time I've ſadly ſaid,
Far better were it I were dead,
Far better ne'er the light to ſee
If I had not this joy in Thee ;
For he who hath not Thee in faith,
His very life is merely death.

7 Jeſus, my Bridegroom and my crown,
If Thou but ſmile, the world may frown
In Thee lie depths of joy untold,
Far richer than her richeſt gold ;
Whene'er I do but think of Thee,
Thy dews drop down and ſolace me ;

8 Whene'er I hope in Thee, my Friend
Thy comfort and Thy peace deſcend ;
Whene'er in grief I pray and ſing,
I feel new courage in me ſpring ;
Thy Spirit witneſſes that this
Is foretaſte of the eternal bliſs.

9 Then while I live this life of care
The croſs for Thee I'll gladly bear
Grant me a patient, willing mood,
I know that it ſhall work my good ;
Help me to do my taſk aright,
That it may ſtand before Thy ſight

10 Let me this fleſh and blood control,
From ſin and ſhame preſerve my ſoul,
And keep me ſteadfaſt in the faith,
Then I am Thine in life and death ;
Jeſus, Conſoler, bend to me,
Ah would I were e'en now with Thee !

(xcix.—„ Balet will ich Dir geben.")

137.

Original Tune.

Fare-well I glad-ly bid Thee, / Thy life is dark and ſin-ful, False, e-vil world, fare-well ! / With thee I would not dwell : In heav'n are joys un-trou-bled, / I long for that bright ſphere Where God re-wards them dou—bled Who ſerv'd Him tru-ly here.

2 Do with me as it pleaſes
Thy heart, O Son of God ;
When anguiſh on me ſeizes,
Help me to bear my load ;
Nor then my ſorrows lengthen,
But take me hence on high ;
My fearful heart, oh ſtrengthen,
And let me calmly die.

3 When all around is darkling,
Thy name and croſs, ſtill bright,
Deep in my heart are ſparkling,
Like ſtars in blackeſt night ;
Appear Thou in Thy ſorrow,
For Thine was woe indeed,
And from Thy croſs I borrow
All comfort heart can need.

4 Thou diedst for me,—oh hide me
   When tempests round me roll;
Through all my foes,.oh guide me,
   Receive my trembling soul:

If I but grasp Thee firmer,
   What matters pain when past?
Hath he a cause to murmur
   Who reaches heaven at last?

5 Oh write my name, I pray Thee,
   Now in the book of life;
So let me here obey Thee,
   And there, where joys are rife,
For ever bloom before Thee,
   Thy perfect freedom prove,
And tell, as I adore Thee,
   How faithful was Thy love.

2
And my soul repineth not,
   Well content whate'er befall her;
Murmurs, wishes, of self-will,
   Doom'd to death, no more enthrall her;
Restless thoughts, that fret and crave,
   Slumber in her Saviour's grave.

138.
Tune.—"Jesus Christ, my sure Defence."

In Thy heart and hands, my God,
Wait-ing pa-tient-ly the end

Calm-ly now my soul re-pos-es,
That Thy aim in all dis-clos-es;

Stripp'd of self, how sweet her rest
On her lov-ing Fa-ther's breast.

3 And my soul doth cease from cares,
   From the thoughts that sore perplex us,
That destroy the inner peace,
   For like sharpest thorns they vex us;
He who made her careth well,
She but seeks in peace to dwell.

4 And my soul despaireth not,
   Loves Him most when sad and lonely;
Grief that wrings and breaks the heart
   Comes to those who hate Him only;
They who love Him still possess
Comfort in their worst distress.

5 And my soul complaineth not,
   For no pain or fears dismay her,
Still she clings to God in faith,
   Trusts Him though He seem to slay her.
'T is when flesh and blood repine,
Sun of joy, Thou canst not shine.

6 Thus my soul is still and waits,
   Every murmuring word she hushes,
Conquering thus the pain or wrong
   That the restless spirit crushes;
Like a silent ocean, bright
With her Maker's praise and light.

139.
Tune.—"Heart and heart together bound."

What with-in me and with-out, Hour-ly on my spi-rit weighs,
Burd-'ning heart and soul with doubt, Dark-'ning all my wea-ry days:
In it I be-hold Thy will,

God, who giv-est rest and peace, And my heart is calm and still, Wait-ing till Thou send re-lease.

2 God! Thou art my rock of strength,
   And my home is in Thine arms,
Thou wilt send me help at length,
   And I feel no wild alarms.
Sin nor Death can pierce the shield
   Thy defence has o'er me thrown,
Up to Thee myself I yield,
   And my sorrows are Thine own.

3 Thou my shelter from the blast,
   Thou my strong defence art ever;
Though my sorrows thicken fast,
   Yet I know Thou leav'st me never;
When my foe puts forth his might,
   And would tread me in the dust,
To this rock I take my flight,
   And I conquer him through trust.

4 When my trials tarry long,
   Unto Thee I look and wait,
Knowing none, though keen and strong,
   Can my faith in Thee abate.
And this faith I long have nurst,
   Comes alone, O God, from Thee;
Thou my heart didst open first,
   Thou didst set this hope in me.

5 Christians! cast on Him your load,
   To your tower of refuge fly;
Know He is the Living God,
   Ever to His creatures nigh.
Seek His ever-open door
   In your hours of utmost need;
All your hearts before Him pour,
   He will send you help with speed.

6 But hast thou some darling plan,
   Cleaving to the things of earth?
Leanest thou for aid on man?
   Thou wilt find him nothing worth.
Rather trust the One alone
   Whose is endless power and love,
And the help He gives His own
   Thou in very deed shalt prove.

7 Yea, on Thee, my God, I rest,
   Letting life float calmly on,
For I know the last is best,
   When the crown of joy is won.
In Thy might all things I bear,
   In Thy love find bitters sweet,
And with all my grief and care
   Sit in patience at Thy feet.

8 O my soul, why art thou vex'd?
   Let things go as e'en they will;
Though to thee they seem perplex'd,
   Yet His order they fulfil.
Here He is Thy strength and guard,
   Power to harm thee here has none;
Yonder will He each reward
   For the works he here has done.

9 Let Thy mercy's wings be spread
   O'er me, keep me close to Thee,
In the peace Thy love doth shed,
   Let me dwell eternally:
Be my All; in all I do
   Let me only seek Thy will,
Where the heart to Thee is true,
   All is peaceful, calm, and still.

(CII.—„Von Gott will ich nicht lassen.")

140.
Original Tune.

From God shall nought di-vide me, For He is true for aye, His ev-er-boun-teous hand
And on my path will guide me, Who else should of-ten stray; By night and day is heed-ful, And gives me what is need-ful, Wher-e'er I go or stand.

If sorrow comes, He sent it,
In Him I put my trust;
I never shall repent it,
For He is true and just,
My life and soul, I owe them
To Him who doth bestow them,
Let Him do as He will.

Whate'er shall be His pleasure
Is surely best for me;
He gave His dearest treasure
That our weak hearts might see
How good His will t'ward us;
And in His Son He gave us
Whate'er could bless and save us;—
Praise Him who loveth thus!

Oh praise Him, for He never
Forgets our daily need;
Oh blest the hour whenever
To Him our thoughts can speed;
Yea, all the time we spend
Without Him is but wasted,
Till we His joy have tasted,
The joy that hath no end.

For when the world is passing
With all its pomp and pride,
All we were here amassing
No longer may abide;
But in our earthy bed,
Where softly we are sleeping,
God hath us in His keeping,
To wake us from the dead.

Then though on earth I suffer
Much trial, well I know
I merit ways still rougher,
And 'tis to heaven I go;
For Christ I know and love,
To Him I now am hasting,
And gladness everlasting
With Him this heart shall prove.

(XCI. Psalm 140, Goudimel.
„Wenn wir in höchsten Nöthen seyn.")

141.

When in the hour of ut---most need
We know not where to look for aid,
Nor help nor coun-sel yet have brought,—

When days and nights of anx-ious thought

For such His will who made us,
The Father seeks our good;
The Son hath grace to aid us,
And save us by His blood;
His Spirit rules our ways,
By faith in us abiding,
To heaven our footsteps guiding;
To Him be thanks and praise.

Then this our comfort is alone,
That we may meet before Thy throne,
And cry, O faithful God, to Thee
For rescue from our misery:

To Thee may raise our hearts and eyes,
Repenting sore with bitter sighs,
And seek Thy pardon for our sin,
And respite from our griefs within:

For Thou hast promised graciously
To hear all those who cry to Thee,
Through Him whose Name alone is great,
Our Saviour and our Advocate.

And thus we come, O God, to-day,
And all our woes before Thee lay,
For tried, forsaken, lo! we stand,
Perils and foes on every hand.

Ah! hide not for our sins Thy face,
Absolve us through Thy boundless grace,
Be with us in our anguish still,
Free us at last from every ill,

That so with all our hearts we may
Once more our glad thanksgivings pay,
And walk obedient to Thy word,
And now and ever praise the Lord.

(CXI.—„Wenn ich in Angst und Noth.")

142.
Original Tune.

When an-guish'd and per--plex'd I lift my wea-ry eyes Up to Thy hills, O

Lord, and tell Thee all that grieves me, Thou heark-en'st to my sighs, And

nev-er com-fort-less Thy in-ner pre-sence leaves me.

2
My help and my defence come, faithful God, from Thee,
By whom were fix'd the heavens, and laid the earth's foundation ;
Man cannot succour me,
Before Thy throne alone is refuge and salvation.

3
Thou watchest that my foot should neither slip nor stray,
Thou guidest me Thyself, though dark the course I travel ;
Thou pointest me the way,
The snares of sin and earth for me Thou dost unravel

4
Guardian of Israel, Thou no rest or sleep dost know,
Thy watchful eye beholds in earth's obscurest regions
Who bravely meets Thy foe,
And bears the Cross on high, still true to our allegiance.

5
And when Thou bidd'st me leave this world of strife and pain,
A steadfast hope in Thee, a quick release, oh grant me,
And let me rise again,
To dwell where death and war no more shall vex and haunt me.

(CVII.—„Warum betrübst du dich.")

143.
Original Tune.

Why art thou thus cast down, my heart ? Why trou-bled, why dost

mourn a-part, O'er nought but earth-ly wealth ? Trust in thy

God, be not a-fraid, He is thy Friend who all things made.

2
Dost think thy prayers He doth not heed ?
He knows full well what thou dost need,
And heaven and earth are His ;
My Father and my God, who still
Is with my soul in every ill.

3
Since Thou my God and Father art,
I know Thy faithful loving heart
Will ne'er forget Thy child ;
See I am poor, I am but dust,
On earth is none whom I can trust.

4
The rich man in his wealth confides,
But in my God my trust abides ;
Then laugh ye as ye will,
I hold this fast that He hath taught,—
Who trusts in God shall want for nought.

5
Yes, Lord, Thou art as rich to-day
As Thou hast been and shalt be aye,
I rest on Thee alone ;
Thy riches to my soul be given,
And 't is enough for earth and heaven.

6
What here may shine I all resign,
If the eternal crown be mine,
That through Thy bitter death
Thou gainedst, O Lord Christ, for me—
For this, for this, I cry to Thee !

7
All wealth, all glories, here below,
The best that this world can bestow,
Silver or gold or lands,
But for a little time is given,
And helps us not to enter heaven.

8
I thank Thee, Christ, Eternal Lord,
That Thou hast taught me by Thy word
To know this truth and Thee ;
O grant me also steadfastness
Thy heavenly kingdom not to miss.

9
Praise, honour, thanks, to Thee be brought,
For all things in and for me wrought
By Thy great mercy, Christ.
This one thing only still I pray,
Oh cast me ne'er from Thee away.

(LXXVII.—„O Chrifte Morgenfterne.")

144.
Original Tune.

O Chrift, Thou bright and Morn-ing Star, Now fhed Thy light a-broad;

Shine on us from Thy throne a-far In this dark place, dear Lord,

With Thy pure glo-rious word.

2
O Jefus, Comfort of the poor,
   I lift my heart to Thee,
I know Thy mercies ftill endure
   And Thou wilt pity me;
I truft alone to Thee.

3
I cannot reft, I may not fleep,
   No joy or peace I know,
My foul is torn with anguifh deep
   And fears a deeper woe;
O Chrift, Thy pity fhow!

4
For Thou didft fuffer for my foul,
   Her burdens to remove;
Oh make me through Thy forrows whole,
   Refrefh me with Thy love;
Lord, help me from above.

5
Then, Jefus, glory, honour, praife,
   I'll ever fing to Thee;
Increafe my faith that Thou wilt raife
   Me once where I fhall fee
Eternal joys with Thee!

(CXIV.—„Wer Gott vertraut hat wohlgebaut.")

145.
Original Tune.

Who puts his truft in God moft juft Hath built his houfe fe-cure-ly;
He who re-lies on Je-fus Chrift, Shall reach His heav'n moft fure-ly;

Then fix'd on Thee my truft fhall be, For Thy truth can-not al-ter; While mine Thou art, not death's worft fmart Shall make my cour-age fal-ter.

2
Though fierceft foes my courfe oppofe,
A dauntlefs front I'll fhow them;
My champion Thou, Lord Chrift, art now,
Who foon fhalt overthrow them!
And if but Thee I have in me
With Thy good gifts and Spirit,
Nor death nor hell, I know full well,
Shall hurt me, through Thy merit.

3
I reft me here without a fear,
By Thee fhall all be given
That I can need, O Friend indeed,
For this life or for heaven.
O make me true, my heart renew,
My foul and flefh deliver!
Lord, hear my prayer, and in Thy care
Keep me in peace for ever.

(Index of Tunes, LXXII.)

146.
Tune.—"Chrift will gather in His own."

Seems it in my an-guifh lone, As though God for-fook His own, Yet I hold this know-ledge faft, God will fure-ly help at laft.

2 Though awhile it be delay'd,
He denieth not His aid;
Though it come not oft with fpeed,
It will furely come at need.

3 As a father not too foon
Grants his child the long'd-for boon,
So our God gives when He will;
Wait His leifure and be ftill.

4 I can reft in thoughts of Him,
When all courage elfe grows dim,
For I know my foul fhall prove
His is more than father's love.

5 Would the powers of ill affright,
I can fmile at all their might;
Or the crofs be preffing fore,
God, my God, lives evermore!

6 Man may hate me caufelefsly,
Man may plot to ruin me,
Foes my heart may pierce and rend,
God in heaven is ftill my Friend.

7 Earth may all her gifts deny,
Safe my treafure ftill on high,
And if heaven at laft be mine,
All things elfe I can refign.

8 I renounce thee willingly,
World, I hate what pleafes thee,
Baneful every gift of thine,
Only be my God ftill mine.

9 Ah Lord, if but Thee I have,
Nought of other good I crave,
Bright is even death's dark road,
If but Thou art there, my God.

(XI.—„Auf meinen lieben Gott.")

147.
Original Tune.

In God, my faith-ful God, I trust when dark my road; Though ma-ny woes o'er—take me, Yet He will not for—sake me; His love it is doth send them, And when 'tis best will end them.

My sins affail me fore,
But I defpair no more;
I build on Chrift who loves me,
From this Rock nothing moves me,
Since I can all furrender
To Him, my foul's Defender.

If death my portion be,
Then death is gain to me,
And Chrift my life for ever,
From whom death cannot fever;
Come when it may, He'll fhield me,
To Him I wholly yield me.

Ah, Jefus Chrift, my Lord,
So meek in deed and word,
Thou diedft once to fave us,
Becaufe Thou fain wouldft have u
After earth's life of fadnefs
Heirs of Thy heavenly gladnefs.

' So be it,' then I fay,
With all my heart each day;
Guide us while here we wander,
Till fafely landed yonder,
We too, dear Lord, adore Thee,
And fing for joy before Thee.

(Index of Tunes, XLIV.)

148.
Tune.—"Lord Jefus, King of Glory."

A pil-grim here I wan-der, On earth have no a-bode, God, For here I jour-ney to and fro,
My fa-ther-land is yon-der, My home is with my God,
There in e-ter-nal reft Will God His gra-cious gift be-ftow On all the toil-op-preff'd.

For what hath life been giving,
From youth up till this day,
But conftant toil and ftriving?
Far back as thought can ftray,
How many a day of toil and care,
How many a night of tears,
Hath pafs'd in grief that none could fhare,
In lonely anxious fears!

3
How many a ftorm hath lighten'd
And thunder'd round my path!
And winds and rains have frighten'd
My heart with fierceft wrath:
And cruel envy, hatred, fcorn,
Have darken'd oft my lot,
And patiently reproach I've born,
Though I deferved it not.

4
Then through this life of dangers
I onward take my way;
But in this land of ftrangers
I do not think to ftay.
Still forward on the road I fare
That leads me to my home,
My Father's comfort waits me there,
When I have overcome.

Ah yes, my home is yonder,
Where all the angelic bands
Praife Him with awe and wonder,
In whofe Almighty hands
All things that are and fhall be, lie,
By Him upholden ftill,
Who cafteth down and lifts on high
At His moft holy will.

6
That home have I defired,
'Tis there I would be gone;
Till I am well-nigh tired,
O'er earth I've journey'd on;
The longer here I roam, I find
The lefs of real joy
That e'er could pleafe or fill my mind,
For all hath fome alloy.

7
The lodging is too cheerlefs,
The forrow is too much;
Ah come, my heart is fearlefs,
Releafe it with Thy touch,
When Thy heart wills, and make an end
Of all this pilgrimage,
And with Thine arm and ftrength defend,
When foes againft me rage.

Where now my fpirit ftayeth
Is not her true abode;
This earthly houfe decayeth,
And fhe will drop its load,
When comes the hour to leave beneath
What now I ufe and have;
And when I've yielded up my breath
Earth gives me but a grave.

9
But Thou, my Joy and Gladnefs,
O Thou, my Life and Light,
Wilt raife me from this fadnefs,
This long tempeftuous night,
Into the perfect gladfome day,
Where bathed in joy divine,
Among Thy faints, and bright as they,
I too fhall ever fhine.

10
There fhall I dwell for ever,
Not as a gueft alone,
With thofe who ceafe there never
To worfhip at Thy throne;
There in my heritage I reft,
From bafer things fet free,
And join the chorus of the bleft
For ever, Lord, to Thee!

(CXVII.—„Wie schön leucht' uns der Morgenstern.")
149.
LOVE TO THE SAVIOUR.

2

Original Tune.

O Morn-ing Star! how fair and bright Thou beam-est forth in
Thou Root of Jes-se, Da-vid's Son, My Lord and Bride-groom,

truth and light! O Sov'-reign meek and low-ly,
Thou hast won My heart to serve Thee   1st Time. sole-ly! 2nd Time.

Ho-ly art Thou, Fair and glo-rious, All vic-to-rious, Rich in bless-ing,

Rule and might o'er all pos-sess-ing.

Thou Heavenly Brightness! Light Divine!
O deep within my heart now shine,
    And make Thee there an altar!
Fill me with joy and strength to be
Thy member, ever join'd to Thee
    In love that cannot falter;
Toward Thee longing Doth possess me,
     Turn and bless me,
     For Thy gladness
Eye and heart here pine in sadness.

3

But if Thou look on me in love,
There straightways falls from God above
    A ray of purest pleasure;
Thy word and Spirit, flesh and blood,
Refresh my soul with heavenly food,
    Thou art my hidden treasure;
Let Thy grace, Lord, Warm and cheer me,
     O draw near me;
     Thou hast taught us
Thee to seek since Thou hast sought us!

4

Here will I rest, and hold it fast,
The Lord I love is First and Last,
    The End as the Beginning!
Here I can calmly die, for Thou
Wilt raise me where Thou dwellest now,
    Above all tears, all sinning:
Amen! Amen! Come, Lord Jesus,
     Soon release us,
     With deep yearning,
Lord, we look for Thy returning!

(XLVIII.—„Ich will dich lieben, meine Stärke.")
150.
Original Tune.

Thee will I love, my Strength, my Tow-er,
Thee in Thy works, with all my pow-er,

Thee will I love, my Hope, my Joy,
With ar-dour Time shall ne'er de-stroy.

Thee will I love, O Light Di-vine,

So long as life is mine!

2

Alas! that I so late have known Thee,
    Who art the Fairest and the Best;
Nor sooner for my Lord could own Thee,
    Our highest Good, our only Rest!
Now bitter shame and grief I prove
     O'er this my tardy love.

3

I wander'd long in willing blindness,
    I sought Thee, but I found Thee not,
For still I shunn'd Thy beams of kindness,
    The creature light fill'd all my thought;
And if at last I see Thee now,
     'T was Thou to me didst bow!

4

I thank Thee, then, true Sun of heaven,
    Whose shining hath brought light to me;
I thank Thee, who hast richly given
    All that could make us glad and free;
I thank Thee that my soul is heal'd
     By what Thy lips reveal'd.

5

Oh keep me watchful, then, and humble,
    And suffer me no more to stray;
Uphold me when my feet would stumble,
    Nor let me loiter by the way;
Fill all my nature with Thy light,
     O Radiance strong and bright!

6

Thee will I love, my Crown of gladness,
    Thee will I love, my God and Lord,
Amid the darkest depths of sadness,
    Not for the hope of high reward,
For Thine own sake, O Light Divine,
     So long as life is mine.

(LIII.— „Jesu meine Freude.")

151.
Original Tune.

Je - su, price - less trea - - sure, Source of
Ah! how long I 've pant - - ed, And my

pur - est plea - sure, Tru - est Friend to me;
heart hath faint - ed, Thirst - ing, Lord, for Thee!

Thine I am, O spot - less Lamb, I will suf - fer nought to hide Thee, Nought I ask be - side Thee.

2

In Thine arm I rest me,
Foes who would molest me
   Cannot reach me here;
Though the earth be shaking,
Every heart be quaking,
   Jesus calms my fear;
Sin and hell in conflict fell
With their bitter storms assail me,
    Jesus will not fail me.

3

Wealth, I will not heed thee,
For I do not need thee,
   Jesus is my choice;
Honours, ye may glisten,
But I will not listen
   To your tempting voice;
Pain or loss, nor shame nor cross,
E'er to leave my Lord shall move me,
    Since He deigns to love me.

4

Farewell, thou who choosest
Earth, and heaven refusest,
   Thou wilt tempt in vain;
Farewell, sins, nor blind me,
Get ye all behind me,
   Come not forth again:
Past your hour, O Pride and Power;
Worldly life, thy bonds I sever,
    Farewell now for ever!

5

Hence, all fears and sadness,
For the Lord of gladness,
   Jesus, enters in;
They who love the Father,
Though the storms may gather,
   Still have peace within;
Yea, whate'er I here must bear,
Still in Thee lies purest pleasure,
    Jesu, priceless treasure!

(Index of Tunes, LXVII.)

152.
Tune.—" Light of Light, enlighten me."

Lov - ing Shep - herd, kind and true,
Seek Thy Lamb as shep - herds do,

Wilt Thou not in pi - ty hear me?
In Thy bo - som gent - ly bear me;

Take me hence from earth's an - noy

To Thy home of end - less joy.

2

See how in this wilderness
   Lost amid its wastes I wander;
Take me hence to dwell in bliss
   With the flock who, gather'd yonder,
Now Thy glory, Lord, behold,
Safe within the heavenly fold.

3

For I fain would gaze on Thee,
   With the lambs, to whom 't is given
That they feed from danger free
   In the happy fields of heaven,
Praising Thee, all terrors o'er,
Never can they leave Thee more.

4

Here I live in sore distress,
   Watching, fearing hour by hour,
For my foes around me press,
   And I know their craft and power;
Lord, Thy lamb can never be
Safe one moment but with Thee.

5

Then, Lord Jesus, let me not
   Fall amid the wolves, but hear me,
As the faithful shepherd ought;
   Help me, keep me ever near Thee,
Till Thou bear me in Thy breast
Homeward to my endless rest.

(Index of Tunes, LXXXIX.)

153.

Tune.—" When the Lord recalls the banished."

Where - fore doſt Thou long - er tar - - ry, Bleſſ - ed ... of the Lord, a - far? Thou my Je - ſus,

Would it were Thy will to en - - ter To my ... heart, O Thou my Star,

Fount of pow'r, Help - er in the need - ful hour!

Sharp - eſt wounds my heart is feel - - ing,

Touch them, Sav - iour, with Thy heal - - ing!

2

For I ſhrink beneath the terrors
   Of the law's tremendous ſway;
All my countleſs crimes and errors
   Stand before me night and day.
     Oh the heavy, fearful load
     Of the righteous wrath of God!
     Oh the awful voice of thunder
     Cleaving heart and ſoul aſunder!

3

Would I then, to ſoothe my ſorrow,
   And my pain awhile forget,
From the world a comfort borrow,
   I but ſink the deeper yet;
     She hath comforts that but grieve,
     Joys that ſtinging memories leave,
     Helpers that my heart are breaking,
     Friends that do but mock its aching.

4

All delight, all conſolation
   Lies in Thee, Lord Jeſus Chriſt,
Feed my ſoul with Thy ſalvation,
   O Thou Bread of Life unpriced.

(♮) Bleſſed Light, within me glow,
   Ere my heart breaks in its woe;
   Oh refreſh me and uphold me,
   Jeſus, come, let me behold Thee.

5

Joy, my ſoul, for He hath heard thee,
   He will come and enter in;
Lo! He turns and draweth toward thee,
   Let thy welcome-ſong begin;
     Oh prepare thee for ſuch gueſt,
     Give thee wholly to thy reſt,
     With an open'd heart adore Him,
     Pour thy griefs and fears before Him.

6

What would ſeem to hurt or ſhame thee
   Shall but work thy good at laſt;
Since that Chriſt hath deign'd to claim thee,
   And His truth ſtands ever faſt;
     And if thine can but endure,
     There is nought ſo fixed and ſure,
     As that thou ſhalt hymn His praiſes
     In the happy heavenly places.

(Index of Tunes, LXXXI.)

154.

Tune.—" O God, Thou faithful God."

O Thou Eſ - ſen - tial Word, Who Thou

With God, for Thou waſt Word, God;

waſt from the be - gin - ing, Choſ - en to ſave our race,

hope of all the ſin - ing,

Wel - come in - deed Thou art, Re - deem - er, Fount of

Grace, To this my long - ing heart.

2

Come, ſelf-exiſtent Word,
   And ſpeak Thou in my ſpirit!
   The ſoul where Thou art heard
   Doth endleſs peace inherit.
     Thou Light that lighteneſt all,
     Abide through faith in me,
     Nor let me from Thee fall,
     And ſeek no guide but Thee.

3

Ah! what hath ſtirred Thy heart,
   What cry hath mounted thither,
   And reached Thy heavenly throne,
   And drawn Thee, Saviour, hither?
     It was Thy wondrous love,
     And my moſt utter need,
     Made Thy compaſſions move,
     Stronger than Death indeed.

4

Then let me give my heart
   To Him who loved me, wholly;
   And live, while here I dwell,
   To ſhow His praiſes ſolely:
     Yes, Jeſus, form anew
     This ſtony heart of mine,
     Make it till death ſtill true
     To Thee, for ever Thine.

5

Let nought be left within
   But what Thy hand hath planted;
   Root out the weeds of ſin,
   And quell the foe who haunted
     My ſoul, and ſet the tares;
     From Thee comes nothing ill,
     O ſave me from his ſnares,
     Make plain my pathway ſtill.

6

Thou art the Life, O Lord,
   And Thou its Light art only!
   Let not Thy bleſſed rays
   Still leave me dark and lonely.
     Star of the Eaſt, ariſe!
     Drive all my clouds away,
     Till earth's dim twilight dies
     Into the perfect day!

(xxxv.—„ Herr Chrift, ber einig' Gott's Sohn.")
155.
Original Tune.

O Thou, of God the Fa-ther The true E-
Of whom 'tis fure-ly writ-ten That Thou with

ter-nal Son, Thou art the bright and Morn-ing Star, Be-
Him art one;

yond all o-ther radi-ance Thy glo-ry ftreams a-far.

2

O let us in Thy knowledge
    And in Thy love increafe,
That we in faith be fteadfaft
    And ferve Thee here in peace;
That fo Thy fweetnefs may be known
    To thefe cold hearts, and teach them
    To thirft for Thee alone.

3

Maker of all! who fhoweft
    The Father's love and might,
In heaven and earth Thou reigneft
    Of Thine own power and right;
So rule our hearts and minds, that we
    Be wholly Thine, and never
    May turn afide from Thee!

(L.—„ In Dir ift Freube.")
156.
Original Tune.

In Thee is glad-nefs A-mid all fad-nefs, Je-fus, Sun-fhine
By Thee are giv-en The gifts of hea-ven, Thou the true Re-

of my heart! Our fouls Thou wakeft, Our bonds Thou breakeft, Who trufts Thee
deem-er art! Our hearts are pin-ing To fee Thy fhin-ing, Dy-ing or

fure-ly Hath built fe-cure-ly, He ftands for ev-er: Hal-le-lu-jah!
liv-ing To Thee are cleaving, Nought can us fev-er: Hal-le-lu-jah!

2

If He is ours
    We fear no powers,
Nor of earth, nor fin, nor death;
    He fees and bleffes
    In worft diftreffes,
He can change them with a breath!
Wherefore the ftory tell of His glory
With heart and voices; all heaven rejoices
    In Him for ever: Hallelujah!
We fhout for gladnefs, triumph o'er fadnefs,
Love Thee and praife Thee, and ftill fhall raife Thee
    Glad hymns for ever: Hallelujah!

(x.—„ Auf, hinauf zu deiner Freude.")

157.
Original Tune.

Up! yes, up-ward to thy glad-ness, Rise, my heart, and soul, and mind! He is thy home,
Caft, oh caft a-way thy fad-ness, Rise where thou thy Lord canft find.

And thy life a-lone is He; Hath the world no place for thee, With Him is room.

2
On, ftill onward, mounting nigher
On the wings of faith to Him;
On, ftill onward, ever higher,
Till the mournful earth grows dim!
God is thy Rock;
Chrift thy Champion cannot fail,
Though thy foes thy life affail,
Fear not their fhock.

3
Hide thee, in His chamber hide thee,
Chrift hath open'd now the door;
Tell Him all that doth betide thee,
All thy forrows there outpour;
He hears thy cry;
Men may hate thee and deceive,
Chrift His own will never leave,
He ftill is nigh.

4
High, oh high, o'er all things earthy,
Raife thy thoughts, my foul, to heaven;
One alone of thee is worthy,
All thou haft to Him be given;
Thy Lord He is
Who fo truly pleads for thee,
Who in love hath died for thee;
Then thou art His.

5
Up then, upwards! feek thou only
For the things that are above;
Sin thou hateft, earth is lonely,
Rife to Him whom thou doft love,—
There art thou bleft;
All things here muft change and die,
Only with our Lord on high
Is perfect reft.

(Index of Tunes, XXXIII.)

158.
Tune.—" Let the earth now praife the Lord."

No-thing fair on earth I fee But I ftraightway think on Thee;

Thou art fair-eft in mine eyes, Source in whom all beau-ty lies!

2
On Thy light I think at morn,
With the earlieft break of dawn;
Think what glories lie in Thee,
Light of all Eternity!

3
When I watch the moon arife
'Mid heaven's thoufand golden eyes,
Then I think, more glorious far
Is the Maker of yon ftar.

4
Or I cry in fpring's fweet hours,
When the fields are gay with flowers,
As their varied hues I fee,—
What muft their Creator be!

5
When along the brook I wander,
Or befide the fountain ponder,
Straight my thoughts take wing and mount
Up to Thee, the pureft Fount.

6
Sweetly all the air is ftirr'd
When the Echo's call is heard;
But no founds my heart rejoice
Like to my Beloved's voice.

7
Take away then what could blind
Unto Thee my foul and mind;
Henceforth ever let my heart
See Thee, Saviour, as Thou art!

III. SPECIAL OCCASIONS.

(LXIX.—„Morgenglanz der Ewigkeit.")

159.
Original Tune.

MORNING.

Day - spring of e - ter - ni - ty! Hide no
Light from Light's ex - hauft - lefs fea, Shine on

more Thy ra - diant dawn - ing! And dif-
us a - frefh this morn - ing!

pel with glo - rious might All our night.

2 Let Thy mercies' morning dew
Roufe our confcience from its blindnefs:
Gladden life's dry plains anew
With the rivers of Thy kindnefs;
Water daily us Thy flock
From the rock.

3 Let the glow of love deftroy
Cold obedience faintly given,
Wake our hearts to love and joy
With the flufhing eaftern heaven;
Let us truly rife ere yet
Life hath fet.

4 Brighteft Star of eaftern fkies!
Grant that at Thy laft appearing
Thefe frail bodies may arife,
Joyfully Thy fummons hearing,
Strong their heavenward courfe to run
As the fun.

5 Through this dark and tearful place
Never be Thy light denied us,
O Thou glorious Sun of grace,
To yon world of gladnefs guide us,
When to joys that never end
We afcend!

(XXXII.—„Gott des Himmels und der Erden.")

160.
Original Tune.

God who mad - - eft and earth and hea - ven,
Who the day and night haft giv - en,

Fa - ther, Son, and Ho - - ly Ghoft,
Sun and moon and ftar - - ry hoft,

All things wake at Thy com - mand,

Held in be - - ing by Thy hand.

2
God, I thank Thee! In Thy keeping
Safely have I flumber'd here;
Thou haft guarded me while fleeping
From all danger, pain, and fear:
And the cunning of my foe
Hath not wrought my overthrow.

3
Let the night of fin that fhrouded
All my life, with this depart;
Shine on me with beams unclouded,
Jefu! In Thy loving heart
Is my help and hope alone,
For the evil I have done.

4
Help me as the morn is breaking,
In the fpirit to arife,
So from carelefs floth awaking,
That when o'er the aged fkies
Shall the morn of Doom appear,
I may fee it free from fear.

5
Lead me, and forfake me never,
Guide my wand'rings by Thy Word;
As Thou haft been, be Thou ever
My defence, my refuge, Lord.
Never fafe except with Thee,
Thou my faithful Guardian be!

6
O my God, I now commend me
Wholly to Thy mighty hand;
All the powers that Thou doft lend me
Let me ufe at Thy command;
Thou my boaft, my ftrength divine,
Keep me with Thee, I am Thine.

7
Thus afrefh with each new morning
Save me from the power of fin,
Hourly let me feel Thy warning
Ruling, prompting me within,
Till my final reft be come,
And Thine angel bear me home.

(Index of Tunes, CXIII.)

161.

Tune.—" Sink not yet my soul to slumber."

As a bird at dawn-ing sing-eth, In the woods or mea-dows fair, So my
Till the lone-ly for-est ring-eth, And it fills the sum-mer air,

heart to Thee would raise, O my God, its song of praise, That the gloom of night is wan-ing, And the Sun once more is reign-ing.

2

Sun of Love, when Thou dost greet me
  All my heart with joy is stirr'd ;
And it upward flies to meet Thee,
  Gladsome as yon little bird.
Shine Thou in me clear and bright,
Till I learn to praise Thee right ;
On the narrow way now speed me,
Let not darkness e'er mislead me.

3

Bless to-day what I am doing,
  Bless whate'er I have and love ;
With the morn my powers renewing,
  Let me ne'er from virtue rove ;
By Thy Spirit strengthen me
In the faith that leads to Thee,
So through life to journey fearless,
Heir of heaven, to glories peerless.

(LXXXVIII.—Psalm 38, Goudimel.)
(„ Seele, bu mußt munter werben.")

162.

Come, my soul, a-wake, 'tis morn-ing, Day is dawn-ing O'er the earth, a-rise and pray ;
Come, to Him who made this splen-dour Thou must ren-der All thy fee-ble pow'rs can pay.

2   3   4   5

Soul, thy incense also proffer;	Bid Him bless what thou art doing,	From God's glances shrink thou never,	Wakenest thou again to sorrow,
Thou shouldst offer	If pursuing	Meet them ever ;	Oh ! then borrow
Praise to Him, who from thy head	Some good aim ; but if there lurks	Who submits him to His grace,	Strength from Him, whose sun-like might
Kept afar the storms of sorrow,	Ill intent in thine endeavour,	Finds that earth no sunshine knoweth	On the mountain-summit tarries,
And the morrow	May He ever	Such as gloweth	And yet carries
Finds the night in peace hath fled.	Thwart and turn thee from thy works.	O'er his pathway all his days.	To the vales their mirth and light.

6

Pray that when thy life is closing,
  Calm reposing
Thou mayst die, and not in pain ;
That, the night of death departed,
  Thou, glad-hearted,
Mayst behold the Sun again.

(XVII.—„Dank fei Gott in der Höhe.")

163.
Original Tune.

While yet the morn is break-ing I
Be-neath whofe care a-wak-ing I

thank my God once more, I thank Him that He calls me
find the night is o'er;

To life and health a-new, I know what-e'er be-

falls me His care will ftill be true.

2

Guardian of Ifrael, hear me,
   Watch o'er me through the day,
In all I do be near me:
   For others too I pray,
To Thee I would commend them,
   Our Church, our youth, our land,
Direct them and defend them
   When dangers are at hand.

3

O gently grant Thy bleffing,
   That we may do Thy will,
No more Thy ways tranfgreffing,
   Our proper tafk fulfil;
With Peter's full affiance
   Let down our nets again,
If Thou art our reliance
   Our toil will not be vain.

4

Thou art the Vine,—oh nourifh
   The branches graft in Thee,
And let them grow and flourifh
   A fair and fruitful tree;
Thy Spirit put within us,
   And let His gifts of grace
To all good actions win us,
   That beft may fhow His praife.

(XII.—..Aus meines Herzens Grunde.")

164.
Original Tune.

My in-moft heart now rai--fes, In this fair morn-ing hour, And as I have be-gun
A fong of thank-ful prai--fes To Thine Al-migh-ty pow'r;

This day, my God, my life fhall be Be-gun and clofed with praife to Thee, Through Chrift Thy on-ly Son.

2

For Thou from me haft warded
   All perils of the night;
From every harm haft guarded
   My foul till morning's light;
Humbly to Thee I cry,
Do Thou in grace the fins forgive
That anger Thee each day I live,
   Have mercy, Lord moft High!

3

And keep me of Thy kindnefs
   From every harm to-day;
Nor let me in my blindnefs
   To Satan fall a prey.
   My cup with good o'erflows,
My foul and body, goods and life,
My home and friends, my child and wife,
   Thy bounteous hand beftows.

4

And fo to Thy good pleafure
   My all I now commend,
And moft, what moft I treafure;
   O Thou Almighty Friend,
Order my courfe for me,
And blefs whate'er I undertake,
Since I in all my choice would make
   As feemeth beft to Thee.

5

Amen! I fay, not fearing
   That God rejects my prayer,
I doubt not He is hearing
   And granting me His care;
And fo I go my way,
And joyfully put forth my hands
To do the work that He commands,
   And ferve Him through the day.

(LXXVI.—„ Nun sich der Tag geendet hat.")

165.
Original Tune.

EVENING.

Now that the sun doth shine no more, And day hath reach'd its close,

They calm-ly sleep who wept be-fore, The wea-ried find re-pose.

2
But Thou, my God, no rest dost know
In Thy unslumb'ring might ;
Thou hatest darkness as Thy foe,
For Thou Thyself art Light.

3
Then 'mid the blackness of these hours
Still think on me for good ;
Refresh me,—let Thy heavenly powers
Now o'er my slumbers brood.

4
I know the evil I have done
Doth cry aloud to Thee ;
But, ah ! the mercy of Thy Son
Hath made amends for me.

5
And therefore now I close my eyes,
And sleep with tranquil breast ;
Why waste the time in fears or sighs ?
God watches o'er my rest.

6
Hence, vain and evil thoughts, depart !
Roam not, my soul, abroad,
For now I build within my heart
A temple to my God.

7
And if this night my last should prove
In this dark land, I pray
Then take me to Thy heaven above,
The home of endless day.

(Index of Tunes, LXXXII.)

166.
Tune.—" Lord Jesus Christ, my Life, my Light."

The hap-py sun-shine all is gone, The gloom-y

night comes swift-ly on ; But shine Thou still, O

Christ our Light, Nor let us lose our-selves in night.

2
We thank Thee, Father, that this day
Thy angels watch'd around our way,
And free from harm and vexing fear,
Have led us on in safety here.

3
Lord, have we anger'd Thee to-day,
Remember not our sins, we pray,
But let Thy mercy o'er them sweep,
And give us calm and restful sleep.

4
Thy angels guard our sleeping hours,
And keep afar all evil Powers ;
And Thou all pain and mischief ward
From soul and body, faithful Lord !

(CXIII.—„ Werbe munter mein Gemüthe.")

167.
Original Tune.

Sink not yet, my soul, to slum-ber, Wake, my heart, go forth and tell
All the mer-cies with-out num-ber That this by-gone day be-fell ; Tell how God hath kept a-

far All things that a-gainst me war, Hath up-held me and de-fend-ed, And His grace my soul be-friend-ed.

Father, merciful and holy,
    Thee to-night I praise and bless,
Who to labour true and lowly
    Grantest ever meet success ;
Many a sin and many a woe,
Many a fierce and subtle foe,
Hast Thou check'd that once alarm'd me,
So that nought to-day has harm'd me.

Now the light, that nature gladdens,
    And the pomp of day is gone,
And my heart is tired and saddens
    As the gloomy night comes on ;
Ah then, with Thy changeless light
Warm and cheer my heart to-night,
As the shadows round me gather
Keep me close to Thee, my Father.

Have I e'er from Thee departed,
    Now I seek Thy face again,
And Thy Son, the loving-hearted,
    Made our peace through bitter pain.
Yes, far greater than our sin,
Though it still be strong within,
Is the Love that fails us never,
Mercy that endures for ever.

Brightness of the eternal city !
    Light of every faithful soul !
Safe beneath Thy sheltering pity,
    Let the tempests past me roll :
Now it darkens far and near,
Still, my God, still be Thou here ;
Thou canst comfort, and Thou only,
When the night is long and lonely.

6

E'en the twilight now hath vanish'd,
  Send Thy blessing on my sleep,
Every sin and terror banish'd,
  Let my rest be calm and deep.
Soul and body, mind and health,
Wife and children, house and wealth,
Friend and foe, the sick, the stranger,
Keep Thou safe from harm and danger.

7

O Thou mighty God, now hearken
  To the prayer Thy child hath made;
Jesus, while the night-hours darken
  Be Thou still my hope, my aid;
Holy Ghost, on Thee I call,
Friend and Comforter of all,
Hear my earnest prayer, oh hear me!
Lord, Thou hearest, Thou art near me.

2

The night is here,
Oh! be Thou near,
Christ, make it light within me;
Chase the darkness from my heart
That to ill might win me.

3

The sun's sweet light
Is sunk in night;
Oh Brightness uncreated,
Shine with joy on us who here
Long for Thee have waited.

4

Each living thing
Is slumbering,
While darkness round is closing;
Work Thou silently in me
While I lie reposing.

5

Ah when shall day
Have perfect sway,
By night no more attended?
When that fairest morn shall break
That shall ne'er be ended.

168.

Tune.—"O darkest woe, ye tears, forth flow!"

The day is done, And, left alone, My heart is fill'd with yearn-ing For the morn when grief and care Shall have no re-turn-ing.

6

For Salem then
Shall ne'er again
Behold her brightness vanish,
Since the Lamb shall be her light,
And all night shall banish.

7

Oh were I there!
Where all the air
With lovely sounds is ringing,
Where the saints Thee, Holy Lord,
Evermore are singing!

8

Lord Jesus, Thou
My rest art now;
Grant me to stand before Thee,
Radiant with Thy light to shine,
And for aye adore Thee!

169.

Tune.—"O World, I now must leave thee."

Now all the woods are sleep-ing, And night and still-ness creep-ing O'er ci-ty, man, and beast; But thou, my heart, a-wake thee, To pray'r a-while be-take thee, And praise thy Ma-ker ere thou rest.

2

O Sun, where art thou vanish'd?
  The Night thy reign hath banish'd,
Thy ancient foe, the Night.
  Farewell, a brighter glory
  My Jesus sheddeth o'er me,
All clear within me shines His light.

3

The last faint beam is going,
  The golden stars are glowing
In yonder dark-blue deep;
  And such the glory given
  When called of God to heaven,
On earth no more we pine and weep.

4

The body hastes to slumber,
  These garments now but cumber,
And as I lay them by
  I ponder how the spirit
  Puts off the flesh t' inherit
A shining robe with Christ on high.

5

Now thought and labour ceases,
  For Night the tired releases,
And bids sweet rest begin:
  My heart, there comes a morrow
  Shall set thee free from sorrow
And all the dreary toil of sin.

6

Ye aching limbs! now rest you,
  For toil hath sore oppress'd you,
Lie down, my weary head:
  A sleep shall once o'ertake you
  From which earth ne'er shall wake you,
Within a narrower, colder bed.

7

My heavy eyes are closing;
  When I lie deep reposing,
Soul, body, where are ye?
  To helpless sleep I yield them,
  Oh let Thy mercy shield them,
Thou sleepless Eye, their guardian be!

8

My Jesus, stay Thou by me,
  And let no foe come nigh me,
Safe shelter'd by Thy wing;
  But would the foe alarm me,
  Oh let him never harm me,
But still Thine angels round me sing!

9

My loved ones, rest securely,
  From every peril surely
Our God will guard your heads;
  And happy slumbers send you,
  And bid His hosts attend you,
And golden-arm'd watch o'er your beds.

(XXII.—„ Die Nacht iſt kommen.")

170.
Original Tune.

2

Let evil thoughts and ſpirits flee before us ;
Till morning cometh, watch, O Maſter, o'er us ;
In ſoul and body Thou from harm defend us,
Thine angels ſend us.

3

Let pious thoughts be ours when ſleep o'ertakes us,
Our earlieſt thoughts be Thine when morning wakes us ;
All day ſerve Thee, in all that we are doing
Thy praiſe purſuing.

Now God be with us, for the night is cloſ - ing ; The light and dark - neſs are of His dis -

After the laſt verſe only.

poſ - ing, And 'neath His ſha - dow here to reſt we yield us, For He will ſhield us. A - men.

4

As Thy beloved ſoothe the ſick and weeping,
And bid the captive loſe his griefs in ſleeping ;
Widows and orphans, we to Thee commend them,
Do Thou befriend them.

5

We have no refuge ; none on earth to aid us,
Save Thee, O Father, who Thine own haſt made us ;
But Thy dear preſence will not leave them lonely,
Who ſeek Thee only.

6

Father, Thy name be praiſed, Thy kingdom given,
Thy will be done on earth as 'tis in heaven ;
Keep us in life, forgive our ſins, deliver
Us now and ever.—Amen.

(XIX.—„ Das alte Jahr vergangen iſt.")

171.
Original Tune.

NEW YEAR.

The old year now hath paſſ'd a - way, We thank Thee, O our God, to - day,

That Thou haſt kept us through the year, When dan - ger and dis - treſs were near.

2

We pray Thee, O Eternal Son,
Who with the Father reign'ſt as One,
To guard and rule Thy Chriſtendom
Through all the ages yet to come.

3

Take not Thy ſaving Word away,
Our ſouls' true comfort and their ſtay ;
Abide with us, and keep us free
From errors, following only Thee.

4

Oh help us to forſake all ſin,
A new and holier courſe begin,
Mark not what once was done amiſs,
A happier, better year be this :

5

Wherein as Chriſtians we may live,
Or die in peace that Thou canſt give,
To riſe again when Thou ſhalt come,
And enter Thine eternal home.

6

There ſhall we thank Thee, and adore,
With all the angels evermore ;
Lord Jeſus Chriſt, increaſe our faith
To praiſe Thy name through life and death

(Index of Tunes, cxv.)

172.
Tune.—" If thou but ſuffer God to guide thee."

Help us, O Lord, be - hold we en - ter Up - on an - o - ther year to - day ;
In Thee our hopes and thoughts now cen - tre, Re - new our cour - age for the way :

New life, new ftrength, new hap-pi-nefs, We afk of Thee,— oh hear and blefs!

2
May every plan and undertaking
  This year be all begun with Thee,
When I am fleeping or am waking,
  Still let me know Thou art with me ;
Abroad do Thou my footfteps guide,
At home be ever at my fide.

3
Be this a time of grace and pardon,
  Thy rod I take with willing mind,
But fuffer nought my heart to harden,
  Oh let me now Thy mercy find ;
In Thee alone, my God, I live,
Thou only canft my fins forgive.

4
And may this year to me be holy,
  Thy grace fo fill my ev'ry thought
That all my life be pure and lowly
  And truthful, as a Chriftian's ought ;
So make me while yet dwelling here
Pious and bleft from year to year.

5
Jefus, be with me and direct me ;
  Jefus, my plans and hopes infpire ;
Jefus, from tempting thoughts protect me ;
  Jefus, be all my heart's defire ;
Jefus, be in my thoughts all day,
Nor fuffer me to fall away !

6
And grant, Lord, when the year is over,
  That it for me in peace may clofe ;
In all things care for me, and cover
  My head in time of fear and woes ;
So may I, when my years are gone,
Appear with joy before Thy throne.

173.

Tune.—" Ah ! God, from heaven look down and fee."

Oh wouldft Thou in Thy glo-ry come,
I count the mo-ment's wea-ry fum

As Thou, Lord, haft fore-told it !
Un-til we may be-hold it ; With

burn-ing lamp, the Church, Thy Bride, Is wait-ing for the

ho-ly tide When Thou, Lord, wilt un-fold it.

2
Yet I would leave it to Thy choice,
  The hour when we fhall meet Thee ;
Though Thou doft love that heart and voice
  Should daily thus entreat Thee,
And henceforth all my courfe fhould be
Still looking on and up to Thee,
  With heart prepared to greet Thee.

3
I joy that from Thy love divine
  No power my foul can fever ;
That I may dare to call Thee mine,
  My Lord, my Friend, for ever ;
That I, O Prince of Life, fhall be
Made wholly one in heaven with Thee,
  In life that endeth never.

4
And therefore do my thanks o'erflow
  That one more year is ended,
And of this Time, fo poor, fo flow,
  Another ftep afcended ;
And with a heart that may not wait
I haften towards the golden gate
  Where long my hopes have tended.

5
And when the wearied hands give way,
  And wearied knees are failing,
Then make Thy mighty arm my ftay,
  Though faith and hope feem quailing ;
That fo my heart drink in new ftrength,
And fear no more the journey's length,
  O'er doubt and pain prevailing.

6
Then on, my foul, with fearlefs faith,
  Let nought to terror move thee,
Nor lift what earthly pleafure faith,
  When fhe would lure and prove thee ;
The eagles' wings of love and prayer
Will bear thee through life's toil and care
  To Him who ftill doth love thee.

(xcv.—„ Seelenbräutigam.")

174.   **MARRIAGE.**

Je-fu, day by day Guide us on life's way; Nought of dan-gers will we rec-kon,
Sim-ply hafte where Thou doft bec-kon, Lead us by the hand To our fa-ther-land.

2
Hard fhould feem our lot,
Let us waver not,
Never murmur at our croffes
In dark days of grief and loffes;
'Tis through trial we
Here muft pafs to Thee.

3
When the heart muft know
Pain for others' woe,
When beneath its own 'tis finking,
Give us patience, hope unfhrinking,
Fix our eyes, O Friend,
On our journey's end.

4
Thus our path fhall be
Daily traced by Thee;
Draw Thou nearer when 'tis rougher,
Help us moft when moft we fuffer,
And when all is o'er,
Ope to us Thy door!

MARRIAGE. OR THE HOUSE.

(cxxi.—„ Wo Gott zum Haus nicht giebt fein' Gunft.")
175.

Oh bleft the houfe, what-e'er be-fall, Where Je-fus Chrift is All in All; Yea, if He were not dwell-ing there, How poor and dark and void it were!

2 Oh bleft that houfe where faith ye find,
And all within have fet their mind
To truft their God and ferve Him ftill,
And do in all His holy will.

3 Bleft, where their prayers fhall daily rife
As fragrant incenfe to the fkies,
While in their lives the world is taught
That forms without the heart are nought.

4 Bleft, where the bufy hands fulfil
Their proper tafk with ready fkill,
While through their different works ye fee
One fpirit run of unity.

5 Bleft fuch a houfe, it profpers well,
In peace and joy the parents dwell,
And in their children's lot is fhown
How richly God can blefs His own.

6 Then here will I and mine to-day
A folemn covenant make, and fay,—
Though all the world forfake Thy Word,
I and my houfe will ferve the Lord.

(Index of Tunes, xxxiii.)

176.   **MISSIONS.**

Tune.—" Let the earth now praife the Lord."

Spread, oh fpread, thou migh-ty Word, Spread the king-dom of the Lord,
Where-fo-e'er His breath has given Life to be-ings meant for heaven.

2
Tell them how the Father's will
Made the world, and keeps it ftill,
How He fent His Son to fave
All who help and comfort crave.

3
Tell of our Redeemer's love,
Who for ever doth remove
By His holy facrifice,
All the guilt that on us lies.

4
Tell them of the Spirit given
Now, to guide us up to heaven,
Strong and holy, juft and true,
Working both to will and do.

5
Word of Life! moft pure and ftrong,
Lo! for Thee the nations long;
Spread, till from its dreary night
All the world awakes to light.

6
Up, the ripening fields ye fee,
Mighty fhall the harveft be,
But the reapers ftill are few,
Great the work they have to do.

7
Lord of harveft, let there be
Joy and ftrength to work for Thee,
Till the nations far and near
See Thy Light, and learn Thy fear.

(LXXV.—„Nun preifet alle.")

177.
Original Tune.

Now let us loud-ly Praife God, the Mer-ci-ful; Chrif-ten-dom proud-ly Tells of His glo-rious rule; Gent-ly He bids thee come be-fore Him, Hafte then, O Is-ra-el, now a-dore Him! Hafte then, O Is-ra-el, now a-dore Him!

2
For the Lord reigneth
Over the univerfe,
All He fuftaineth,
All things His praife rehearfe;
The hoft of angels round Him dwelling,
‖:Pfalter and harp of His praife are telling.:‖

3
Rife then, ye nations,
Caft off your mournfulnefs:
Into His paftures
Will ye not gladly prefs?
For there His Word abroad is founded,
‖:Pardon for finners, and grace unbounded.:‖

4
Richly he feeds us,
Always and everywhere;
Gently He leads us
With a true Father's care;
The late and early rains He fends us,
‖:Daily His blelling, His love attends us.:‖

5
Sing we His praifes
Who is thus merciful;
Chriftendom raifes
Songs to His glorious rule!
Rejoice! no foe fhall now alarm us,
‖:He will protect us, and who can harm us?:‖

(Index of Tunes, VII.)

178.
Tune.—" Hark! a voice faith, All are mortal." SCHOOLS.

Je-fu, when Thou once re-turn-edft From the tem-ple of the Lord,
Where His ho-ly will Thou learn-edft, Glad-ly to Thy home re-ftored,
Thou waft rea-dy to ful-fil, As a child, Thy pa-rents' will;
Grace and fweet hu-mil-i-ty, in Thee.
Ev-er-more were feen in Thee.

2
See Thy little flock difperfing
From their fchool with joyous hearts;
Here Thy leffons oft rehearfing,
Train them for life's bufy parts;
Lord, at home or by the way,
Lonely, or in merry play,
Be our Pattern ne'er forgot;
Friend of children, leave us not !

179.

Tune.—" O bleft the houfe, whate'er befall."

Lord Je-fus Chrift, we come to Thee, For Thou haft deign'd on earth to be A pi-ous and a lov-ing child, Whom nev-er fin nor guilt de-filed.

We afk but one thing for our lot,   Oh put Thy Spirit in our breaft,
O Lord, deny Thy children not,—   Help us to learn with childlike zeft,
Teach us to reft upon Thy will,   That we may lay the one true ground,
And take Thee for our Pattern ftill.   And evermore in Thee be found.

180.   ON A JOURNEY.

Tune.—" Ere yet the dawn hath fill'd the fkies."

In God's name let us on our way! The Fa-ther's help and grace we pray; His love fhall guard us round a-bout From foes with-in and harms with-out. Hal-le-lu-jah.

And Chrift, be Thou our Friend and Guide,
Through all our wanderings at our fide,
Help us all evil to withftand
That wars againft Thy leaft command.
     3   Hallelujah

The Holy Spirit o'er us brood
With all His gifts of richeft good,
With hope and ftrength when dark our road,
And bring us home again in God!
     Hallelujah.

181.   HARVEST.

Tune.—" Oh would, my God, that I could praife Thee."

Come, Chrif-tians, praife your Mak-er's good-nefs, Re-joice in Him and in His gift;
To-day be-fore the Lord of har-veft, In hap-py fongs your voi-ces lift;
For He who cared for us of yore Hath blefs'd our fields and homes once more.

Accept, O Lord, our thankful praifes   Thou feedeft us in pure compaffion;   Open Thy bounteous hands in bleffing   Preferve to us what Thou haft fent us,
For all our Father's bleffing gives;   Teach us to care for others' need;   Thus to refrefh us, year by year;   And grant us calm and peaceful days
May it increafe our faith, and lead us   Let each, as he is able, comfort   Provide for us through all life's journey,   And grateful hearts, that we may ufe it
To praife Thee by obedient lives,   The fick and poor, the hungry feed: And make us faithful ftewards while here   In quiet gladnefs to Thy praife:
That every deed and word may prove   O Father Thou of all below,   Of all that to our care is given,   And while our bodies thus are fed,
We feel and truft our Father's love.   On each, what moft he needs, beftow.   That greater gifts be ours in heaven.   O grant our fouls the Living Bread!

(xxiv.—„Du Friedefürst, Herr Jesu Christ.")

182.
Original Tune.

WAR AND PEACE.

Lord Je - su Christ, the Prince of Peace, True
Might - y to help in life and death, O
God and Man art Thou! hear and help us now! 'Tis through Thy name a -
lone we claim The mer - cy of Thy Fa - ther!

The times are fore and perilous
With heavy woes and wars,
Whence no man can deliver us
But Thou! Oh plead our caufe,
That God may lay His wrath away,
Nor deal with us in anger!
·6·

We have deferved, and patiently
Would bear, whate'er Thou wilt,
But grace is mightier far with Thee
Than all our fin and guilt;
Forgive us then, dear Lord, again,
Thy love is ever faithful.

(Danger and grief around us ftand,
When plagues are in the air;
But far more wretched is the land
When cruel war is there;
Men fcorn the good, in recklefs mood
All holy things defpifing.

There law and judgment yield to force,
None afketh what is right;
Thy Word is hinder'd in its courfe,
And quench'd its bleffed light;
Then drive afar this harmful war,
Help, fave us from its terrors.)

And let Thy grace, O Lord, control
Our minds and hearts, that none
Should make a fport, that kills the foul,
Of evils war hath done.
'Tis Thou alone who from Thy throne
Canft rule us thus, and fave us!

2

(Index of Tunes, LXX.)

183.
Tune.—" Now thank we all our God."

Lord God, we wor - fhip Thee! In
We praife Thy love and pow'r, Whofe
loud and hap - py cho - rus, To heav'n our fong fhall
good - nefs reign - eth o'er us!
foar, For ev - er fhall it be Re -
found - ing o'er and o'er; Lord God, we wor - fhip Thee!

Lord God, we worfhip Thee!
For Thou our land defendeft,
Thou poureft down Thy grace,
And ftrife and war Thou endeft;
Since golden Peace, O Lord,
Thou granteft us to fee,
Our land with one accord,
Lord God, gives thanks to Thee!

3

Lord God, we worfhip Thee!
Thou didft indeed chaftife us,
Yet ftill Thy anger fpares,
And ftill Thy mercy tries us;
Once more our Father's hand
Doth bid our forrows flee,
And Peace rejoice our land;
Lord God, we worfhip Thee.

4

Lord God, we worfhip Thee!
And pray Thee, who haft bleft us,
That we may live in peace,
And none henceforth moleft us;
O crown us with Thy love;
Fulfil our cry to Thee,
O Father, grant our prayer;
Lord God, we worfhip Thee!

184.

Tune.—" My foul, now praife thy Maker."

Thank God it hath re-found-ed, The blefs-ed voice of joy and Peace!
And murder's reign is bound-ed, And fpear and fword at laft may ceafe.

Bright hope is break-ing o'er us, A-rife, my land, once more,

And fing in full-ton'd cho - - rus Thy hap-py fongs of yore;

Oh raife thy heart to God and fay: Thy covenants, Lord, en - dure,

Thy mer-cies do not pafs a - way, Thy pro-mi - fes are fure.

2

O welcome day, that brought us
This precious noble gift of Peace!
For war hath deeply taught us
What forrows come where fhe doth ceafe;
In her our God now layeth
  All hope, all happinefs;
Who woundeth her, or flayeth,
  Doth, like a madman, prefs
The arrow to his own heart's core,
  And quench with impious hand
The golden torch of Peace once more,
  That glads at laft our land.

3

This ye could teach us only,
So dull and hard thefe hearts of ours,
  Ye homes, now ftripp'd and lonely,
Ye wafted cities, ruin'd towers;
  Ye fields, once fairly blooming,
  With golden harveft graced,
  Where forefts now are glooming,
  Or fpreads a dreary wafte;
Ye graves, with corpfes piled, where lies
  Full many a hero brave,
Whofe like no more fhall meet our eyes,
  Who died, yet could not fave.

4

O man, with bitter mourning
Remember now the by-gone years,
  When thou haft met God's warning
With carelefs fcoff, not contrite tears;
  Yet like a loving Father
  He lays afide His wrath,
  And feeks with kindnefs rather
  To lure thee to His path;
He tries if love may yet conftrain
  The heart that hath withftood
His rod;—oh let Him not in vain
  Now ftrive with Thee for good

5

Thou carelefs world, awaken!
Awake, awake, all ye that fleep,
Ere yet ye be o'ertaken
With ruin fudden, fwift, and deep!
But he who knows Chrift liveth,
  May hope and fear no ill,
The Peace that now He giveth
  Hath deeper meaning ftill,
For He will furely teach us this:
  " The end is nigh at hand,
When ye in perfect reft and peace
Before your God fhall ftand."

185.

Tune—" If thou but fuffer God to guide thee."

FOR THE SICK AND DYING.

I know the doom that muft be-fall me, But know not
It may be that my God will call me To - day, to -

when, or where, or how; Ere yet this pre - fent hour is
mor - row, nay, or now;

fled This liv - ing bo - dy may be dead.

2

Lord, let me die to felf each hour,
  And at the laft Thy prefence give,
Then Death may try his utmoft power,
  He can but make me truly live;
Then welcome my laft hour fhall be
When, where, and how it pleafes Thee.

(ᵛ.—„Chriſtus der iſt mein Leben.")
(„Ach bleib' mit Deiner Gnade.")

186.
Original Tune.

My life is hid in Je - ſus, And death is gain to me; Then when - ſo - e'er He

plea - - ſes, I meet it will - ing - ly.

2 For Chriſt, my Lord and Brother,
  I leave this world ſo dim,
  And gladly ſeek that other
  Where I ſhall be with Him.

3 My woes are nearly over,
  Though long and dark the road;
  My ſins His merits cover,
  And I have peace with God.

4 Then when my powers are failing,
  My breath comes heavily,
  And words are unavailing,
  Oh hear my ſighs to Thee !

5 When mind, and thought, O Saviour,
  Are flickering like a light,
  That to and fro doth waver
  Ere 'tis extinguiſhed quite;

6 In that laſt hour, oh grant me
  To ſlumber ſoft and ſtill,
  No doubts to vex or haunt me,
  Safe anchor'd on Thy will;

7 And ſo to Thee ſtill cleaving
  Through all death's agony,
  To fall aſleep believing,
  And wake in heaven with Thee.

(ᶜˣᵛ¹.—„Wer weiß wie nahe mir mein Ende.")

187.
Original Tune.

Who knows how near my end may be?
How ſwift - ly, ah! how ſud - den - ly,
Time ſpeeds a - way, and Death comes on;
May Death be here, and Life be gone!
My God, my God, for

Je - ſu's ſake I pray Thy peace may bleſs my dy - ing day.

8
From Him can nought my ſoul divide,
  Nor life nor death can part us now;
I lay my hand upon His ſide,
  And ſay, My Lord and God art Thou;
My God, for Jeſu's ſake I pray
Thy peace may bleſs my dying day.

9
In holy baptiſm long ago
  I join'd me to the living Vine,
Thou loveſt me in Him, I know,
  In Him Thou doſt accept me Thine;
My God, for Jeſu's ſake I pray
Thy peace may bleſs my dying day.

10
And I have eaten of His fleſh
  And drunk His blood,—nor can I be
Forſaken now, nor doubt afreſh,
  I am in Him and He in me;
My God, for Jeſu's ſake I pray
Thy peace may bleſs my dying day.

11
Then death may come or tarry yet,
  I know in Chriſt I periſh not,
He never will His own forget,
  He gives me robes without a ſpot;
My God, for Jeſu's ſake I pray
Thy peace may bleſs my dying day.

12
And thus I live in God at peace,
  And die without a thought of fear,
Content to take what God decrees,
  For through His Son my faith is clear,
His grace ſhall be in death my ſtay,
And peace ſhall bleſs my dying day.

2
The world that ſmiled when morn was come
  May change for me ere cloſe of eve;
So long as earth is ſtill my home
  In peril of my death I live;
‖: My God,:‖ for Jeſu's ſake I pray
Thy peace may bleſs my dying day.

3
Teach me to ponder oft my end,
  And ere the hour of death appears,
To caſt my ſoul on Chriſt her Friend,
  Nor ſpare repentant cries and tears;
My God, for Jeſu's ſake I pray
Thy peace may bleſs my dying day.

4
And let me now ſo order all,
  That ever ready I may be
To ſay with joy, whate'er befall,
  Lord, do Thou as Thou wilt with me;
My God, for Jeſu's ſake I pray
Thy peace may bleſs my dying day.

5
Let heaven to me be ever ſweet,
  And this world bitter let me find,
That I, 'mid all its toil and heat,
  May keep eternity in mind;
My God, for Jeſu's ſake I pray
Thy peace may bleſs my dying day.

6
O Father, cover all my ſins
  With Jeſu's merits, who alone
The pardon that I covet wins,
  And makes His long-ſought reſt my own;
My God, for Jeſu's ſake I pray
Thy peace may bleſs my dying day.

7
His ſorrows and His croſs I know
  Make death-beds ſoft, and light the grave,
They comfort in the hour of woe,
  They give me all I fain would have;
My God, for Jeſu's ſake I pray
Thy peace may bleſs my dying day.

(Index of Tunes, LV.)

188.

Tune.—" Jesus Christ, my sure Defence."

Go and dig my grave to-day! Wea-ry of my cease-less roam—ing, An-gel voi-ces
Now from earth I pass a-way, Heav'n-ly peace a-waits my com-ing,

from a-bove Call me to their rest and love.

Go and dig my grave to-day!
 Homeward now my journey tendeth,
And I put my staff away,
 Here where all earth's labour endeth,
And I lay my weary head
In the only painless bed.

3 What is there I yet should do
 If in this dark vale I linger?
Proud our schemes, and fair to view,
 Yet they melt beneath Time's finger
Like the sand before the wind,
That no power of man can bind.

4 Farewell earth, then! I am glad
 That I now in peace may leave thee;
For thy very joys are sad,
 And thy hopes do but deceive thee;
Fading is thy beauty's gleam,
False and transient as a dream.

5 Sun and moon and stars so bright,
 Farewell all your golden splendour!
Here I loved you, but your light
 Gladly will I now surrender
For the glories of that day,
Where ye all must fade away.

6 Farewell, O ye friends I love!
 Though awhile ye journey grieving,
Comfort cometh from above
 To the hearts in Christ believing;
Weep not o'er a passing show,
To th' eternal world I go.

7 Weep not that this earth I leave,
 Mourn not that I am exchanging
Errors that here closely cleave,
 Empty ghosts and shadows ranging
Through a world of nought and night,
For a land of truth and light.

8 Weep not! dearest to my heart
 Is my Saviour, He doth cheer me;
And I know that I have part
 In His pains, and He is near me;
For He shed His precious blood
For the whole world's highest good.

9 Weep not, my Redeemer lives!
 From the dust, Hope ever vernal
Looks to Heaven and upward strives;
 Fearless Faith and Love eternal
Now are softly whispering nigh,
" Child of God, fear not to die!"

(LXXXV.—„ O Welt ich muß dich laffen."
 „ Nun ruhen alle Wälder."

189.

Original Tune.   FOR THE DYING.

O world, I now must leave thee, But lit-tle doth it grieve me, I seek my na-tive land;
True life I there in-her-it, And here I yield my spi—rit With joy to God's all-gra-cious hand.

So on His Word relying,
I know while I am dying
 I soon shall see His face
Through Christ whose death hath bought me,
The Father's love He brought me,
 And now prepares for me a place.

The grave hath lost its terrors
Since for my sins and errors
 My Saviour doth atone:
My works can nought avail me,
But His work cannot fail me,
 I rest in faith on Him alone.

My service cannot merit
That I should e'er inherit
 Eternal life with Christ:
But He hath freely given
A share with Him in heaven
 Of that fair heritage unpriced.

And so I hence am going
In peace, full surely knowing
 With Him is perfect rest;
I feel Death's icy finger,
My soul here cannot linger,
 Nor would I stay—to go is best.

6
O world, I yet would teach thee
That Death will surely reach thee,
 That thou must follow me;
Then while thy days are lengthen'd,
Pray that thy faith be strengthen'd,
 That God have mercy too on thee!

(LXXXII.—„O Jesu Christ mein Lebenslicht.")

190.
Original Tune.

FOR THE SICK AND DYING.

Lord Je - sus Christ, my Life, my Light, My strength by day, my trust by night,

On earth I'm but a pass - - ing guest, And sore - ly with my sins op - press'd.

Far off I see my fatherland,
Where through Thy grace I hope to stand,
But ere I reach that Paradise
A weary way before me lies.

Oh let Thy sufferings give me power
To meet the last and darkest hour;
Thy cross the staff whereon I lean,
My couch the grave where Thou hast been.

And when the last great Day is come,
And Thou our Judge shalt speak the doom,
Let me with joy behold the light,
And set me then upon Thy right.

3

My heart sinks at the journey's length,
My wasted flesh has little strength,
Only my soul still cries in me,
Lord, fetch me home, take me to Thee!

5

Since Thou hast died, the Pure, the Just,
I take my homeward way in trust,
The gates of heaven, Lord, open wide,
When here I may no more abide.

7

Renew this wasted flesh of mine,
That like the sun it there may shine
Among the angels pure and bright,
Yea, like Thyself in glorious light.

8

Ah then I have my heart's desire,
When singing with the angels' choir,
Among the ransomed of Thy grace,
For ever I behold Thy face!

(LXIII.—„Mach's mit mir Gott nach Deiner Güt'.")

191.
Original Tune.

FOR THE DYING.

Deal with me, God, in mer - cy now,
Thine ear to me in pi - ty bow;

Oh help me in my ut - - ter woe,
When hence my soul must quick - ly go,

Re - ceive her, as her God and Friend,

For all is right if right the end.

2

Now, O my Lord, I follow Thee,
Safe where Thy steps I plainly trace;
Ah, now Thou art not far from me,
Though Death is with me face to face,
And I must leave the friends most dear
Who loved me well and truly here.

3

The body calmly sleeps in earth,
To Thee the spirit spreads her wings,
And in Thy hands, a second birth
She finds in death, to life she springs;
Here was a land of tears and woe,
Where toil and care are all we know.

4

Now Death and Satan, hell and sin,
And this world, all have lost their power,
The grace and hope Thou, Lord, didst win
For me, uphold me in this hour;
For on the Son my debts were laid,
And He my ransom freely paid.

5

Why mourn, then, that I now go hence?
Surely a blessed lot is mine;
Clothed in His spotless innocence,
Before Him as a bride I shine;
Farewell, thou evil world, farewell!
With God I rather choose to dwell.

(Index of Tunes, c.)

192.

Tune.—" Our Father, Thou in heaven above."

O Lord my God, I cry to Thee, In my dif-trefs Thou help-eft me; To Thee myfelf I all com-mend, Oh fwift-ly now Thine an-gel fend To guide me home, and cheer my heart,
Since Thou doft call me to de-part.

O Jefu Chrift, Thou Lamb of God,	O Holy Spirit, at the end,
Once flain to take away our load,	Sweet Comforter, be Thou my Friend!
Now let Thy crofs, Thine agony,	When death and hell affail me fore,
Avail to fave and folace me,	Leave me, oh leave me, nevermore,
Thy death to open heaven, and there	But bear me fafely through that ftrife,
Bid me the joy of angels fhare.	As Thou haft promifed, into life!

(cxii.—„Wenn ich in Tobesnöthen bin.")

193. FOR THE SICK AND DYING.

When my laft hour is clofe at hand,
Do Thou, Lord Je-fus, by me ftand,
And I muft hence be-take me,
Nor let Thine aid for-fake me; To Thy bleft
hands I now com-mend My foul, at this my earth-ly end, And Thou wilt fafe-ly keep it.

My fins, dear Lord, difturb me fore,	That I was graft into the Vine,	Since Thou didft leave the grave again,	To Thee I now ftretch out mine arms,
My confcience cannot flumber,	Hence will I comfort borrow;	It cannot be my dwelling;	And gladly hence betake me;
But I will cleave to Thee the more,	For Thou wilt furely keep me Thine	Thou art in heaven—this foothes my pain,	I fleep at peace from all alarms,
Though they the fands outnumber;	Through fear, and pain, and forrow;	All fear of death difpelling,	No human voice can wake me.
I will remember Thou didft die,	Yea, though I die, I die to Thee,	For Thou wilt have me where Thou art,	But Chrift is with me through the ftrife,
Will think on Thy moft bitter cry,	And Thou through death didft win for me	And fo with joy I can depart	And He will bear me into life,
Thy fufferings fhall uphold me.	The right to life eternal.	To be with Thee for ever.	And open heaven before me.

(Index of Tunes, LXXVI.)

194. FOR THE DYING.

Tune.—" Now that the fun doth fhine no more."

My God, to Thee I now com-mend My foul, for Thou, O Lord, Doft live and love me with-out end, And wilt per-form Thy word.

2
To whom else fhould I make my plea,
That heavenly life be mine?
All fouls, my God, belong to Thee,
My foul is alfo Thine.

3
Thou gav'ft my fpirit at my birth,
Take back what Thou haft given;
And with the Lord I ferved on earth
Grant me to live in heaven.

4
Faith fpreads her wings, fhe fees reveal'd
The fhining walls above;
My fpirit knows that fhe is feal'd,
Redeem'd from death by love

5
Thou my Deliverer waft of yore,
From fin Thou mad'ft me free,
Now, faithful God, doft Thou once more
In death deliver me.

6
Thou liv'ft and loveft without end,
And doft perform Thy word;
My paffing foul I now commend
To Thee, my God and Lord !

(LII.—„Jerufalem, bu hochgebaute Stabt.")

195.
Original Tune.

THE LIFE TO COME.

Je - ru - fa - lem, thou ci - ty fair and high,

Would God I were in thee! My long - ing heart

fain, fain to thee would fly, It will not ftay with me;

Far o - ver vale and moun - tain, Far o - ver field and plain,

It haftes to feek its Foun-tain And quit this world of pain.

4 Oh Zion, hail! Bright city, now unfold
The gates of grace to me!
How many a time I long'd for thee of old,
Ere yet I was fet free
From yon dark life of fadnefs,
Yon world of fhadowy nought,
And God had given the gladnefs,
The heritage I fought.

5 Oh what the tribe, or what the glorious hoft,
Comes fweeping fwiftly down? [moft,
The chofen ones on earth who wrought th
The Church's brighteft crown,
Our Lord hath fent to meet me,
As in the far-off years
Their words oft came to greet me
In yonder land of tears.

6 The Patriarchs' and Prophets' noble train,
With all Chrift's followers true,
Who bore the crofs, and could the worft
That tyrants dared to do, [difdain
I fee them fhine for ever,
All-glorious as the fun,
'Mid light that fadeth never,
Their perfeft freedom won.

7 And when within that lovely Paradife
At laft I fafely dwell, [rife,
From out my foul what fongs of blifs fhall
What joy my lips fhall tell,
While holy faints are finging
Hofannas o'er and o'er,
Pure Hallelujahs ringing
Around me evermore.

8 Innumerous choirs before the fhining throne
Their joyful anthems raife,
Till heaven's glad halls are echoing with the tone
Of that great hymn of praife,
And all its hoft rejoices,
And all its bleffed throng
Unite their myriad voices
In one eternal fong!

2 Oh happy day, and yet far happier hour,
When wilt thou come at laft? [er,
When fearlefs to my Father's love and pow-
Whofe promife ftandeth faft,
My foul I gladly render,
For furely will His hand
Lead her with guidance tender
To heaven her fatherland.

3 A moment's fpace, and gently, wondroufly,
Releafed from earthly ties,
The fiery car fhall bear her up to thee
Through all thefe lower fkies,
To yonder fhining regions,
While down to meet her come
The bleffed angel legions,
And bid her welcome home.

(v.11.—„ Alle Menſchen müſſen ſterben.")

196.
Original Tune.

Hark! a voice ſaith, All are mor-tal, Yea, all fleſh muſt fade as graſs, And this bo-dy form'd of clay,
On - ly thro' Death's gloom - y por - tal, To a bet - ter life ye paſs,
in light.

Here muſt lan-guiſh and de - cay, Ere it riſe in glo - rious might, Fit to dwell with ſaints in light.

2 Therefore, ſince my God doth chooſe it,
Willingly I yield my life,
Nor I grieve that I ſhould loſe it,
For with ſorrows it was rife;
And my Saviour ſuffer'd here
That I might not faint nor fear,
Since for me He bore my load
And hath trod the ſame dark road.

3 For my ſake He went before me,
And His death is now my gain;
Peace and hope He conquer'd for me,
So without regret or pain
To His lovely home I go,
From this land of toil and woe,
Glad to reach that bleſt abode
Where I ſhall behold my God.

4 There is joy beyond our telling
Where ſo many ſaints are gone;
Thouſand thouſands there are dwelling,
Worſhipping before the throne,
There the ſeraphim on high
Brightly ſhine, and ever cry
" Holy, Holy, Holy, Lord!
Three in One for aye adored! "

5 O Jeruſalem, how clearly
Doſt Thou ſhine, Thou city fair!
Lo! I hear the tones more nearly,
Ever ſweetly ſounding there!
Oh what peace and joy haſt thou!
Lo the ſun is riſing now,
And the breaking day I ſee
That ſhall never end for me!

6 Yea, I ſee what here was told me,
See that wondrous glory ſhine,
Feel the ſpotleſs robes enfold me,
Know a golden crown is mine;
So before the throne I ſtand
One amid that glorious band,
Gazing on that joy for aye
That ſhall never paſs away!

(lxxxvi.—„ O wie ſeelig ſeid ihr boch ihr Frommen.")

197.
Original Tune.

Oh how bleſt are ye be - yond our tell - - ing Who have paſs'd through death, with God are dwell - - ing,

For ev - er riſ - en From the trou - bles of our earth - ly pri - - ſon.

2 Here as in a dungeon grief hath bound us,
Cares and fear and terrors ſtill ſurround us,
Our beſt endeavour
But in toil and heart-ache iſſues ever.

3 While that ye are in your manſions reſting,
Safe and free at laſt from all moleſting,
No croſs or ſadneſs
There can hinder your untroubled gladneſs.

4 Chriſt doth wipe away all tears and crying,
Ye poſſeſs what we muſt ſeek with ſighing;
To you are chanted
Songs that ne'er to mortal ears were granted.

5 Oh who would not for that home of joyance
Gladly leave a land of dark annoyance?
Who loves delaying
'Mid a world of ſhadows and decaying?

6 Come, we pray Thee, from our poſt releaſe us;
Quickly guide us to Thy heaven, Lord Jeſus:
In Thee the ſpirit
Can alone true joy and reſt inherit!

(cx.—„Welt abe, ich bin bein mübe.")

198.
Original Tune.

World, fare-well! Of thee I'm tir-ed, Now t'ward heav'n my way I take;

There is peace the long-de-fir-ed, Lof-ty calm that nought can break:

World, with thee is war and ftrife, Thou with cheat-ing hopes art rife,

But in heav'n is no al-loy, On-ly peace and love and joy.

2 When I reach that home of gladnefs
I fhall feel no more this load,
Feel no ficknefs, want, or fadnefs,
Refting in the arms of God.
In the world woes follow faft,
And a bitter death comes laft,
But in heaven fhall nought deftroy
Endlefs peace and love and joy.

3 Here is nought but care and mourning,
Comes a joy, it will not ftay ;
Fairly fhines the fun at dawning,
Night will foon o'ercloud the day ;
World, with thee we weep and pine,
Gnawing care and grief are thine ;
But in heaven is no alloy,
Only peace and love and joy.

4 Well for him whom death has landed
Safely on yon bleffed fhore,
Where, in joyful worfhip banded,
Sing the faithful evermore ;
For the world hath ftrife and war,
All her works and hopes they mar,
But in heaven is no annoy,
Only peace and love and joy.

5 Time, thou fpeedeft on but flowly,
Hours, how tardy is your pace,
Ere with Him, the High and Holy,
I hold converfe face to face :
World, with partings thou art rife,
Fill'd with tears and ftorms and ftrife ;
But in heaven can nought deftroy
Endlefs peace and love and joy.

6 Therefore will I now prepare me,
That my work may ftand His doom,
And when all is finking round me,
I may hear not " Go "—but " Come ! "
World, the voice of grief is here,
Outward feeming, care, and fear,
But in heaven is no alloy,
Only peace and love and joy !

(LXXXIX. PSALM 42, Goudimel.)

199.

When the Lord re-calls the ban-ifh'd, Frees the cap-tives all at laft ;
Ev'-ry for-row will have van-ifh'd, Like a dream when night is paft ;

Then fhall all our hearts re-joice, And with glad re-found-ing voice We fhall praife the Lord who fought us,

For the free-dom He hath wrought us.

2
Lift Thy hand to aid us, Father,
Look on us who widely roam,
And Thy fcatter'd children gather
In their long'd-for promifed home.
Steep and weary is the way,
Shorten Thou the fultry day :
Faithful warriors haft Thou found us,
Let Thy peace for aye furround us.

3
In that peace we reap in gladnefs
What was fown in tearful fhowers :
There the fruit of all our fadnefs
Ripens,—there the palm is ours ;
There our God upon His throne
Is our full reward alone.
They who all for God furrender,
Bring their fheaves in heavenly fplendour.

(CVI.—„Wachet auf ruft uns die Stimme.")
200.
Original Tune.

2

Zion hears the watchmen finging,
And all her heart with joy is fpringing,
   She wakes, fhe rifes from her gloom ;
For her Lord comes down all-glorious,
The ftrong in grace, in truth victorious,
   Her Star is rifen, her Light is come !
      Ah come, Thou bleffed Lord,
      O Jefus, Son of God,
         Hallelujah !
We follow till the halls we fee
Where Thou haft bid us fup with Thee.

3

Now let all the heavens adore Thee,
And men and angels fing before Thee,
   With harp and cymbal's cleareft tone ;
Of one pearl each fhining portal,
Where we are with the choir immortal
   Of angels round Thy dazzling throne ;
      Nor eye hath feen, nor ear
      Hath yet attain'd to hear
         What there is ours,
But we rejoice, and fing to Thee
Our hymn of joy eternally.

APPENDIX.

I.   [See No. 189.

„O Welt ich muß dich laffen," as it appears both in melody and harmony in the " Mufæ
Sioniæ Michaelis' Prætorii," vol. viii. 1610.

II. [See No. 93.

Johann Crüger's tune to „Schmücke bich, o liebe Seele," as it appears, both in melody and harmony, in his „Geistliche Kirchenmelobien." Leipzig, 1649.

Deck thy-self, my soul, with glad-ness,
Come in-to the day-light's splen-dour,
Leave the gloom - y
There with joy thy

haunts of sad - ness,
praif - es ren - der
Un - to Him whose grace un - bound - ed
Hath this won-drous ban - quet found - ed;

High o'er all the heav'ns He reign-eth, Yet to dwell with thee He deign - eth!

III. [See No. 199.

Goudimel's Melody to Psalm xlii., " *Comme on voit un cerf qui brâme*," known in Germany under the title, „Freu bich sehr o meine Seele," as it is found, both in melody and harmony, in Samuel Marfhall's edition of the Whole Book of Pfalms. Bafle, 1594.*

O my foul, be glad and cheer-ful,
From this earth fo dark and tear-ful,
Now for-get thy mif - e - ry;
Chrift the Lord is call - ing thee.

Out of for-rows, fears, and woe, To that joy thou now fhalt go;

Which our thought may pic-ture nev - er, But we know it lafts for ev - er.

* In this reprint of Goudimel's Pfalmody (French) 1565, the melody is, for the firft time, given to the higheft voice. In Goudimel's original work the melody is entrufted to the tenor, as was cuftomary in his time.

IV.   [See No. 51

Hans Leo Haffler's tune, „ Herzlich thut mich verlangen," as it appears, both in melody and
harmony, in J. H. Schein's Cantional, 1627.*

1st Time.

My heart is fill'd with long - ing   To pafs a - way in peace;
For woes are round me throng - ing,   And tri - als will not

2nd Time.

ceafe. Oh fain would I be haft - ing   From thee, dark world of gloom,

To glad - nefs ev - er - laft - ing;   O Je - fus! quick-ly come!

* The harmonies, as printed here for *four voices*, are from Schein's " Cantional," and are a
reduction from the Compofer's original fcore of *five voices*, as publifhed by him in 1601 to the
words „ Mein Gemüth ist mir verwirret."

V.   [See No. 88.

Pfalm cxxxiv. (in England called the Old 100th). The Melody is given below, as it is
found on its firft appearance (without harmonies) in the work: " *Les Pfeaumes mis en rime
Françaife par Cl. Marot et Theodor de Bèze; à Lyon par Jan de Tournes pour Antoine Vincent,*
MDLXIII."* (Preface dated Geneva, June 10, 1543.)

PSEAUME CXXXIIII.—Th. de BE (Theo. de Beza).

Or fus fer - vi - teurs du Seig-neur Vous qui de . nuit en fon hon - neur

De - dans fa mai-fon le fer - vez Lou - ez le et fon nous ele - vez.

Subfequently this tune (as above, without any alteration) appears to " Pfalm C. Jubilate
Deo, J. H." in Sternhold and Hopkins' edition of the Whole Book of Pfalms, London, 1604,
and later in Ravenfcroft's " Whole Booke of Pfalmes, London, 1621;" fet for four parts, once
on the words of the 100th Pfalm, and a fecond time to harmonies by Ravenfcroft, as given
below. The melody is affigned to the Tenor, as was ufually done at that period.

CANTUS.
MEDIUS.

Be - hold now give heede, fuch as be

TENOR, or Faburden.
BASS.

the Lords ferv - ants faith - full and true: Come praife the Lord

eve - ry de - gree, With fuch fongs as to him are due.

* There is a fine copy of this book at the Britifh Mufeum.   24

VI.

Luther's tune and hymn „Wir glauben all an Einen Gott," as it appears for the first time in Johann Walter's „Geiſtliches Geſangbüchlein." Wittemberg, 1524. The harmonies are taken from the tune book publiſhed by command of the „Eiſenach Kirchenconfereng," by G. v. Tucher and others (Stuttgart, 1854), and are probably ſelected from old editions.

1

We all be-lieve in One true God,

Mak-er of the earth and hea-ven; The Fa-ther, who to us in love

Hath the claim of chil-dren giv-en. He in ſoul and bo-dy feeds us,

All we want His hand pro-vides us; Thro' all ſnares and per-ils leads us,

Watch-es that no harm be-tides us; He cares for us,

Cares for us by day and night, All things are go-vern'd by His might.

2

And we believe in Jeſus Chriſt,
    His Only Son, our Lord, poſſeſſing
An equal Godhead, throne and might,
    Through whom deſcends the Father's bleſſing;
Conceivèd of the Holy Spirit,
    Born of Mary, virgin mother;
That loſt man might life inherit
    Made true man, our Elder Brother,
Was crucified for ſinful men,
And raiſed by God to life again.

3

And we confeſs the Holy Ghoſt,
    Who from Son and Father floweth,
The Comforter of fearful hearts,
    Who all precious gifts beſtoweth;
In whom all the Church hath union,
Who maintains the Saints' Communion;
    We believe our ſins forgiven,
    And that life with God in heaven,
When we are raiſed again, ſhall be
Our portion in eternity.

This hymn and tune was intended by Luther to be ſung as the Creed during the morning ſervice, and remained in uſe as ſuch for a long time. Though omitted by the Editors in the body of this work, being conſidered by them unſuitable for England, they have inſerted it here as an intereſting ſpecimen of hymnology.

INDEX OF FIRST LINES.

INDEX OF FIRST LINES.

INDEX OF FIRST LINES.

INDEX OF FIRST LINES.

INDEX OF TUNES,
WITH HISTORICAL NOTES.* ✱

This Index applies strictly only to the Melodies of the Tunes; their Harmonies in the foregoing work (where they are not the Editors') are derived from various sources.

Tune.	Set to Hymns.	Composer or Origin.	First Appearance in Print.
i. Ach bleib' bei uns Herr Jeſu Chriſt Ich bleib' mit Deiner Gnade, see Chriſtus der iſt mein Leben.	18	—	„Harmoniſches Chor- und Figural-Geſangbuch, u. ſ. w.," edited by L. Erhardi, Frankfurt a/M. 1659.
ii. Ach Gott und Herr	107	—	J. H. Schein's „Cantional," Leipzig, 1627.
iii. Ach Jeſu Dein Sterben	50	Dr. Fr. Layriz, about 1850.	„Kern des deutſchen Kirchengeſanges," ed. by Dr Layriz, Noerdlingen, 1854.
iv. Ach was ſoll ich Sünder machen	110, 39, 106, 131	J. Flittner, 1618—1678.	„Muſikaliſches Weckerlein," ed. by J. Flittner, Greifswald, 1661.
v. Allein Gott in der Höh' ſei Ehr'	1	Baſed upon a Chorale of the Latin Church.	In the preſent form (and probably arranged by the Editor of the following work): "Concentus novi," &c. &c., ed. by Hans Kugelmann, Augsburg, 1540. Simultaneouſly in „Geiſtliche Lieder und Pſalmen," Magdeburg, 1540. M. Lotther, Printer.

✱ * Should any errors of detail in this liſt be detected hereafter, they will be corrected in any later edition.

INDEX OF TUNES.

Tune.	Set to Hymns.	Composer, or Origin.	First appearance in Print.
vi. Allein zu Dir, Herr Jesu Chrift	112	On a broadsheet in 1541. Nuremberg.	„Geiſtliche Lieder." 2nd Part. Leipzig, 1545. Val. Babſt, Printer.
vii. Alle Menſchen müſſen ſterben	196, 63, 178	J. Rosenmüller, 1610—1680, or J. Hintze, 1622—1695.	„Praxis Pietatis Melica." 24th edition. Ed. by Jacob Hintze, Berlin, 1690.
viii. Alles iſt au Gottes Segen	130	—	„Harmoniſcher Lieder-ſchatz," &c. &c. Ed. by J. B. König, Frankfurt a|M., 1738.
ix. An Dir allein, an Dir hab' ich geſündigt	42	J. C. Kühnau, 1735—1805.	„Vierſtimmige alte unb neueChoralgeſänge." Ed. by J. C. Kühnau. Part I. Berlin, 1786.
x. Auf, hinauf zu beiner Freube	157	Adaptation of a tune by Joh. Rud. Ahle, „Seele was iſt Schönres wohl" (1662).	In this form: „Geiſt-reiches Geſangbuch." Ed. by J. A. Freylinghauſen. Vol. I. Halle, 1704.
xi. Auf meinen lieben Gott	147	Adaptation of a well-known fecular tune of the XVI. Century, probably by J. H. Schein.	In this form: J. H. Schein's „Cantional," &c. Leipzig, 1627.
xii. Aus meines Herzens Grunde	164, 22	Probably an adaptation of what was previoufly a fecular tune.	In this form: „Neu Catechiſmusgeſangbuch," by Dav. Wolder. Hamburg, 1598; to „Herz-lich thut mich erfreuen."
xiii. Aus tiefer Noth ſchrei ich zu Dir	40	—	„Geiſtliches Geſang-büchlein." Wittenberg, 1524.
xiv. Chriſt lag in Todesbanden	60	Luther's adaptation of the Eaſter Hymnus, „Chriſt iſt er-ſtanben." See No. XVI.	In this form (simul-taneously): „Enchiri-bion,"&c. Erfurt, 1524; and „Geiſtliches Geſang-büchlein." Wittenberg, 1524.
xv. Chriſtus ber iſt mein Leben. (Later known as „Ach bleib' mit Deiner Gnabe.")	186, 68	Melchior Vulpius, 1560—1616.	„Ein ſchön geiſtlich Ge-ſangbuch u. ſ. w., burch M. Vulpius." 2nd Edition. Erfurt, 1609.
xvi. Chriſtus iſt erſtanben	58	In use in the Church before the Reforma-tion, probably dating from the XII. Cent.	In this form: (ber Böh-miſchen Brüber) „Ein neu Geſangbuch," &c. Ed. by Michael Weiß, 1531.
xvii. Da Jeſus an bem Kreuze ſtunb	53, 121	From the XV. Cen-tury.	„Geiſtliche Lieder," Leipzig, 1545. V. Babſt, Printer.
xviii. Dank ſei Gott in der Höhe	163	J. S. Bach, 1685—1750.	J. S. Bach's „Vier-ſtimmigeChoralgeſänge," compiled by his ſon, Ph. E. Bach. Vol. I. 1765 } Berlin & Vol. II. 1769 } Leipzig.
xix. Das alte Jahr vergaugen iſt	171	J. Crüger, 1598—1662.	„Geſangbuch Augsbur-giſcher Confeſſion," ed. by J. Crüger, Berlin, 1640.
xx. Der Du, Herr Jeſu, Ruh unb Raſt	55	—	(ber Böhmiſchen Brü-ber) „Ein neu Geſang-buch," &c. &c. Ed. 1531 (where it appears, but in a different form, un-der the name „O Jeſu Chriſte Gottes Sohn").
xxi. Der Tag bricht an unb zeiget ſich	17	Melchior Vulpius, 1560—1616. See XV.	„Ein ſchön geiſtlich Ge-ſangbuch, u. ſ. w., burch M. Vulpius." 2nd edi-tion, Erfurt, 1609.
xxii. Die Nacht iſt kommen, b'rin wir ruhen ſollen	170	—	„Der Böhmiſchen Brü-ber Kirchengeſang," &c. Edition 1566.
xxiii. Dir, Dir Jehovah will ich ſingen	117, 87	—	„Geiſtreiches Geſang-buch," ed. by J. A. Frey-linghauſen. Vol. II. Halle, 1714.

INDEX OF TUNES.

Tune.	Set to Hymns.	Composer, or Origin.	First Appearance in Print.
xxiv. Du Friedefürst, Herr Jesu Christ	182	J. Crüger, 1598—1662.	„Gesangbuch Augsburgischer Confession." Ed. by J. Crüger. Berlin, 1640.
xxv. Du keusche Seele Du	82	Joh. Rud. Ahle, 1625—1673.	J. R. Ahle's „Festandachten." Mühlhausen, 1662.
xxvi. Ein' feste Burg ist unser Gott	124	Martin Luther, 1483—1546.	*? („Geistliche Lieder.") Printed by J. Klug. Wittenberg, 1529; and „Augsburger Gesangbuch," 1530. ✳
xxvii. Erhalt uns Herr bei Deinem Wort	103, 123,	—	„Geistliche Lieder." Printed by J. Klug. Wittenberg, 1543.
xxviii. Erschienen ist der herrlich' Tag	57, 35, 126, 180	Nicolaus Heermann, died 1560.	„Die Sonntagsevangelia in Gesänge verfasset," &c. Von Nic. Heermann. Nürnberg, 1559—60.
xxix. Es ist das Heil uns kommen her Freu' dich sehr o meine Seele, see Psalm 42. Goudimel.	2, 64	—	„Etlich Christlich Lieder, Lobgesang, und Psalm," &c. Wittenberg, 1524.
xxx. Freut euch ihr lieben Christen	32	—	„Weihnachtsliedlein," von Leonhard Schröter. Helmstädt, 1587.
xxxi. Freuet euch ihr Christen alle	33	Andreas Hammerschmidt, 1611—1675.	„Musikalische Andachten." Von A. Hammerschmidt. Freiberg, 1646. (Part IV.)
xxxii. Gott des Himmels und der Erden	160	Heinrich Albert, born 1604.	H. Albert's „Arien oder Melobien." Vol. V. Königsberg, 1642—43.
xxxiii. Gott sei Dank durch alle Welt	176, 24, 158	—	„Geistreiches Gesangbuch," &c. Ed. by J. A. Freylinghausen. Halle, 1704.

✳ * There is some uncertainty about the exact title of this book, the title-page being wanting in the few copies now known, which however contain the printer's name and date at the close.

Tune.	Set to Hymns.	Composer, or Origin.	First Appearance in Print.
xxxiv. Heil'ger Geist du Tröster mein	69	—	„Praxis Pietatis Melica." Ed. by Joh. Crüger. Wittenberg, 1656.
xxxv. Herr Christ der einig' Gott's Sohn	155, 48	Adapted from a secular tune: „Ich hört ein Fräulein klagen."	In this form: „Enchiridion," &c. Erfurt, 1524.
xxxvi. Herr ich habe mißgehandelt	44	J. Crüger, 1598—1662.	Joh. Crüger's „Geistliche Kirchenmelodien." Berlin, 1649.
xxxvii. Herr Jesu Christ dich zu uns wend	13, 118	—	"Cantionale sacrum," &c. 2nd edition. Gotha, 1651.
xxxviii. Herr nun laß in Friede	26	J. S. Bach, 1685—1750.	„Musikalische Kirch- und Haus-Ergötzlichkeit. Von D. Vetter." Vol. II. Leipzig, 1713.
xxxix. Herzlich lieb hab' ich Dich o Herr	119	—	„Dresdner Gesangbuch," 1593; and Seth Calvisius's "Harmoniæ Cantionum Ecclesiasticarum." Leipzig, 1597.
xl. Herzlich thut mich verlangen. (O Haupt voll Blut und Wunden.)	51, 98, 108 App. iv	Hans Geo. Haßler, to a secular song, "Mein Gemüth ist mir verwirret." 1601.	As a sacred song (to the words „Herzlich thut mich verlangen") "Harmoniæ sacræ." 3rd edition. Görlitz, 1613.
xli. Herzliebster Jesu was hast Du verbrochen	52	Joh. Crüger, 1598—1662.	„Gesangbuch Augsburgischer Confession." Ed. by J. Crüger. Berlin (Runge), 1640.
xlii. Hochheilige Dreieinigkeit	76	—	„Geistreiches Gesangbuch." Ed. by J. A. Freylinghausen. Halle, 1704.
xliii. Höchster Priester, der Du Dich	129	—	Ditto.

INDEX OF TUNES.

Tune.	Set to Hymns.	Composer, or Origin.	First Appearance in Print.
✱ xliv. Ich banť Dir lieber Herre	37, 148	16th Century, probably of secular origin.	In a Magdeburg Hymn Book. 1540.
xlv. Ich hab' mein' Sach' Gott heimgestellt	127	Said to be of secular origin.	As a sacred song: „Neu Catechismusgesangbuch." Von Dav. Wolder. Hamburg, 1598. In the present form from Vopelius' „Neu Leipziger Gesangbuch." Leipzig, 1682. ✱?(„Geistliche Lieder"), gedruckt zu Wittenberg, durch Joseph Klug. 1535.
xlvi. Ich ruf' zu Dir, Herr Jesu Christ	116	—	

✱ • See note on No. xxvi.

xlvii. Ich steh' in Angst und Pein	28	H. Albert, born 1604.	H. Albert's „Arien oder Melodien," &c. Vol. IV. Königsberg, 1641.
xlviii. Ich will Dich lieben, meine Stärke	150	—	„Harmonischer Liederschatz." Ed. by J. B. König. Frankfurt a|M., 1738.
xlix. In Dich hab' ich gehoffet, Herr	120	—	H. Finken's „Schöne auserlesene Lieder." Nürnberg, 1536. Subsequently „Straßburger GroßKirchengesangbuch." 1560.
l. In Dir ist Freude	156	G. G. da Caravaggio, 1591 (to a Madrigal).	As a sacred tune to this hymn: " Cantionale sacrum." Gotha, 1646.
li. In natali Domini	4	From the Latin Church, probably XIV. Century.	„Ein Gesangbuch der Brüder in Böhmen und Mähren." Nürnberg, 1544. Joh. Günther, printer.
lii. Jerusalem, du hochgebaute Stadt	195	? Melchior Frank, 1580—1639.	„Christlich neu vermehrtes u. s. w. Gesangbuch." Erfurt, 1663. Published by J. Brand.
liii. Jesu meine Freude	151	Joh. Crüger, 1598—1662.	„Praxis Pietatis,"&c. Ed. by J. Crüger. Wittenberg, 1656. And simultaneously „Dresdner Gesangbuch." Dresden, 1656. (Published by C. & M. Berg.)
liv. Jesu meines Lebens Leben	49, 66, 73	17th Century.	In the present form taken from „Hauschoralbuch." 4th edition. Gütersloh, 1855.
lv. Jesus meine Zuversicht	59, 38, 65, 138, 188	Joh. Crüger (perhaps his adaptation of a tune originally composed by the author of the hymn: The Electress Luise Henriette of Branbenburg).	" Psalmodia sacra." Ed. by Joh Crüger. Berlin, 1658.
lvi. Komm Heiden Heiland, Lösegeld	23	From the Latin Church (Ambrosius) IV. Century ?	In this form: J. H. Schein's „Cantional." Leipzig, 1627.
lvii. Komm heiliger Geist, Herre Gott	72	In use in the Church before the Reformation, probably 15th—16th Century.	In this form: „Enchiribion," &c. Erfurt, 1524. And simultaneously „Geistliches Gesangbüchlein." Wittenberg, 1524.
lviii. Komm, o komm, du Geist des Lebens	74	?Joh. Chr. Bach, 1643—1703.	„Geistreiches Gesangbuch." Ed. by J. A. Freylinghausen. Halle, 1704.

INDEX OF TUNES.

Tune.	Set to Hymns.	Composer, or Origin.	First Appearance in Print.
lix. Laßt uns alle fröhlich sein	29	—	„Neu Leipziger Gesangbuch." Ed. by Gottfried Vopelius. Leipzig, 1682.
lx. Lasset uns den Herren preisen	10, 85	Johann Schop (about 1640).	„Himmlische Lieder." Ed. by Johann Rist. Lüneburg, 1641.
lxi. Liebster Jesu, wir sind hier	12, 90	Joh. Rud. Ahle, 1625—1673.	J. R. Ahle's „Sonntagsandachten." Sondershausen, 1664. (The tune is found here to its original hymn: „Ja er ist's, das Heil der Welt.")
lxii. Lobe den Herren, den mächtigen König der Ehren	9	—	„Praxis Pietatis Melica, vermehrt und verbessert von Peter Sohr." Frankfurt a/M., 1668. To the words: „Hast du denn, Jesu, dein Antlitz gänzlich verborgen."
lxiii. Mach's mit mir Gott nach Deiner Güt'	191, 47, 78, 133	J. H. Schein, 1586—1630.	J. H. Schein's „Cantional," &c. 2nd edition. Leipzig, 1645.
lxiv. Macht hoch die Thür, die Thor' macht weit	25	? Joh. Crüger.	„Praxis Pietatis Melica." 3rd Frankfurt edition. Frankfurt a/M., 1666. Chr. B. Wust, Printer.
lxv. Mein Jesu, dem die Seraphinen	67, 113	—	„Geistreiches Gesangbuch," &c. Ed. by J. A. Freylinghausen. Halle, 1704.
lxvi. Meine Hoffnung stehet feste	8	J. Neander, 1610—1680.	„Joachimi Neandri Glaub und Liebesübung," &c. Bremen, 1680.
lxvii. Meinen Jesum laß ich nicht	19, 152	? J. S. Bach, 1685—1750.	„J. S. Bach's vierstimmige Choralgesänge." Compiled by his son, Ph. E. Bach. Vol. I. 1765 } Berlin & Vol. II. 1769 } Leipzig
lxviii. Mit Frieb' und Freud' ich fahr' dahin	81	—	„Geistliches Gesangbüchlein." Wittenberg, 1524.
lxix. Morgenglanz der Ewigkeit	159	—	„Geistreiches Gesangbuch." Ed. by J. A. Freylinghausen. Halle, 1704.
lxx. Nun danket alle Gott	11, 183	Joh. Crüger, 1598—1662.	Joh. Crüger's „Geistliche Kirchenmelodien." Berlin, 1649.
lxxi. Nun freut euch lieben Christeng'mein — Known in England as " Luther's Hymn."	101, 173	—	*? („Geistliche Lieder"). Gedruckt zu Wittenberg durch Joseph Klug. (Wittenberg), 1535. ✳
lxxii. Nun komm der Heiden Heiland	99, 146	After the Latin Hymnus, " Veni redemptor gentium," from the IV. Century. Ambrosius?	In this form : „Enchiridion,"&c. Erfurt, 1524.
lxxiii. Nun laßt uns den Leib begraben	96, 97	—	„123 neue deutsche geistliche Gesänge," &c. Wittenberg, 1544. Georg Rhaw, Printer.
lxxiv. Nun lob' mein' Seel' den Herren	7, 94 184	? Johann Kugelmann about 1540.	"Concentus novi, &c. Durch Hans Kugelmann gesetzt." Augsburg, 1540.
lxxv. Nun preiset alle — Nun ruhen alle Wälder. See O Welt ich muss dich lassen.	177	W. A. von Löwenstern, 1594—1648.	„Vollständige Kirchen und Hausmusik." Breslau (? 1644). ("Baumann's Erben," Printer.)
lxxvi. Nun sich der Tag geendet hat	165, 14, 194	—	„Geistreiches Gesangbuch." Darmstadt, 1698.

✳ * See note on No. xxvi.

INDEX OF TUNES.

Tune.	Set to Hymns.	Composer, or Origin.	First Appearance in Print.
lxxvii. O Chriſte Morgenſterne	144	—	B. Geſius's Vol. II. of an earlier work, called, „Geiſtliche deutſche Lieder Luther's," &c. (1601.) Frankfurt a|O., 1605.
lxxviii. O baß ich tauſend Zungen hätte	5, 6, 181	—	„Harmoniſcher Lieder-ſchatz," &c. Ed. by J. B. König. Frankfurt a' Main, 1738. To the words, „Ach ſagt mir nichts von Gold und Schätzen."
lxxix. O der Alles hätt' verloren	132	—	„Geiſtreiches Geſang-buch." Darmſtadt, 1698
lxxx. O geſegnetes Regieren	105, 111 139	—	„Choralbuch der Brü-bergemeinen (Gnadau)." 1784.
lxxxi. O Gott du frommer Gott. O Haupt voll Blut und Wunden. See Herzlich thut mich ver-langen.	115, 154	—	J. G. Chr. Störl's „Für Würtemberg herausgege-benes Geſangbuch." Stutt-gart, 1711.
lxxxii. O Jeſu Chriſt, mein's Lebens Licht. Alſo called, Herr Jeſu Chriſt, mein's Lebens Licht	190, 100 166	—	"Pſalmodia nova," &c. Von Joſ. Claudero. Leipzig, 1630.
lxxxiii. O Lamm Gottes unſchuldig	46	—	„Geiſtliche Lieder und Pſalmen." Magdeburg, 1540. M. Lotther, Printer.
lxxxiv. O Traurigkeit, O Herzeleid	54, 56, 168	—	„Himmliſche Lieder." Ed. by Joh. Riſt. Lüne-burg, 1641.
lxxxv. O Welt ich muß dich laſſen. Later, Nun ruhen alle Wälder	189, 169 App. i.	Printed as a ſecular ſong to the words, "Insbruck ich muß dich laſſen," in the year 1539.	To the hymn, „O Welt ich muß dich laſſen." „Neu Catechis-musgeſangbuch." Von Dav. Wolder. Ham-burg, 1598.
lxxxvi. O wie ſeelig ſeid ihr doch, ihr Frommen	197	Joh. Crüger. 1598—1662.	„Geiſtliche Kirchen-meſodien." Ed. by Joh. Crüger. Berlin, 1649.
lxxxvii. Pſalm 8. Goudimel.	43, 45	One or more of theſe Pſalm tunes are probably of ſecular origin, and may have appeared in Th. de Beza's edition of 1562, or even earlier. As a whole they are firſt found in Goudimel's work of 1565.	Contained in Claude Goudimel's edition of the whole of the Pſalms. Paris, 1565. 1ſt German edition by Lobwaſſer. Leipzig, 1573.
lxxxviii. Pſalm 38. Goudimel. Later known as, Seele du mußt munter werden.	162, 109		Ditto.
lxxxix. Pſalm 42. Goudimel. Later known as, Freu dich ſehr o meine Seele.	199, 83, 153 App. iii.		Ditto.
xc. Pſalm 134. Goudimel. Known in England as the "Old Hundredth."	88, 3, 79 App. v.		Ditto.
xci. Pſalm 140. Goudimel.	141		Ditto.
xcii. Pſalm 88. Ravenſcroft.	61	With Ravenſcroft called a Scotch Tune, and named "Abbey."	Ravenſcroft's book of Pſalms. London, 1621.＊

＊ ＊ Received into this work from being also found in German hymn-books. 25

xciii. Ringe recht, wenn Gottes Gnade	128, 104	—	„Choralbuch der Brü-bergemeinen." 1735. (Gnadau.)
xciv. Schmücke dich, o liebe Seele Seele du musst munter werden, see Pſalm 38. Goudimel.	93 App. ii.	Joh. Crüger, 1598—1662.	Joh. Crüger's „Geiſt-liche Kirchenmeſodien." Berlin, 1649.
xcv. Seelenbräutigam	174, 91	A. Dreſe, 1630—1718.	„Geiſtreiches Geſang-buch." Darmſtadt, 1698.
xcvi. Sieh, hier bin ich, Ehrenkönig	122	? J. Neander.	Ditto.

INDEX OF TUNES.

Tune.	Set to Hymns.	Composer, or Origin.	First Appearance in Print.
xcvii. Straf mich nicht in Deinem Zorn	41, 125	? J. Rosenmüller, 1610—1686.	„ Hundert geistliche Arien," &c. Dresden, 1694.
xcviii. Unser Herrscher, unser König	15, 77	J. Neander, 1610—1680.	„ Joachimi Neandri Glaub- und Liebes-übung," &c. Bremen, 1680.
xcix. Balet will ich bir geben	137, 80 95	Melchior Teschner, about 1600.	On a broadsheet headed : „ Ein andächtiges Gebet, u. f. w. ; gestellt durch Val. Herberger." Leipzig, 1615.
c. Vater unser im Himmelreich	114, 136 192	— (Luther ?)	„ Geistliche Lieber und Psalmen." Magdeburg, 1540. M. Lotther, Printer.
ci. Veni Creator spiritus	86	From the Latin Church.	In this form (and probably altered by Luther) *? („ Geistliche Lieber), gedruckt zu Wittenberg, durch Joseph Klug." 1535.
cii. Von Gott will ich nicht lassen	140, 84,	(According to C. von Winterfeld) J. Eccard (?) 1533—1611.	„ Christliche und tröstliche Tischgesänge, u.f.w., durch J. Magdeburg." Erfurt, 1572.
ciii. { Von Gott will ich nicht lassen { 2nd Tune.	71, 89	Joh. Crüger, 1598—1662.	„ Neu u. f. w. Gesangbuch Augsb. Confession." Von Joh. Crüger. Berlin, 1640.
civ. Vom Himmel hoch da komm' ich her	30, 20	—	„ Geistliche Lieber,"&c. Magdeburg, 1540 (Lotther) ; and „ Geistliche Lieber." Wittenberg, 1543 (Jos. Klug).

※ * See note on No. xxvi.

Tune.	Set to Hymns.	Composer, or Origin.	First Appearance in Print.
cv. Wach' auf, wach' auf, du sich're Welt	27	—	„ Geistreiches Gesangbuch," &c. Ed. by J. A. Freylinghausen. Halle, 1704.
cvi. Wachet auf, ruft uns die Stimme	200	? Philipp Nicolai, 1556—1608.	Phil. Nicolai's „ Freudenspiegel des ewigen Lebens." Frankfurt a|M., 1599.
cvii. Warum betrübst du dich, mein Herz	143	—	" Cantica sacra." Ed. by Fr. Eler. Hamburg, 1588.
cviii. Warum sollt' ich mich denn grämen	31	J. G. Ebeling, 1620—1672.	„ P. Gerhard's Geistliche Andachten mit neuen Melodien." Von J. G. Ebeling. Berlin, 1666-67.
cix. Was Gott thut das ist wohlgethan	135, 62, 102	? J. Pachelbel, 1653—1706.	„ Nürnbergisches Gesangbuch " (preface by Feuerlein). Nürnberg, 1690.
cx. Welt ade, ich bin kein müde	198	J. Rosenmüller, 1610—1680.	„ Neu Leipziger Gesangbuch." Ed. by Gottfried Vopelius. Leipzig, 1682.
cxi. Wenn ich in Angst und Noth	142	M. A. von Löwenstern, 1594—1648.	„ Vollständige Kirchen- und Hausmusik." Breslau (? 1644). (Baumann's Erben, printer.)
cxii. Wenn ich in Todesnöthen bin	193	Melchior Franck, 1580—1639.	" Psalmodia sacra," &c. Von Melchior Franck. Nürnberg, 1631.
cxiii. Werde munter mein Gemülthe	167, 161	Johann Schop, (about 1640).	„ Himmlische Lieber," &c. Ed. by Johann Rist. Lüneburg, 1642.

INDEX OF TUNES.

Tune.	Set to Hymns.	Composer, or Origin.	First Appearance in Print.
cxiv. Wer Gott vertraut hat wohl-gebaut	145	—	"Musae Sioniae." Edited by Michael Prätorius. Part VIII. Wolfenbüttel. Subsequently in Crüger's „Gesangbuch Augsb. Confession." Berlin, 1640.
cxv. Wer nur den lieben Gott läßt walten	134, 92, 172, 185	G. Neumark, 1621—1681.	Georg Neumark's „Musikalisch - poetischer Lustwald." Jena, 1657.
cxvi. Wer weiß wie nahe mir mein Ende	187	—	„ Choralbuch für die evang.-luther. Gemeinde im Großherzogthum Berg." 1809.
cxvii. Wie schön leucht' uns der Morgenstern	149, 36, 70	? Philipp Nicolai, 1556—1608.	Phil. Nicolai's „Freudenspiegel des ewigen Lebens." Frankfurt a|M., 1699.
cxviii. Wie soll ich Dich empfangen	21	Joh. Crüger, 1598—1662.	„Luther's und anderer u. s. w. geistliche Lieder." Ed. by Johann Crüger. Berlin, 1653.
cxix. Wir Christenleut'	34	—	(Broadsheet, 1589.) „Dresdner Gesangbuch." 1594.
cxx. Wir glauben all an Einen Gott, Vater	75	Doubtful.	Here taken from Hiller's „Choralbuch." 1793.
Wir glauben all an Einen Gott, Schöpfer.	App. vi.	Luther.	
cxxi. Wo Gott zum Haus nicht giebt sein' Gunst	175, 16, 179	—	* ?(„Geistliche Lieder), gedruckt zu Wittenberg, durch Joseph Klug." 1535. ✳

✳   * See note on No. xxvi.

TITLES IN FULL

OF SOME OF THE PRINCIPAL WORKS QUOTED IN EXTRACT IN THE PREVIOUS INDEX OF TUNES, AND A FEW REMARKS CONCERNING THEM.

„Enchiridion, oder ein Handbüchlein, einem jeglichen Christen fast nützlich bei sich zu haben; zur stetter Uebung und Trachtung geistlicher Gesänge und Psalmen, rechtschaffen und künstlich vertheutscht. MCCCCCXXIIII." On the last page of the book: Gedruckt zu Erffordt (Erfurt) zum Schwarzen Horn, bei der Kremerbrucken. MDXXIIII. Jar. (Containing No. XIV, XXXV, LVII, and others in the present work.)

(„ Geistliche Lieder . . .") ? The title page lost and title only conjectured. On the last page: Gedruckt zu Wittemberg, durch Joseph Klug. One edition, 1529, containing for the first time Luther's „Ein' feste Burg," No. XXVI. Another, 1535, containing No. XLVI, LXXI, &c. &c., in the present work.

TITLES IN FULL, ETC.

a. „Ein neu Gefangbüchlein." MDXXXI. Edited by M. Weiſs. And:

b. „Ein Gefangbuch der Brüder in Böhmen und Mähren, die man aus Haß und Neid Pickarden, Waldenſer u. ſ. w. nennt. Von ihnen auf ein Neues (ſonderlich vom Sacrament des Nachtmahls) gebeſſert, und etliche ſchöne neue Gefänge hinzugethan. MDXLIII. Gedruckt zu Nürnberg durch Joh. Günther. 1544." Later edition of the firſt-named book of 1531. From it No. XVI, XX, LI, in this book. Another edition—conſiderably enlarged—of the above work, under a new title (Kirchengeſang u. ſ. w.), appeared in 1566. From it No. XXII.

„Freuden-Spiegel des ewigen Lebens; das iſt: Gründliche Beſchreibung des herrlichen Weſens im ewigen Leben u. ſ. w.; aus Gottes Wort richtig und verſtändlich eingeführt u. ſ. w., durch Philippum Nicolai, der heiligen Schrift Doctor und Diener am Wort Gottes zu Hamburg. Gedruckt zu Frankfurt am Mayn. 1599." Reprinted 1617. (This was a tract written at a moment when the plague raged in the place where the author lived (Unna in Weſtphalia), and an appendix contains the two tunes and hymns introduced here under No. CVI and CXVII (200 and 149).

„Cantional, oder Gefangbuch Augsburgiſcher Confeſſion, in welchem des Herrn Dr. Martini Lutheri und andrer frommen Chriſten, auch des Autors eigene Lieder und Pſalmen, ſamt etlichen Hymnis und Gebetlein u. ſ. w. So im Churfürſtenthümern Sachſen, inſonderheit aber in beiden Kirchen und Gemeinen allhier zu Leipzig gebräuchlich. Verfertigt, und mit 4, 5 und 6 Stimmen componiret, von Johan Hermano Schein, Grünhain, Directore der Muſic baſelbſten. 1627." A later edition of the ſame work ſlightly augmented. 1645. From this Cantional No. II, XI (LVII), LXIII. The greater part of Schein's work was ſubſequently incorporated in Gottfried Vopelius' „Neu Leipziger Gefangbuch u. ſ. w. Leipzig, 1682." From Vopelius No. LIX, CX in the preſent work.

„Geiſtliche Kirchen-Melodeien über die von Herrn D. Luthers ſelbſt und andern vornehmen und gelehrten Leuten aufgeſetzte geiſt- und troſtreiche Gefänge und Pſalmen. Der göttlichen Majeſtät zu Ehren und nützlichem Gebrauch ſeiner chriſtl. Kirchen in 4 Vocal- und 2 Inſtrumental-Stimmen, als Violinen und Cornetten, überſetzet von Johanne Crügern, Gub. Luſato, Directore der Muſik in Berlin ad Div. Nicol. Cum privilegio. Leipzig, in Verlegung Daniel Reichels, Buchhändlers zu Berlin. Gedruckt bei Timotheo Ritzſchen. Anno Chriſti 1649." (From it No. XXXVI, LXX, LXXXVI, XCIV in this book.) Crüger's „Geiſtliche Kirchenmelodien," juſt named, is preceded in 1640 by his „Neues Vollkömmliches Gefangbuch Augsburgiſcher Confeſſion," and followed in 1658 by his "Praxis pietatis melica," the titles of both of which, being rather lengthy and bombaſtic, are not given here at full length. Of hymnological works of that period theſe are among the moſt important, and before the cloſe of the 17th century the laſt-named had gone through nearly 30 editions. From theſe three works No. VII, XXIV, XXXVI, LIII, CIII, and others in this book.

„Geiſtreiches Gefang-Buch. Vormahls in Halle gedruckt, nun aber allhier mit Noten der unbekannten Melodien und 123 Liedern vermehret, wie auch von vielen im vorigen gefundenen Druckfehlern verbeſſert; zur Ermunterung gläubiger Seelen, mit einer von guten Freunden verlangten Vorrede Eberhard Phillip Zuehlens, jüngeren Stadtpredigers baſelbſt u. ſ. w. Darmſtadt, im Drucke Sebaſtian Griebels. 1698." This book is generally quoted by the name of Zuehlen, who wrote the preface. No copy, and conſequently no title, is known of the work to which it refers as its predeceſſor, and as having been printed at Halle. From it No. LXXVI, LXXIX, XCV, XCVI in this book.

---

a. „Geiſtreiches Gefangbuch, der Kern alter und neuer Lieder. Wie auch die Noten der unbekannten Melodeyen, und dazu gehörige nützliche Regiſter in ſich haltend, ſamt einer Vorrede zur Erweckung heiliger Andacht u. ſ. w. Herausgegeben von Joh. Anaſt. Freylinghauſen. Halle, im Waiſenhauſe. 1704."

b. „Neues geiſtreiches Gefangbuch, auserleſene, ſo alte als neue, geiſtliche und liebliche Lieder, nebſt den Noten der unbekannten Melodeien in ſich haltend u. ſ. w. Herausgegeben von Joh. Anaſt. Freylinghauſen. Halle, im Waiſenhauſe. 1714." b forms the 2nd part of a, and after having ſeparately gone through many editions their contents were united into one, and publiſhed together in 1741—two years after the death of the original editor—by his ſon-in-law G. A. Francke. From that period it appeared under the name „Joh. Anaſt.

Freylinghaufen's ꝛc. Geiſtreiches Gefangbuch u. ſ. w.," and contained about 1600 hymns to 600 tunes; it was reprinted at as late a date as 1771, and muſt doubtleſs be confidered as the moſt important hymnological book of the 18th century. On its appearance it was looked upon as typifying the ſpirit pervading the claſs of Chriſtians at that period, deſignated in Germany as the "Pietiſten," and confequently became much attacked by the orthodox party, to the extent of the theological faculty of Wittenberg iſſuing an official warning againſt the uſe of the book (1716). From the different editions of Freylinghaufen No. X, XXIII, XXXIII, XLII, LVIII, and feveral others in the prefent work are taken.

TABLE OF GERMAN HYMNS.

1 Allein Gott in der Höh' ſei Ehr'.
2 Sei Lob und Ehr' dem höchſten Gut.
3 Himmel, Erde, Luft und Meer.
4 Auf den Nebel folgt die Sonn'.
5 O daß ich tauſend Zungen hätte.
6 Lob ſei Dir, treuer Gott und Vater.
7 Nun lob' mein' Seel' den Herren.
8 Meine Hoffnung ſtehet feſte.
9 Lobe den Herrn, den mächtigen König der Ehren.
10 Sollt' ich meinem Gott nicht ſingen.
11 Nun danket Alle Gott.
12 Liebſter Jeſu, wir ſind hier.
13 Herr Jeſu Chriſt, Dich zu uns wend'.
14 Ach bleib' mit Deiner Gnade.
15 Thut mir auf die ſchöne Pforte.
16 Brunn alles Heils, dich ehren wir.
17 Es geht daher des Tages Schein.
18 Ach bleib' bei uns, Herr Jeſu Chriſt.
19 Licht von Licht, erleuchte mich.
20 Ihr Himmel tröpfelt Thau in Eil'.
21 Wie ſoll ich dich empfangen.
22 Auf, auf, ihr Reichsgenoſſen.
23 Komm, Heiden Heiland, Löſegeld.
24 Gott ſei Dank durch alle Welt.
25 Macht hoch die Thür, das Thor macht weit.
26 Gottes Sohn iſt kommen.
27 Wach auf, wach auf, du ſich're Welt.
28 Ich ſteh' in Angſt und Pein.
29 Laßt uns alle fröhlich ſein.
30 Vom Himmel hoch da komm' ich her.
31 Fröhlich ſoll mein Herze ſpringen,
32 Freut euch, ihr lieben Chriſten.
33 Freuet euch, ihr Chriſten alle.
34 Wir Chriſtenleut' han jetzo Freud'.
35 Wir ſingen Dir, Immanuel.
36 Wie herrlich ſtrahlt der Morgenſtern.
37 O König aller Ehren.
38 Werde Licht, du Stadt der Heiden.
39 Wer im Herzen will erfahren.
40 Aus tiefer Noth ſchrei ich zu Dir.
41 Straf' mich nicht in Deinem Zorn.
42 An Dir allein, an Dir hab' ich geſündigt.
43 Hier lieg' ich, o mein Gott, zu Deinen Füßen.
44 Herr, ich habe mißgehandelt.
45 Bin ich allein ein Fremdling auf der Erden.
46 O Lamm Gottes, unſchuldig.
47 Liebe, die du mich zum Bilde.
48 Wenn meine Sünd' mich kränken.
49 Jeſu, meines Lebens Leben.
50 Ach Jeſu, Dein Sterben.
51 O Haupt voll Blut und Wunden.
52 Herzliebſter Jeſu, was haſt Du verbrochen.
53 Da Jeſus an dem Kreuze ſtund.
54 O Traurigkeit, o Herzeleid.
55 Der Du, Herr Jeſu, Ruh und Raſt.
56 Nun gingſt auch du.
57 Frühmorgens, da die Sonn' aufgeht.
58 Chriſtus iſt erſtanden.
59 Jeſus, meine Zuverſicht.
60 Chriſt lag in Todesbanden.

TABLE OF GERMAN HYMNS.

PUBLISHED REVIEWS OF *THE CHORALE BOOK FOR ENGLAND*.

These reviews in the press were found in an 1863 printing of *The Chorale Book for England*, at the end of the book:

"We might seem extravagant to some were we to express our full sense of the piety, poetry, and music of this most charming volume of sacred verse and harmony. All the hymns have considerable merit (which can be said perhaps of no other collection). Some of them are most touching, especially when well sung: but they need to be *well* sung. They need a degree of executive skill which will not be found in parish churches as a rule. It is a book, in a word, for which all hymn-lovers must be grateful: it must tend powerfully to refine the taste of the Christian public where it is known. Most of the hymns, although translations, read with all the freshness of originals." LITERARY CHURCHMAN.

"Of the *Chorale Book* as a whole we may speak most favourably. From the hands of such musical editors nothing that could offend the most critical could be expected to appear. . . . . Many of the tunes are as beautiful as they are new to the English ear. They are all derived from the German sources, though the origin of many, dating before the Reformation, is European rather than locally national. The variety of their metres is welcome, after the uniform stiffness to which we are accustomed in England. Two-thirds of the hymns themselves are familiar to us from their appearance in Miss Winkworth's *Lyra Germanica*; those which have been added are translated by the same accomplished pen, and are characterized by the same merits. . . . . Dr. Bennett and Mr. Goldschmidt have done good service by undertaking this compilation; and we can honestly recommend it to every choir that loves sound and sterling music." SATURDAY REVIEW.

"The editors have, in many cases, retained the harmonies of the authors of the tunes, and in general have striven to preserve, as far as possible, the character belonging to the period of their composition: thus, the melodies of the sixteenth and eighteenth century called for different styles of harmony, clearly indicated by their different flow in respect of distances. The editors say that they have in all cases endeavoured to combine solemnity with simplicity, and to give harmonies which, though offering no difficulty in execution, should yet approach the strength and purity peculiar to the best Church music of all times. . . . . The *Chorale Book* is really a beautiful and highly valuable work, and it will be found to administer admirably to musical taste when directed to holy and devout themes." CLERICAL JOURNAL.

"It is gratifying to find two such distinguished musicians as Professor Sterndale Bennett and Mr. Otto Goldschmidt co-operating in work which deserves to take high rank as a standard collection of Church tunes, admirable alike in selection and arrangement. . . . It is with much satisfaction that we welcome the appearance of the *Chorale Book*, as a collection of some of the grandest and purest old tunes associated with religious purposes. . . . . . This work, viewed in its musical aspect, is likely to cause a healthy reaction in English Psalmody." LONDON REVIEW.

"The names of the editors of this book are a sufficient guarantee for the value of its contents. Professor Bennett is well known to have devoted much of his attention to the old German school of sacred music, and the English public are mainly indebted to his exertions for such knowledge as they possess of the most illustrious masters of that school. Mr. Otto Goldschmidt is one of the most learned and accomplished German musicians of our time, and a fitting coadjutor with Professor Bennett in such a work as the present. . . . . . This volume contains many of the finest German, French, and Flemish tunes. The harmonies are excellent, and the entire volume is of great value. . . . . In regard to the harmonisation, the editors have endeavoured to combine solemnity with simplicity, and to give harmonies which, though offering no difficulty in execution, should yet approach the strength and purity peculiar to the best church music of all times. In the execution of this task they have availed themselves of the labours of Sebastian Bach; and their *Chorale Book* contains a body of ecclesiastical harmony which, in antique and venerable grandeur, plain and simple style, freedom from chromatic crudities, and fitness to be sung by large numbers of voices, is unequalled by any work of this class that has ever appeared in England." DAILY NEWS.

"The general arrangement of this book carries with it tokens of an amount of diligent research which, in connexion with the musical learning of its editors, would make it an impertinence for any one not specially devoted to the archaeology of German sacred music to criticise the selection. . . . . The arrangements of the tunes are worthy of all praise. The harmony is essentially vocal. It is quite a luxury to follow even with the eye the bold, free movement of the parts which distinguishes every page of the book, contrasting so pleasantly with the prevalent or lately prevalent style of hymn-book harmony. . . . . The independent melodic treatment of each part is preserved, tenfold interest being thereby given to the work of each individual singer. The universal use of keyed instruments has somewhat dulled the popular perception of the beauty of vocal harmony; and a piano-forte-player falls insensible into the habit of regarding harmony as succession of chords. These chorales are just the thing to counteract this tendency. They should be sung, not played. They are essentially vocal music. So treated, this collection will be, all association apart, a source of delight to all part-singers who can enjoy real harmony in its purest forms." READER.

www.ingramcontent.com/pod-product-compliance
Lightning Source LLC
Chambersburg PA
CBHW081212020426
42331CB00012B/3004